Artificial Neural Networks: Electronic Implementations

Edited by Nelson Morgan

Professor Frankenstein turns to 20th century methods.

Artificial Neural Networks: Electronic Implementations

Edited by Nelson Morgan

IEEE Computer Society Press
Los Alamitos, California

Washington • Brussels • Tokyo

Artificial neural networks / [edited by] Nelson
Morgan.
p. cm.
Includes bibliographical references (p.).
ISBN 0-8186-2029-3 (pbk.). -- ISBN 0-8186-6029 (microfiche)
1. Neural computers. 2. Artificial intelligence. I. Morgan,
Nelson.
QA76.5.C6183 1990
006.3--dc20 89-046431
CIP

Published by IEEE Computer Society Press
10662 Los Vaqueros Circle
P.O. Box 3014
Los Alamitos, CA 90720-1264

Cover designed by Jack I. Ballestero

Printed in the United States of America

IEEE Computer Society Order Number 2029
Library of Congress Number 89-46431
IEEE Catalog Number 90EH0309-5
ISBN 0-8186-2029-3 (paper)
ISBN 0-8186-6029-5 (microfiche)
ISBN 0-8186-9029-1 (case)
SAN 264-620X

Additional copies can be ordered from:

IEEE Computer Society Press
Customer Service Center
10662 Los Vaqueros Circle
P.O. Box 3014
Los Alamitos, CA 90720-1264

IEEE Computer Society
13, Avenue de l'Aquilon
B-1200 Brussels
BELGIUM

IEEE Computer Society
Ooshima Building
2-19-1 Minami-Aoyama,
Minato-Ku
Tokyo 107, JAPAN

IEEE Service Center
445 Hoes Lane
P.O. Box 1331
Piscataway, NJ 08855-1331

THE INSTITUTE OF ELECTRICAL AND ELECTRONICS ENGINEERS, INC.

Preface

This volume is a continuation of the Computer Society series begun by V. Vemuri in the field of Artificial Neural Networks (ANNs). The focus here is on design issues for electronic ANN systems, with an emphasis on functioning integrated circuits. These circuits are necessarily experimental, since ANN algorithms are still in an early stage, so that the optimal implementations cannot yet be known.

The papers that have been included are both historically and technically fundamental. The first paper, written by researchers at Caltech (Sivilotti et al), is what we believe to be the first published description of an artificial neural network IC. The Caltech group has designed continuous-time analog circuits, primarily for associative memory (as in this paper) and emulation of the sensory input paths for the human central nervous system (the Lyon and Mead paper from this volume for the auditory sense; other Mead papers are concerned with the visual system).

The second paper, by J. Sage and R.S. Withers of Lincoln Laboratory at MIT, is an example of the use of discrete-time analog technology (CCDs) for high speed computation, in combination with analog nonvolatile storage of synaptic weights. The chip described may also have been the first ANN chip to include on-chip learning.

The next two papers are a sampling of the ANN hardware developed at AT&T Bell Labs. The Graf et al paper describes an analog Hopfield network with three values of weights permitted (-1, +1, 0), which are stored in digital RAM. The Schwartz et al paper describes a new chip with relatively high resolution weights (10 bits worst case), achieved by representing each weight as the difference in voltage between two capacitors -- a far more accurate technique than simply using a single capacitor or floating gate to hold the weight.

Paper 5, by Holler et al from Intel, is a good recent example of the use of floating-gate technology for the representation of synaptic weights. CMOS EEPROM technology has been used for this work.

The next paper, from Murray and Smith at the University of Edinburgh, describes a new set of techniques which falls somewhere between digital and analog implementations. Digitally stored weights gate the pulsed outputs (modeled after axonal firings of biological neurons) from source units into each target unit, which itself then generates a pulse stream if the integrated excitatory inputs are greater than the integrated inhibitory inputs. This is one of the more unusual of the ANN implementations. In more recent work, the authors have further modified this method to use pulse-width modulation.

The seventh paper, from Bell Communications Research (Alspector et al), describes the first chip specifically designed to implement a Boltzmann machine algorithm, including learning [Ackley et al, 1985]. Besides including analog amplifiers to act as "neurons", and 5-bit registers as synapses, this chip employes noise amplifiers for the simulated annealing. Additional correlation logic tests the similarity of neuron outputs for training.

The eighth paper is the work of Richard Lyon and Carver Mead, who have implemented an electronic analog of the human cochlea (inner ear). These authors are specifically interested in building electronic models of biological function. The technology that they have used can also be seen as an extremely low-power/high-density way of building audio-frequency processing for which low noise operation is not required.

We include one more paper from AT&T Bell Labs, this one from Mackie and Denker at Holmdel. This paper is of particular interest with respect to the claims of many neural network researchers, who have suggested that the reason for the high speed of their circuits is the analog computation. This chip is a special-purpose bit-serial digital design which implements 5 billion elementary decisions per second. Because of the distributed and dedicated nature of the hardware, essentially all of it is busy with useful computation at any given time. It is this characteristic of special-purpose designs in general which gives them their speed. This is the only fully digital ANN IC represented in this volume, but the reader is directed to other reports about digital CMOS ANNs [Weinfeld et al, 1988; Duranton and Sirat, 1989].

The last three papers suggest directions for future large ANN systems. Raffel et al from MIT Lincoln Labs show how an existing wafer-scale technology can be applied to the interconnection of multiplying digital-to-analog converters (MDACs) to implement fairly large ANNs (they estimate 10,000 summing nodes on a 4-inch wafer using 2-micron design rules). Research by Bailey and Hammerstrom at the Oregon Graduate Center asserts the need for multiplexed systems for large ANNs. Finally, Kung and Hwang show that a wide variety of ANN algorithms can be mapped efficiently to a digital ring architecture.

Due to space restrictions, much significant work could not be included. For instance, the entire volume could have been devoted to the efforts of the Caltech group, particularly the work of Carver Mead and his students and co-workers †. We have confined their contribution to papers on associative memories and the cochlear chip, thus missing, among other works, the artificial retina. An important early paper from Moopen et al, 1987, was included in the first volume of this series. Graf and Henderson have recently reported a writable ANN chip capable of 3×10^{11} single-bit connections using a mixed analog-digital approach; their paper [Graf and Henderson, 1990] was slightly too late for this book. Papers describing general-purpose simulation machines such as the Mark II and IV from TRW, the Anza from Hecht-Nielsen, the Odyssey from Texas Instruments, or the Ring-Array-Processor (RAP) multiprocessor from ICSI in Berkeley [Morgan et al, 1990] are also not included. A final and major omission is the entire body of work in optical and electro-optical realizations of artificial neural networks. This is a large enough area to merit a separate volume.

†An excellent volume describing this work is *Analog VLSI and Neural Systems* by Carver Mead.

Table of Contents

Artificial Neural Networks: Electronic Implementations

Introduction

1: Background

Computer scientists and designers have long been interested in comparisons between artificial automata and the human brain [Von Neumann, 1957]. Mental activity is often characterized as the result of the parallel operation of large numbers of relatively simple elements ($\tilde{}10^{11}$ for the human brain). These elementary biological units are called *neurons*. Neurons interact electrochemically on a time scale of milliseconds, and are jointly capable of significant feats of pattern recognition (such as recognizing a friend wearing an unusual costume). These commonplace human achievements are currently unattainable by large electronic computers built from components with characteristic delays in the nanosecond range. Artificial neural network (ANN) researchers hope that simplified functional models of nervous tissue can help us to design algorithms and machines that are better than conventional computers for difficult problems in machine perception and intelligence.

Physiological neurons are actually quite complex, and the true mechanisms of memory and cognition are still poorly understood. Nonetheless, it is undoubtedly true that the amazing performance of the brain must partly be due to the extreme parallelism of the simultaneous activity of widespread elements of its nervous tissue. Despite the technological advances of Very-Large-Scale-Integrated (VLSI) circuits, the solution of difficult problems in pattern recognition and signal processing is expected to require machines with far more computational capability than can be provided from any single integrated circuit or uniprocessor. Although ANN algorithms may not be faithful models of the real mechanisms of neural behavior, they may show how to map these problems to the parallel systems that will be required for machine perception and intelligence.

It is not yet clear what biological systems will reveal about the design of physical hardware for performing ANN algorithms. Electronic systems are characterized by high speeds, few elements, and low connectivity. A typical gate may feed only a few others, although the actual fan-out depends primarily on wire space constraints, as well as drive and load characteristics and speed requirements. Nervous systems are primarily composed of elements that operate at low speeds†, although some little-understood mechanisms may operate at high speed. Much nervous tissue is composed of a large number of heavily interconnected neurons; a pyramidal cell in the cerebral cortex can have 50,000

†Individual axonal firings, which could be considered to be elementary "decisions," occur on a time scale of milliseconds. However, the simultaneous neural integration of 50,000 inputs in this period corresponds to 10^{-7} seconds/synaptic "operation". This computational rate is not slow, even by 1989 supermicro standards.

EH2029-3/90/0000/0001$01.00 © 1990 IEEE

inputs. Silicon systems are primarily two-dimensional. "Wiring" in the nervous system is three-dimensional† and relatively "cheap" (in the sense that point-to-point wiring is ubiquitous locally, and common over long distances). Given these differences in design components, dissimilar implementations have developed for natural and synthetic "computing" systems.

Despite these differences, many researchers are attempting to manipulate the style and content of their hardware designs to imitate, to some small degree, the mechanisms observed in biological nervous systems. This book is a collection of some of the first significant papers describing the application of IC technology to the implementation of ANNs.

2: IC Technology and Artificial Neural Networks

Networks of artificial neural-like elements have been used in the fields of adaptive signal processing and pattern recognition by many researchers since the early '60s [Widrow, 1960; Nilsson, 1965]. In particular, working algorithms with multiple layers of nonlinear weighted-sum elements (perceptrons) have been in use for a variety of practical applications [Viglione, 1970]. Multi-layered perceptrons continued to be used for difficult problems in biomedical signal processing in the 1970s and 1980s [Gevins and Morgan, 1986, 1988]. However, the recent resurgence of interest in this area has sparked many new research developments. One of the most important differences between what is possible with ANN research today and what was possible 25 years ago is the huge improvement in technological capability. A single high-performance microprocessor can contain over a million transistors and is capable of arithmetic performance exceeding that of the largest mainframes of the early '60s. It is now feasible to propose designs with thousands or even millions of connected silicon-based elements.

Despite these impressive developments, there is no clear consensus on how to exploit VLSI capabilities for massively parallel ANN algorithms. Because they are in flux, most of these algorithms are still implemented in software on general-purpose computers. It is not currently possible to determine with any assurance the best way to perform ANN calculations for any given application. Whether ANN or more conventional approaches are used, the run-time for real engineering problems is frequently dominated by operations that are quite different from the ubiquitous multiply-accumulate. Additionally, ANN learning algorithms continue to be developed. One common algorithm, error back-propagation [Rumelhart et al, 1986], requires a wide dynamic range for the weights, as well as a backward path through the network. Other networks such as structured connectionist models [Feldman et al, 1988] attempt to incorporate knowledge in the structure of the network itself. Efficient implementation of each of these approaches requires a different type of computation.

Computational circuits may be classified as either continuous-time or discrete-time. They also are considered analog or digital, depending on whether the range of

†It is true that tissue such as cortex is, roughly speaking, a sheet. However, the third dimension is still important in these systems, since fibres can connect between widely distant areas, and because even the sheet has a depth of multiple layers of cells (six for the neocortex).

permissible amplitudes is continuous or discrete. For instance, an active filter (composed of fixed connections of resistors, capacitors, and op-amps) is an analog (continuous-valued) continuous-time circuit. A microprocessor is a digital, discrete-time machine. There are many examples of circuits that fall somewhere between these extremes. Switched-capacitor filters are both analog and discrete-time, as are analog multiplexers. Multiplying digital-to-analog converters (MDACs) generate an analog voltage that is the product of a digital multiplier and an analog multiplicand.

Most ANN implementations have used analog, continuous-time hardware (in imitation of the nervous system), although some have used a discrete-time model because of the high communication costs in a non-multiplexed silicon system. Many designs use digital weights, which may be useful even for an otherwise analog system when high-resolution adaptations are required. While low-resolution components can be used for many kinds of collective computation [Hopfield, 1988], gradient learning algorithms currently in use can require a dynamic range of 12-16 bits for convergence [Baker and Hammerstrom, 1988; Duranton and Sirat, 1989]. A few implementations of ANNs use completely digital hardware, capitalizing on recent developments in semi-custom CAD, and on the rapid rate of circuit improvement for digital VLSI systems. Such an approach ignores the neural net model as a guide to hardware design, and merely implements the algorithms in the most efficient way available. A preliminary example is a recent 6-bit implementation of a sigmoid nonlinearity in 2 micron CMOS [Morgan, 1990]. This circuit was roughly the size of an op-amp, and operated at 20 MHz. Special-purpose chips for digital signal processing (DSP) suggest the computational capabilities of today's digital VLSI. For instance, a commercial 64-tap FIR filter has been reported that computes over 10^9 8-bit multiplications and 10^9 24-bit accumulations per second, using a purely digital design with a 1.5 micron CMOS process [Ruetz, 1989]. Sub-micron versions of these circuits would be an order of magnitude faster, and two orders of magnitude smaller.

Analog circuits are widely used for high-speed signal processing, such as the high-speed amplification, demodulation, and filtering required in a television set. They are frequently more efficient than digital implementations when the computational operation required is one that is naturally performed by physical processes, such as the Kirchoff's Law current summation performed at a node. High-frequency analog circuit error is dominated by thermal ($\frac{kT}{C}$) noise, which can be expected to be much worse for submicron circuits. Of course, key circuits can be made larger to reduce this effect. For low frequencies, most error is due to 1/f noise, which may not be worse for smaller dimensions if fabrication technology continues to improve. Additionally, bipolar technologies typically provide lower noise, and are now resurfacing in VLSI designs in the form of BiCMOS, a process which includes both bipolar and MOS transistors. Process variations across the surface of a chip result in transistor threshold variations and amplifier offset problems. All of these analog design problems are being attacked using clever circuit designs and algorithms which are resistant to noise.

The ultimate "analog-vs-digital" question cannot be answered until one knows what algorithms (and their corresponding accuracies, etc.) are required for artificial neural network applications. Study of application-specific integrated circuits (ASICs) reveals that extremely high throughput can be achieved using either analog or digital technologies given a sufficient restriction on the functionality of the design [Brodersen, 1989].

3: Literal vs. Virtualized Implementations

The previous section introduced some of the factors affecting the choice between analog or digital implementations of ANN algorithms. However, even analog processing elements can implement multiple computations in a time-multiplexed manner. Regardless of whether analog or digital hardware is used, the choice of a literal or a time-multiplexed implementation of ANN algorithms remains a significant design issue. In other words, how many virtual neurons should be implemented on each physical processor? The extreme cases are the serial implementation of an ANN algorithm on a general-purpose uniprocessor (fully virtualized), and the fully parallel implementation of one processing element per algorithmic neuron (no virtualization). The discussion which follows should show that this range of design choices is ultimately dependent on communication capabilities provided by the technology.

As mentioned previously, one of the fundamental differences between the building blocks available to nature and to silicon designers is the capability for connectivity. This may change with new techniques for multi-layer wafer-scale integration, or anisotropic etching (which could provide up to thousands of connections out of each die)[Tuckerman, 1987]. However, the massive interconnections which are routine in the brain are probably impossible in forseeable future electronic systems. Given the current connectivity restrictions, we have considered limitations to the number of physical processors which can be usefully employed to implement an ANN. If plausible limits can be inferred, highly virtualized systems with powerful processors implementing many virtual units would appear to be preferable to large, finely grained, massively parallel systems.

3.1: The Random Connection Problem: Some Assumptions

For simplicity, we only consider the spreading activation of a network, and ignore learning. Additionally, we assume a simple, one-cycle broadcast capability for communication from any unit to all others. Technologies that permitted direct point-to-point connection between all communicating processing elements would invalidate the following arguments, which are aimed at considering the consequences of the connectivity constraints of today's silicon systems. We also assume that the number of connections from each unit is a constant (smaller than the number of units), and that the units are randomly scattered over the available processors. Fully connected networks are impossible for a large number of units, since the connection weights will take up a prohibitive amount of memory, so having a partially connected network is a reasonable assumption. Finally, we initially assume that the speed of the broadcast bus is roughly the same as the speed of one elementary computation (e.g., multiply-accumulate) on a processor. This "fast" processor requirement will be relaxed after the next section.

3.2: The Fast Processing Case

Suppose there are U units (e.g., 100,000), and the number of connections out of each of them is C (e.g., 1000). In each step, a different unit broadcasts to all of the others, and only C of the units will need to receive this value. If there are P physical processors, then the probability that a particular connection will not be implemented on a processor is

$$p(miss/conn) = \frac{P-1}{P}$$

and the probability that none of the C connections made in a single broadcast step are implemented on this processor is

$$p(miss) = \left[\frac{P-1}{P} \right]^C$$

This probability is essentially an inefficiency factor. Note that, for P = C, this probability is approximately equal to 1/e, since

$$\lim_{x \to \infty} \left[\frac{x}{x-1} \right]^x \approx \lim_{x \to \infty} \left[\frac{x+1}{x} \right]^x = e$$

Thus, asymptotic performance (total useful computation within 37% of the maximum achievable by an infinite number of processors) is reached for a number of processors comparable to the number of connections out of each unit.

A further consideration is the predictability of the number of connections that will be implemented in each processor. Small variability is important both for minimization of buffering requirements for each processor, and for the reduction of lost cycles waiting for processors to finish up. Assuming a normal approximation to the binomial distribution, the variance of the number of connections to a processor is

$$\sigma^2 = \#connections \times p(connection\ in\ P) \times p(no\ connections\ in\ P)$$

$$\approx \#connections \times p(connection\ in\ P) = \frac{CU}{P} = mean$$

where the factor of the probability of an individual connection not landing in a processor is ignored, since it is close to 1 for P >> 1. To have a small standard deviation of connections per processor, expressed as a fraction of the average number of connections per processor, we should minimize

$$\frac{\sigma}{mean} = \frac{\sqrt{\frac{CU}{P}}}{\frac{CU}{P}} = \frac{\sqrt{P}}{\sqrt{CU}}$$

Since the number of processors is the only part of this relation that can be varied for a given problem, it should be minimized. Thus, both for reasons of efficiency and predictability, the number of "fast" processors should not be any greater than the average number of connections from each unit. Much fewer than C processors, however, would imply inefficient usage of memory circuitry, as well as a significantly reduced computational throughput.

3.3: The Slow Processing Case

While similar behavior should be observed for other simple architectures†, a major sticky assumption is that the processing units are as fast as the bus. Certainly this biases the argument against fine-grained elements; one could easily imagine many slower elements operating in parallel replacing the fast coarse-grained elements. In fact, the complex processors that make up the fast units can themselves be viewed as a collection of parallel and pipelined simple units. For instance, a fast parallel multiplier is more or less a large group of one bit adders (with the appropriate carry logic). If each slow computational unit has its own memory, then it is a truly fine-grained system. Potentially, the upper bound on processors described in the previous section can be magnified by a factor S, which is the speed ratio between broadcast and processing elements. On the average, one broadcast per S cycles would be relevant for any particular processor, which could take S cycles to compute the weighted input. Some buffering capability might also be required.

Unfortunately for this scheme, any broadcast value must, in some sense, be examined for its relevance to the local unit. This "examination" could be as simple as a table look-up on the identity of the sender (which is assumed to be broadcast along with the data). However, the computation required is not negligible, since the identification must take place at the speed of the broadcasts. Since short word-length multiplications are fairly comparable to table look-ups (and in fact can be done with table look-ups using squares or logarithms), it is unlikely that any great advantage in silicon resources could be gained by deliberately designing the computational units to be slow. Certainly an S factor over 10 is not likely to be useful.

3.4: Conclusions about Virtualization

The cost of receiving and interpreting a broadcast should be shared over multiple units per processor. This, along with the need to minimize the probability of a processor being idle in a broadcast step, and to minimize the variability in connections per processor, pushes us towards implementations with a moderate number of high-speed processors, at least for a broadcast-based architecture. Of course, specific ANN algorithms may permit architectures which are more highly parallel than is suggested by this casual analysis of a random network.

Assuming the validity of the suggested limitations, can we ever implement truly massive networks with high speed? If a large network is divided into some number of smaller networks that all obey the restrictions suggested above, the subnetworks can be connected with one another in a limited way (i.e., with C connections). Such a hierarchical structuring could be extended to other levels. The division into subnetworks is not unreasonable, since all practical problems successfully tackled by network algorithms (biological signal processing, speech analysis, meteorological pattern recognition, etc.) have used a moderate number of "neural" units. Larger networks are trained with great difficulty, and are unlikely in general to converge to good solutions. One would expect, however, that larger problems could be handled by collections of smaller networks. The

†Joachim Beer of ICSI has performed a similar analysis of full crossbar architectures to show the high likelihood of conflicts at terminals of the crossbar for the random connection problem.

hierarchical solution, then, is both a good match to real applications and to the communication requirements of multiprocessor systems.† Finally, the lower levels of subnetwork might be small enough to permit many point-to-point interconnections and thus remove some of the arguments for heavy virtualization.

4: Further Reflections on Analog vs Digital Implementations

Analog ANN hardware is frequently built to mimic neurobiology. Analog circuits can sometimes offer particularly efficient solutions for engineering problems. However, the discussions above suggest some difficult limitations for fully analog approaches to ANN implementations. While some ANN systems are not adaptive learning machines, many rely on estimation of the gradients of some error criterion. If gradient algorithms are used, synaptic weights may require 12-16 bits worth of dynamic range (i.e., the smallest weight change needs to be 4000-64000 times smaller than the largest weight). This is impractical for sub-micron Ultra-Large-Scale-Integrated (ULSI) circuits of the late 1990's unless weights are implemented as digital coefficients. If the ANN elements are heavily interconnected, multiplexing is required for currently available electronic technologies. Multiplexing imposes a discrete-time requirement for at least part of the system. If the number of connections per unit is small compared to the number of units, which is probably the only practical assumption to make for large systems, then the arguments in the previous section suggest that each physical processing element may need to implement many virtual neurons (assuming at best a single-bus broadcast capability). It is true that all of these difficulties can be handled with a hybrid digital-analog system (such as the MDAC-based neurons used by a number of the authors in this volume). However, the digital control logic to multiplex the processing element may dominate the silicon resources, so that it may ultimately be advantageous to implement the entire system digitally. Furthermore, the large dynamic range required for weights in gradient error-correction systems would mean that a large range in analog circuit element values would be required for an MDAC.

Because of these considerations, it is likely that submicron digital ANN implementations may be the best match to the gradient algorithms that are widely used for ANN-style pattern recognition and signal processing, much as they increasingly dominate adaptive linear processing for communications applications. However, gradient algorithms, while eminently practical for some engineering problems, are not likely to be particularly good models of the way biological systems function. Nervous systems certainly are composed of massively parallel, low-resolution, noisy, analog elements (with the exception of axonal communication, which is pulse-like). Despite these limitations, nervous tissue learns, recalls, and recognizes. If non-gradient ANN algorithms that behave more like neural masses can be applied successfully to significant engineering problems, then analog solutions will become much more attractive. Furthermore, the practical advantages of low power, compatibility with sensor outputs, and high-speed operation for some simple functions (as evidenced by the continued use of analog circuits in high-speed signal processing applications) may continue to inspire designers to find clever

† See the Bailey and Hammerstrom paper in this volume for further discussions about the effects of virtualization vs. direct implementation on silicon area.

solutions to the difficulties described above. Nonetheless, significantly different connection technologies will be needed to eliminate the need for time multiplexing of signals or the virtual implementation of multiple algorithmic neurons on each physical processing element (for large systems).

5: A Caveat about ANN Claims

New fields have frequently been undermined by the backlash from early, exaggerated expectations that could not be realized. The papers included in this volume demonstrate that ANN hardware can implement ANN algorithms with a throughput far exceeding what can be achieved with a general-purpose computer. However, the reader should take care not to jump to conclusions that the authors themselves may not intend. In particular, be wary of the following common traps:

"His benchmark showed the hardware to be umpty-zillion times faster than a general-purpose computer."

An old joke says that there are liars, damned liars, and statisticians. In addition there are benchmarks. Despite the best intentions of authors, there is no simple way to judge the speed of an ANN chip in any but the grossest manner (for instance, by connections/second). There is also no simple way to describe the speed of a general-purpose computer for an ANN algorithm, since run-time can be so strongly implementation dependent (1-2 orders of magnitude variation is not uncommon). This does not mean that the authors are making things up. It does mean that, in the absence of widely accepted benchmark programs (comparable to LINPACK, a linear algebra package commonly used to rate a computer's capabilities for numerical calculations), reported speedups should be taken as qualitative descriptions of the advantage of the special-purpose hardware.

"His hardware runs this fast because it is analog/continuous time."

As pointed out above, fast digital application-specific integrated circuits (ASICs) now have roughly comparable capabilities to some of the fastest analog ANN chips. It is frequently the dedicated character of custom circuits, either analog or digital, which provides the high performance. In many cases, the authors are choosing analog implementations for exploratory reasons, not because they believe that it is the only way to get the throughput. In Mead's work, for instance, both low power and biological modeling are major design goals, neither of which are handled well by a digital design that might even be faster.

"His hardware is this amazing because it is a neural network"

We do not know how to build nervous tissue. At the moment, even the most literal circuit implementations are still combinations of conventional analog and/or digital elements. Therefore, the factors controlling the effectiveness of the hardware are the same as for other computational circuits: how narrowly can we restrict required characteristics (bandwidth, signal-to-noise, circuit function or programmability) and map them to available circuit elements?

ANNs are fundamentally a mainstream development of the fields of computer science and pattern recognition. Historic precedents [Viglione, 1970; Gevins and Morgan, 1988] have shown the utility of ANN algorithms for difficult problems in pattern recognition and signal processing. There are, therefore, obvious advantages to efficient implementations of these algorithms in hardware. The papers in this volume represent some of the best early work in this new area of hardware design. The coming years will probably see both the development of algorithms that can effectively exploit the capability of analog circuits, and of digital circuits that can efficiently implement gradient error-correction algorithms for nonlinear engineering problems.

6: Acknowledgments

The development of this volume benefited directly and indirectly from the comments and suggestions of numerous people. In particular, I wish to thank Eric Allman, J Beer, J Beck, J Bilmes, J Wawrzynek, S Omohundro, and George and Molly Csicsery for their many comments and suggestions. Jerry Feldman and the International Computer Science Institute provided financial, intellectual, and moral support. Finally, my thanks to Pamela Sichta for her cartoon design and support on many levels.

7: References

Ackley, D.H., Hinton, G.E., and Sejnowski, T.J., 1985. "A learning algorithm for Boltzmann machines," Cognitive Science 9 (1985), pp.147-169.

Baker, T., and Hammerstrom, D., 1988, "Modifications to Artificial Neural Networks Models for Digital Hardware Implementation," Oregon Graduate Center Technical Report No. CS/E 88-035.

Beck, J., Morgan, N., Allman, E., Beer, J., 1989. "A Multi-DSP Ring Array for Connectionist Simulations," Proceedings of the 1989 Asilomar Conference on Signals, Systems, and Computers.

Brodersen, R.W., 1989. "Evolution of VLSI Signal Processing Circuits," *Advanced Research in VLSI,* Proceedings of the 1989 Decennial Caltech Conference, Charles Seitz, editor.

Duranton, M., and Sirat, J.A., 1989. "Learning on VLSI: A General Purpose Digital Microchip," Proceedings of 1989 International Neural Network Society Conference

Feldman, J.A., Fanty, M.A., Goddard, N., and Lynne, K., 1988. "Computing with Structured Connectionist Networks," *Communications of the ACM,* 1988.

Gevins, A. and Morgan, N. (1986) "Classifier-directed signal processing in brain research". *IEEE Transactions on Biomedical Engineering, BME-33* (12), pp. 1054-1068.

Gevins, A., and Morgan, N., 1988. "Applications of Neural Network (NN) Signal Processing in Brain Research," IEEE Transactions on Acoustics, Speech, and Signal Processing, July, 1988.

Graf, H., and Henderson, D., 1990. "A Reconfigurable CMOS Neural Network", 1990 IEEE International Solid-State Circuits Conference, San Francisco, pp 144-145

Hopfield, J.J., 1988. "Artificial Neural Networks," IEEE Circuits and Devices Magazine, Vol. 4, No. 5, September, 1988.

Morgan, N., Beck, J., Allman, E., and Beer, J., 1990. "RAP: A Ring Array Processor for Multilayer Perceptron Applications" *Proc. IEEE Intl. Conf. on Acoustics, Speech, & Signal Processing,* Albuquerque, New Mexico, 1990.

Morgan, N., 1990. "Considerations for the Electronic Implementation of Artificial Neural Networks", ICSI Technical Report TR-90-003

Nillson, N.J., 1965. *Learning Machines,* McGraw-Hill, New York, 1965.

Ruetz, P., 1989. "The Architectures and Design of a 20-MHz Real-Time DSP Chip Set," IEEE Journal of Solid State Circuits, April, 1989.

Rumelhart, D.E., Hinton, G.E. and Williams, R.J., 1986. "Learning Internal Representations by Error Propagation," in *Parallel Distributed Processing*. vol. 1: Foundations, Ed. D.E.Rumelhart and J.L.McClelland, MIT Press, 1986.

Tuckerman, D.B., "Laser-patterned interconnect for thin-film hybrid wafer-scale circuits," IEEE Elec. Dev. Let., EDL-8, No. 11, p.540, Nov. 1987

Viglione, S.S., 1970, "Applications of pattern recognition technology," in *Adaptive Learning and Pattern Recognition Systems,* J.M. Mendel and K.S.Fu, Eds., New York, Academic Press, 1970, pp. 115-161.

Von Neumann, J., 1957. *The Computer and the Brain* New Haven and London, Yale University Press.

Weinfeld, M., Dreyfus, G., Johannet, A., Personnaz, L., 1988. " A Fully Digital CMOS Integrated Feedback Network Including the Learning Process," Proceedings of Neural Networks for Computing, Snowbird, Utah, 1988.

Widrow, B. and Hoff, M.E., 1960. "Adaptive Switching Circuits," *WESCON Convention Record,* 4:96-104.

A Novel Associative Memory Implemented Using Collective Computation

Massimo Sivilotti, Michael Emerling, and Carver Mead

Department of Computer Science
California Institute of Technology, Pasadena

Abstract

A radically new type of associative memory, the ASSOCMEM, has been implemented in VLSI and tested. Analog circuit techniques are used to construct a network that evolves towards fully restored (digital) fixed-points that are the memories of the system. Association occurs on the whole source word, each bit of which may assume a continuous analog value. The network does not require the distinction of a search *key* from a *data* field in either the source or target words. A *key* may be dynamically defined by differentially weighting any subset of the source word. The key need not be exact; the system will evolve to the closest memory. In the case when the key is the whole input word, the system may be thought of as performing error correction.

1 Introduction

Conventional digital associative memories [1,2,3] have two characteristic shortcomings: (i) the association occurs on an a priori defined key, which must be supplied exactly, (ii) resolution of multiple matches often demands an additional serial polling algorithm (slow). In addition, they only work on digital (restored) data, and thus are useless for recognition of patterns with grey scale. We have designed and tested a radically new genre of associative memory. In the ASSOCMEM, association takes place on the word as a whole; the result is the word stored in memory that is *closest* to the supplied word. There is no distinction made between *key* and *data*. The convergence of the association process is guaranteed by theory. The length of time required to perform the association depends, in some sense, on the *distance* between the input and the result.

"A Novel Associative Memory Implemented Using Collective Computation" from *1985 Chapel Hill Conference on Very Large Scale Integration/A Novel Associative Memory Implemented Using Collective Computation.* Edited by Henry Fuchs. Authors M. Sivilotti et. al.

This novel behaviour is obtained through the use of analog circuit techniques to perform a "collective computation" [4]. Each bit of the word is represented by the state of an active element (amplifier). These elements are interconnected in a way to make the desired memory contents stable states of the network. An association consists of setting the initial conditions of the network to a neutral state, then letting the network evolve to a fixed-point.

A very simple example of such a network is the flip-flop illustrated in Fig. 1. It may be considered to operate in a continuous range between the signal rails $+1$ and -1. The neutral state is the well-known "hung" condition where both inputs and outputs are equal. When the system is released, any difference between the inputs will cause the flip-flop to evolve to the closest stable state. This particular system may be thought of as having two memories, $(+1,-1)$ and $(-1,+1)$.

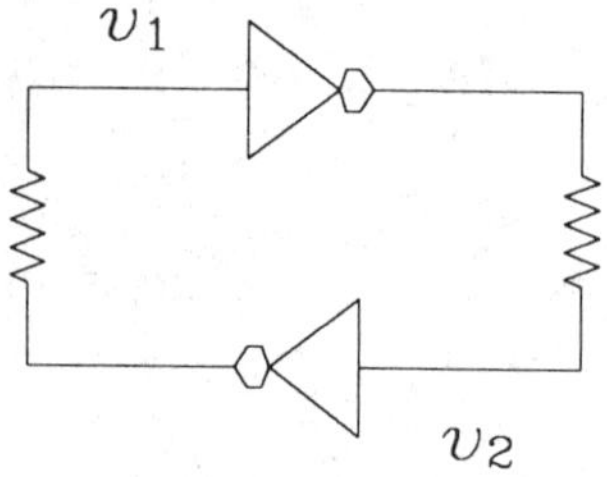

Figure 1: Simple Flip-Flop.

In general, a network will be represented by an interconnection matrix, as in Fig. 2. A considerable amount can be said about the behavioural properties of such a system: J. Hopfield has shown [5] that a symmetric interconnect matrix guarantees the existence of stable states (i.e. that the network will not oscillate, but will ultimately reach convergence), and has developed a synthetic technique for deriving a matrix with specified stable states [6]. This technique consists, in essence, of setting up a matrix such that every active element reinforces every other active element, when the system is in the stable state. The stable state vector is represented by $\vec{v}$, $(v_i \in \{-1,+1\})$, and the connection between the output of amplifier j and the input of amplifier i represented by T_{ij}. The connection matrix may be obtained by taking the outer product $\vec{v} \times \vec{v}$ (See Fig. 3). This matrix is guaranteed to have the desired symmetry property (i.e. $T_{ij} = T_{ji}$).

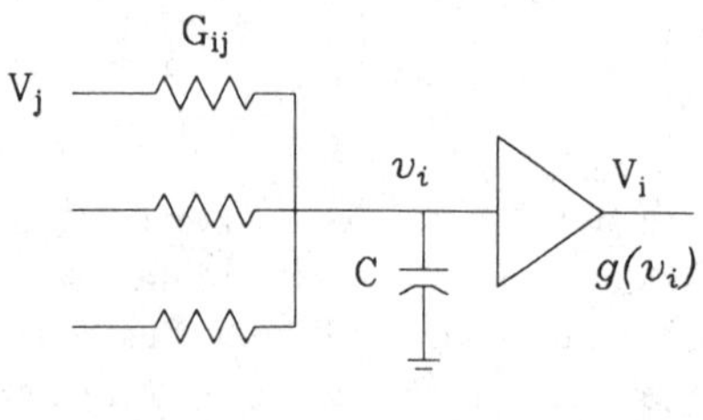

$$C \cdot \frac{dv_i}{dt} = \sum_{j=1}^{N} G_{ij}(\pm V_j - v_i)$$
$$= \sum_{j=1}^{N} G_{ij}(\pm g(v_j) - v_i)$$

Figure 2: Interconnection of active elements, and dynamic behaviour of system.

$$\vec{v} \text{ X } \vec{v} = \begin{bmatrix} +1 & -1 & -1 \\ -1 & +1 & +1 \\ -1 & +1 & +1 \end{bmatrix}$$

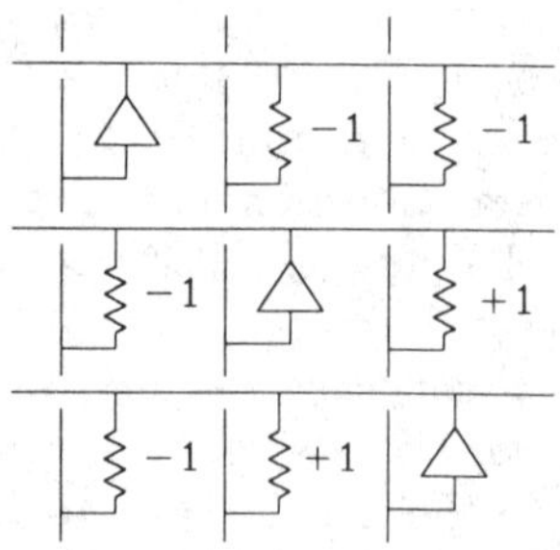

Figure 3: Reinforcement of stable state with matrix generated by outer product technique.

$\vec{v} = (+1,-1,-1)$

The evolution of the state of such a network with time is interpreted as an association in progress. Hopfield has proven the existence of an energy function [5] that the system minimizes. The local minima of this function constitute the fixed-points, or memories, of the network.

Such associative memories have several appealing features. First, it is possible to indicate *confidence* on a bit-by-bit basis, by setting the initial conditions appropriately, i.e. by making certain bits weigh more heavily, if desired. This property allows the ASSOCMEM to accept analog inputs, thus permitting it to process image or sound data. Secondly, all the bits are treated uniformly. The device may be thought of as an error-correcting machine, where randomly-occurring bit errors are corrected. Thirdly, the actual memories are *stored in the interconnect* in a highly redundant fashion, making this architecture naturally fault tolerant. Simulation results have indicated that 10% to 20% of all connections may be destroyed with practically no loss of functionality. If a small number of amplifiers are non-functional, they can still be "out-voted" by the rest of the network, and errors limited to those bits only.

2 The Chip: Design and Fabrication

The first version of the ASSOCMEM was designed in 4μm nMOS technology, and has a dynamically programmable full interconnect. Consequently, every amplifier must be connectable to every other amplifier, dictating a mesh topology with the amplifiers on the diagonal, and their input and output lines running orthogonal to each other. At each off-diagonal node, an interconnection "conductance", G_{ij}, is located. This topology (used in Fig. 3) produces a two-dimensional embedding of the interconnect graph implied by Fig. 2.

2.1 Design of the active elements

In order to achieve a general computation, both positive and negative signals and interconnect values must be representable. It is not possible to fabricate negative resistances, as would be implied by a negative matrix element. The solution was to design the amplifiers to take differential inputs and generate complementary outputs. These inputs may be thought of as excitatory and inhibitory (ie. non-inverting and inverting). This duality allows us to represent "negative" V_j's while using only positive signals. Also, it guarantees symmetry between "positive" and "negative" V_j's, since they are in fact the same voltage, merely on different lines (Fig. 4). The matched parameters of VLSI devices ensure a high CMRR for this configuration.

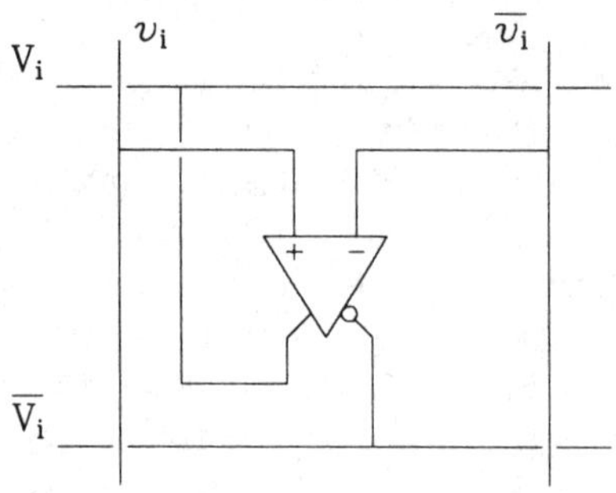

Figure 4a: Dual-rail signal representation

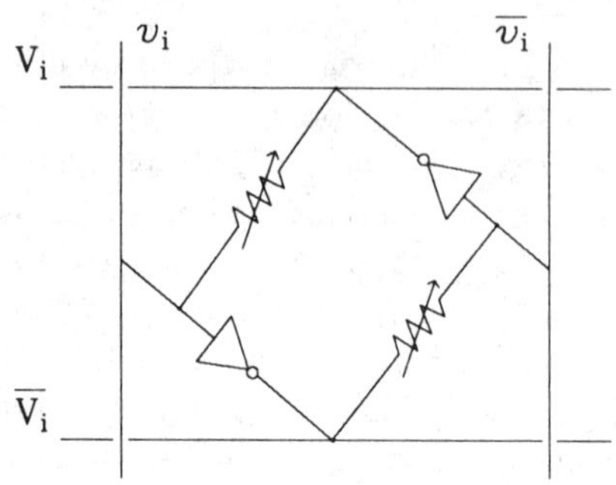

Figure 4b: Variable Feedback in T_{ii}

This dual-rail voltage representation on both input and output to the active elements greatly simplifies their design. The only constraint on the transfer function $g(v_j)$ is monotonicity (to guarantee convergence, by the energy theorem), and that the gain be sufficiently large. A loop gain of greater than 1 is required to create distinct stable states; a high gain guarantees that all outputs will be driven to the rails. We chose to implement the amplifiers with the simplest circuit element possible: an nMOS depletion-load inverter. Two inverters are required for each amplifier: one between the non-inverting input and the complemented output, and one between the inverting input and the uncomplemented output. Note that feedback through the *matrix* is required to ensure that the amplifier outputs are indeed complementary. If the two inverters are replaced by a pair of cross-coupled NOR gates (i.e. a simple SR flip-flop), this complementarity can be enforced at each diagonal (T_{ii}) element.

The design that was implemented allowed for both modes of operation to be tested, by providing a variable strength cross-connection (CROSS_COUPLE) between the two inverters. The circuit diagram for the T_{ii} element is shown in Fig. 5. Two pass transistors, gated on ϕ_1, allow the inputs of the amplifier to be latched. This capability is required for programming the interconnection matrix, and is desirable to halt the operation of the memory, for test purposes.

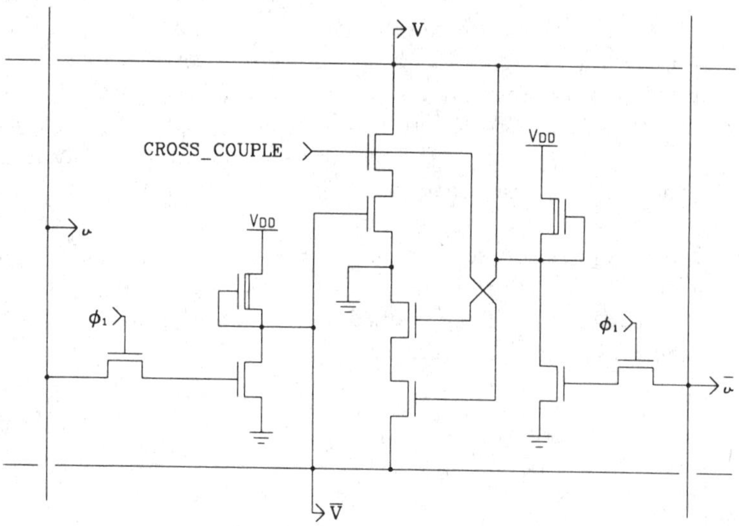

Figure 5: T_{ii} Element Schematic

2.2 Resistive Interconnect

The resistive coupling, representing the G_{ij} matrix, is provided by pass transistors, which constitute the functional part of the "G_{ij} Element" (Fig. 6), located at every off-diagonal location of the chip. These pass transistors are controlled by the tri-flop T_{ij} cell, which provides three interconnection strengths (+1, 0, −1). When $T_{ij} = +1$, the + output of amplifier j is connected to the + input of amplifier i (excitation), and the − output is connected to the − input of the respective amplifiers (negative inhibition $\Rightarrow$ excitation); the opposite is true for $T_{ij} = -1$. If $T_{ij} = 0$, all transistors are disconnected, and amplifier j has no *direct* influence on amplifier i. Each pass transistor is in series with an ENABLE transistor that allows the matrix to be selectively disengaged, providing a "single-step" operation.

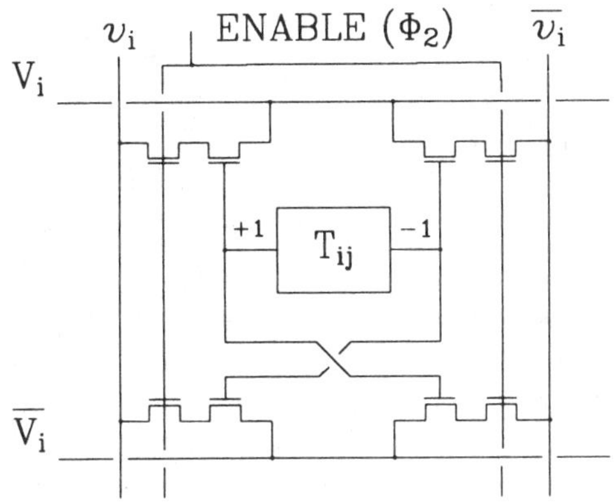

Figure 6: Resistive Interconnect

2.3 Programming the T_{ij} Elements

The associative memory can be programmed to have a particular vector as a stable state by adding the outer product of that vector with itself to the existing T matrix. In the ASSOCMEM, this operation is a primitive of the hardware, and has been generalized to allow taking outer products of any two vectors. The components of the outer product are produced in place at the T_{ij} element where they are required, by placing one vector on the horizontal signal lines, and the other on the vertical lines. This calculation requires only a 1-bit by 1-bit multiplication (for vectors containing +1 and −1 exclusively), which can be implemented by an AND structure (Fig. 7). The result of the correlation is added to the present contents of the T_{ij} cell, and the result is stored in the tri-flop T_{ij} latch.

The addition operation is truncated, and the behaviour is described in Table 1. It should be noted that this operation is *not* associative (the final matrix depends on the order in which the memories were added); however, the symmetry of the final matrix is guaranteed (since all intermediate sums comprised symmetric matrices, in the case of outer products taken of a vector with itself).

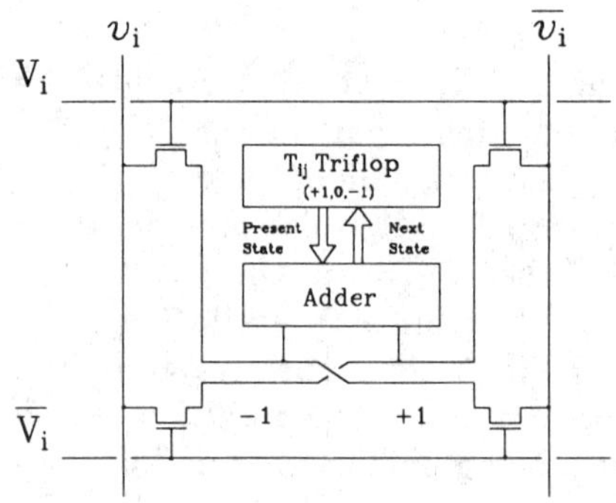

Outer Product \ Present State	−1	0	+1
+1	0	+1	+1
0	−1	0	+1
−1	−1	−1	0

Next State

Figure 7 and Table 1: Programming the matrix

The effect of truncating the matrix in this fashion was one aspect of the theory we were interested in investigating. Software simulation of this scheme indicated that little functionality would be lost, in the case of uncorrelated memories (memories sufficiently far apart in Hamming space, so that no small number of bits become crucial in differentiating between them).

The complete schematic of the T_{ij} element, and the interconnection "resistors", is shown in Fig. 8. It should be pointed out that all but four of the transistors are required just to implement the *programmability* of the ASSOCMEM. In many applications, the interconnect matrix could be determined a priori, and the chip fabricated to this specification. We estimate that 100 times as many active elements could be fabricated within the same die size, for a predetermined function.

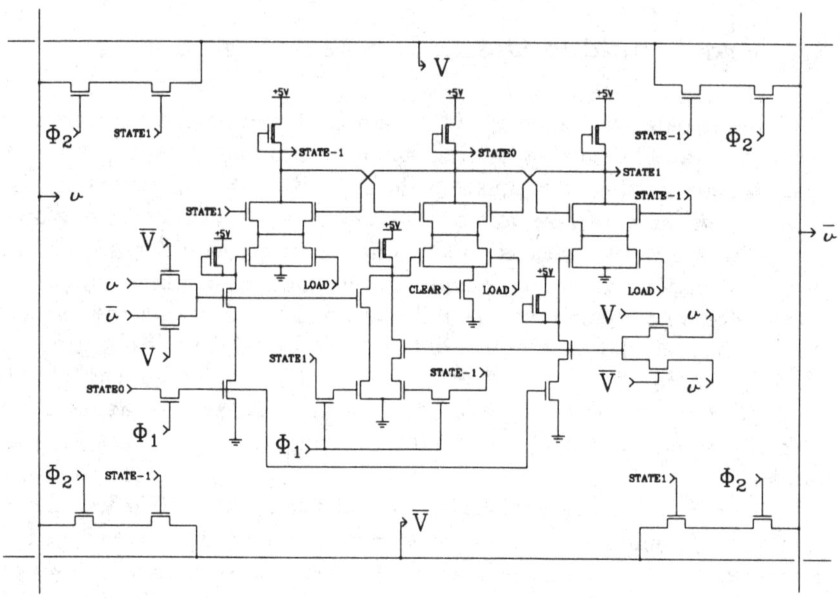

Figure 8: Schematic of T_{ij} element

3 Fabrication History

The first version of this chip was fabricated by MOSIS, the ARPA chip broker, on run M41U, in December 1983. It consisted of a 22 × 22 matrix, measuring 6700μm × 5700μm, and containing over 20,000 transistors (Fig. 9). The ASSOCMEM required 53 pads, as both inputs of each amplifier were brought out to pads. This redundancy was incorporated to increase flexibility in testing the chip. Only one input per amplifier is required, as the complement could be generated on-chip.

A second version of the chip was fabricated in May 1984, correcting some defects that made sections of the first chip non-functional and non-observable. This redesign yielded testable chips; however, the chips were returned unbonded, and only a few could be bonded locally and tested. The yield was low, and no single project was fully functional.

The desire for a larger sample size of chips prompted a third resubmission, which incorporated a set of minor modifications making it possible for MOSIS to package and bond the ASSOCMEM. This set of chips was returned in November 1984, and is currently being tested.

Figure 9: The ASSOCMEM

4 Experimental Results

The ASSOCMEM was tested on a dedicated, workstation-based functional tester. The first sets of experiments were designed to measure the input-output characteristics of the active elements. The input of a single T_{ii} element was connected, (via T_{ij} elements) to the outputs of the other amplifiers. The output of this element was monitored for 220,000 randomly chosen input vectors (this operation corresponds to taking the inner product of the random input vector with a vector that is all 1s).

The resulting output was plotted as a function of the arithmetic sum of the input bits (i.e. the number of $+1$'s in the input vector minus the number of -1's), as shown in Fig. 10. The symmetry of the graph demonstrates that the output is unbiased and the input sum to the active element is balanced for an input vector containing equal numbers of $+1$'s and -1's.

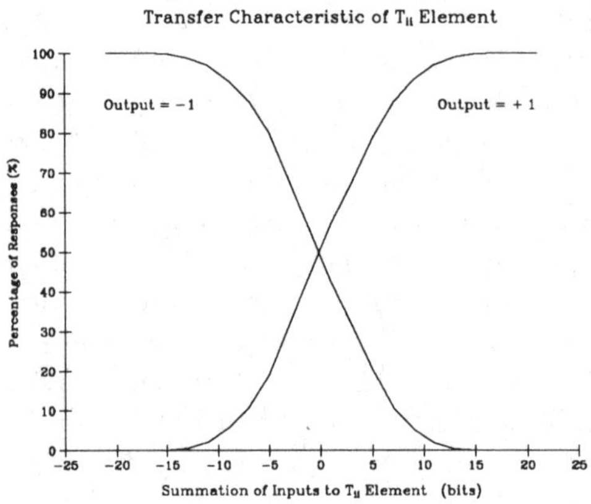

Figure 10: T_{ii} Transfer Characteristic

The ability to arbitrarily set a single T_{ij} element confirmed the functionality of the adder elements and tri-flops within each T_{ij} element. Several ring oscillators were programmed into the matrix, ranging from 3 stages to 19 stages. A typical waveform is shown in Fig. 11. The results in Fig. 12 indicate a characteristic propagation delay of 510ns per stage. The ring oscillators required an asymmetric connection matrix, as oscillatory behavior is excluded for symmetric matrices.

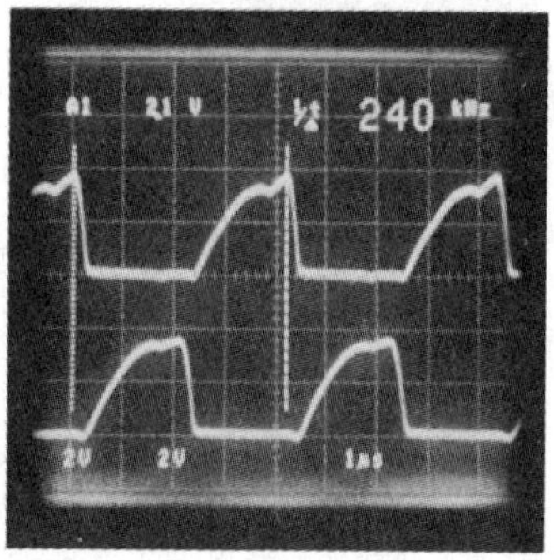

Figure 11: Ring Oscillator

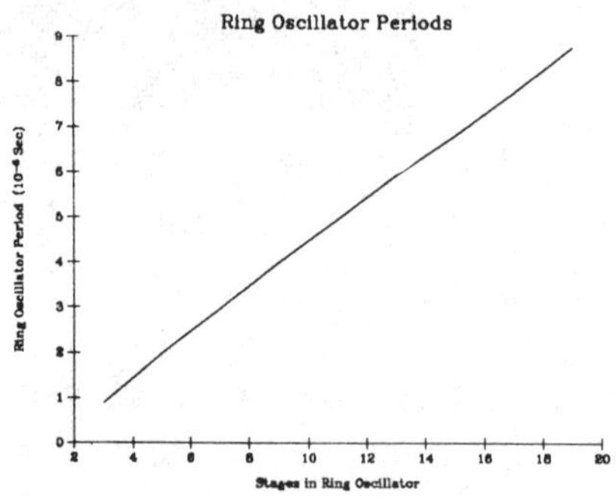

Figure 12: Ring Oscillator Periods

The next experiment was to perform an actual association. Two random memories were programmed into the matrix, via the on-chip outer product and adder mechanisms, and were observed to be, in fact, fixed points of the network. Due to the fast T_{ii} elements, the convergence of the network, including the driving of the output pads, was generally completed within a few microseconds.

If the function of the ASSOCMEM is considered to be that of an error-correcting code, it is useful to consider the final stable state as a function of the bit-errors in the initial state. Typical experimental results demonstrating the distinct regions of convergence for a two memory system are shown in Fig. 13. Effectively, this system always converges to the memory nearest in Hamming space to the initial condition.

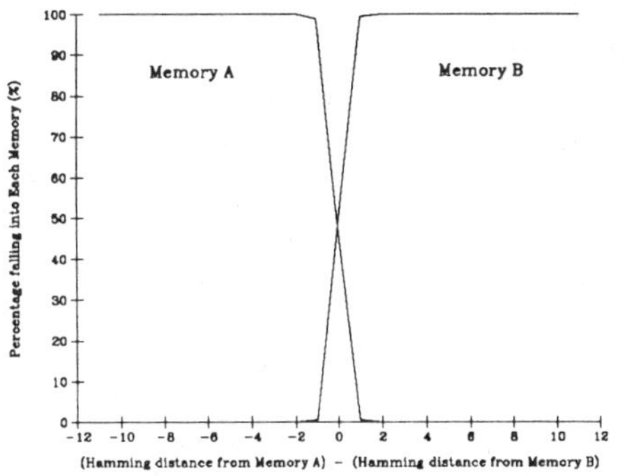

Figure 13: Convergence Properties

By using ϕ_1 and ϕ_2 as non-overlapping "clocks" to successively engage and disengage the connection matrix and T_{ii} elements, it is possible to "single-step" through the convergence operation. Each step corresponds to the network synchronously performing an inner product calculation to obtain the next state from the present state. It can be proven that a network which converges in synchronous-update mode will also do so asynchronously (i.e. ϕ_1 and ϕ_2 ON simultaneously), although the converse is *not* true. For networks that do converge in single-step mode, it is interesting to observe the process in action (see Fig. 14). In this illustration, note that the intermediate results are restored approximations to the analog voltages within the ASSOCMEM, and that although two iterations appear identical, the convergence is not yet complete.

Simulation results [6] have suggested an empirical limit on the number of uncorrelated memories that can be programmed into a Hopfield network to be approximately 15% of the number of active elements. Beyond this, spurious stable states begin to appear, often displacing desired memories. Since the network is based on mutual inhibition and reinforcement, any correlation between memories causes some bits to be weighted more heavily than others. Statistical orthogonality between memories minimizes this effect.

A second limitation on the number of stable states arises due to the clipped nature of the T_{ij} matrix. Hopfield and Feinstein [7] showed that the "attraction" of stable states decays exponentially with the number of memories subsequently added to the matrix.

For the ASSOCMEM, it was found that up to three stable states could be reliably programmed, along with their complements (which appear due to the symmetry of the system). At all stages of the experimentation, consistency with simulation results was observed.

Of the ten chips returned by MOSIS, all were found to be functional to the extent of permitting at least two stable states. A cif defect made a particular T_{ij} element malfunction in all chips. On some chips, sizeable numbers of T_{ij} elements were inoperative. A sample map, from a particularly bad chip, is shown in Fig. 15 ("*" represent good T_{ij} elements). Since care was taken to keep the CLEAR circuit simple, and the matrices on all chips were observed to clear correctly (and totally), it is postulated that the primary failure mode was T_{ij} stuck-at-zero faults. Since null T_{ij}'s do not contribute *detrimentally* to the operation of the network, even the ASSOCMEM of Fig. 15 was capable of memorizing two stable states, and associating to them.

```
Incremental Association:

(stable states  (hex): 0F0F0F, 000FFF)
(vector written (hex): 00000F)

Iteration 0: V = 000000000000000000001111
Iteration 1: V = 000000000011110000001111
Iteration 2: V = 000000000011110000001111
Iteration 3: V = 000101000011110000001111
Iteration 4: V = 001111000011110000001111
```

Figure 14: Single-Step Association

```
I                  ***
*I***********
  I
***I*
    I
*****I
      I
****** I
        I
******   I
          I        ***
***********I*
            I     ****
*************I
              I
***************I* ****
****************I ****
*****************I****
***************** I***
***************** *I**
***************** **I*
***************** ***I
```

Figure 15: T_{ij} Yield Map

5 Conclusions

The ASSOCMEM represents a novel computational metaphor for VLSI. Both the implementation and the functional behaviour of this chip are radically different from conventional digital architectures and algorithms. By implementing a well understood system, such as associative memories, with collective circuit design, we have produced a functional component demonstrating the usefulness of these architectures for solving ill-defined problems. Collective circuits are ideally suited to VLSI, as they require very large numbers of individually simple elements.

In the future, we expect to apply this approach to other applications, including analysis of "fuzzy" sensory data. Development of alternate circuit techniques is also proceeding, with the recent fabrication of a CMOS associative memory based on slightly different principles.

Acknowledgements

This research was funded by the System Development Foundation. One of us (MS) was also partially supported by the Natural Sciences and Engineering Research Council (NSERC) of Canada.

The authors are indebted to Dr. John Hopfield, David Feinstein, and John Platt for many hours of stimulating discussions concerning the nature and properties of collective systems.

References

1. Hayes, J.P., Computer Architecture and Organization, McGraw-Hill, 1978, Sec. 5.3.3.
2. Parhami, B., "Associative Memories and Processors: An Overview and Selected Bibliography", *(1973) Proc. IEEE, Vol. 61*, 722-723.
3. Weems, C. et al, "TITANIC: A VLSI Based Content Addressable Parallel Array Processor", *(1982) Proc. IEEE ICCC*, 236-239.
4. Hopfield, J. J., "Collective Processing and Neural States," *Modelling and Analysis in Biomedicine*, 371-389.
5. Hopfield, J. J., "Neurons with graded response have collective computational properties like those of two-state neurons," *(1982) Proc. Natl. Acad. Sci. USA 81*, 3088-3092.
6. Hopfield, J. J., "Neural networks and physical systems with emergent collective computational abilities," *(1982) Proc. Natl. Acad. Sci. USA 79*, 2554-2558.
7. Feinstein, D. and Hopfield, J. J., private communication.

ANALOG NONVOLATILE MEMORY FOR NEURAL NETWORK IMPLEMENTATIONS

Jay P. Sage and Richard S. Withers
Massachusetts Institute of Technology
Lincoln Laboratory
Lexington, MA 02173-0073

Abstract

This paper describes a technology for implementing electronic neural networks which include on-chip learning capability. The synaptic weight parameters are stored using analog nonvolatile MNOS memory that is written using a special charge controlled technique. Charge-coupling techniques are also used to perform the neural computations.

1 Introduction

Since this paper is the first in a mini-series dealing with the implementation of electronic neural networks using dual-dielectric devices, we will begin by providing a brief tutorial on the subject of neural networks. Since our implementation of neural networks uses metal-nitride-oxide-silicon (MNOS) devices for analog nonvolatile storage in combination with charge-coupled devices (CCDs) for computation and control, we will next briefly describe their operating principles, concentrating on the aspects that relate to the neural network implementation. Of particular interest will be the method developed at Lincoln Laboratory for charge-controlled writing of analog information into nonvolatile MNOS memory. Finally, we will describe how this technique was used to implement a simple neural network that uses the Hopfield model to perform associative memory.

2 Neural Network Basics

In this section we will begin with a working definition of neural networks and a discussion of where neural networks fit in the overall field of information processing. We will then discuss the basic building block — the neuron. Next we will describe how these neurons are assembled into networks, and finally we will discuss the very important subject of learning in neural networks.

2.1 A Definition

Unless we explicitly indicate otherwise, when we talk about neural networks in this paper, we are referring not to real, biological neural networks but to what is perhaps more precisely denoted by terms such as artificial neural networks or neuromorphic systems. It is not easy to define this subject precisely, but, to facilitate discussion, participants in the DARPA Neural Network Study settled on a three-part definition which, slightly modified, reads as follows:

> A system composed of many simple processors, fully or sparsely connected, whose function is determined by the connection topology and strengths.
>
> This system is capable of a high level function such as adaptation or learning with or without supervision as well as lower level functions such as vision and speech preprocessing.
>
> The function of the simple processors and the structure of the connections are inspired by the study of biological nervous systems.

One key idea in the first paragraph of the definition is that, unlike conventional computers, which have a small number of very powerful processors, neural networks have relatively large numbers of generally very simple processors. We will look at those processors in more detail in a moment.

A second key idea in that paragraph concerns how the functionality of the network is determined. With conventional computers, the functionality is established by the program that is loaded into memory and executed. One of the great strengths of conventional computers is their ability to change their function simply by loading a different program. With neural networks, the functionality derives primarily from the architecture of the network and the connection strengths between the elements.

The functionality of a neural network may also depend in a very critical way on the rules according to which the connection strengths are modified during operation of the network. This issue is covered in the second paragraph of the definition, where it is noted that neural networks may learn or adapt based on the data they receive and that learning may or may not be augmented using information from a teacher. Alternatively, the parallel processing power of nonadaptive neural networks may be exploited for preprocessing sensory data.

Finally, the third paragraph indicates that neural network research is motivated — to greater or lesser degrees — by biological nervous systems. This motivation stems to a considerable degree from the fact that biological nervous systems demonstrate unequivocally the ability to perform information processing tasks that we very much want to perform in artificial systems.

2.2 Neural Networks as Information Processors

Neural networks do not offer the only approach to information processing. Indeed, for the past couple of decades, another approach associated with the name "artificial intelligence" or AI has dominated the field. Perhaps because of that dominance and the concomitant low level of support for neural network research from the early 1960s until very recently, there has been an unfortunate tendency to portray neural networks and AI in an adversarial relationship. In fact, it would appear likely that the solution of significant problems like speech and vision will require combinations of the two approaches.

While neither AI nor neural networks is rigidly defined, as generally practiced they tend to have different flavors, as indicated in Table 1. AI generally operates on symbolic representations, while neural networks operate on patterns of activation. AI proceeds deductively based on logic and rules, while neural networks seek inductive, statistical correlations. The rules used in AI tend to be fixed, determined by prior analysis of the problem, perhaps including information obtained from experts. With neural networks, the human effort is devoted to designing the network architecture and learning rules; specific problems are then solved by allowing the network to adapt to training data presented to it.

AI	NN
deductive	inductive
rule based	statistical
based on symbols	based on patterns
based on logic	based on correlation
fixed	adaptive
serial	parallel

Table 1: The different information processing flavors of artificial intelligence (AI) and neural network (NN) approaches.

It is worth repeating that neither AI nor neural networks are circumscribed by these characterizations. There is nothing about AI, for example, that precludes its use of rules that modify themselves based on experience. Conversely, not all neural networks are adaptive; some have fixed weights determined *a priori*. On the other hand, neural networks by their nature are amenable to massively parallel implementation, something that is not obviously possible in all cases with AI approaches.

2.3 The Neuron

The basic building block out of which neural networks are constructed is the neuron. We will be considering three different kinds of neurons: the biological neuron, the mathematical neuron, and the electronic neuron. The last of these will be the main subject of this paper; the other two we will discuss briefly now.

2.3.1 The Biological Neuron

The biological neuron, which serves as the inspiration and motivation for the other two, is illustrated in Fig. 1. The important components to notice are: (1) the neural body, or soma, where it is thought decisions are made; (2) the axons which carry the output signal from the soma; (3) the dendrites that bring signals into the soma; and (4) the synapses that couple axons bringing signals from other neurons to the dendrites of this neuron. Biological neurons actually come in many different forms, so this picture should be taken only as a guide to the nomenclature and basic functioning of the neuron.

2.3.2 The Mathematical Neuron

A mathematical neuron is a model and a set of mathematical equations that try to capture at least some of the features — one hopes the essential ones — of the biological neuron.

A fairly general model of a mathematical neuron is shown in Fig. 2. On the right hand side of the figure, the corresponding biological structures are indicated. According to this model, axonal signals $x_i, i = 1 \ldots n$, arrive at the synapses ji of neuron j and are acted on by nonlinear functions F_{ji} which depend on the input signal x_i and the synaptic weight parameter W_{ji}. The resulting dendritic signals arrive at the neural soma, where they are combined and processed according to G_j, a general nonlinear function of all the inputs F_{ji}. This result is carried by the axons to other neurons.

This mathematical model appears to be highly general. Indeed, it is so general as to be *intractable* without the introduction of some simplifying assumptions. However, at the same time it is by far *not general enough* to describe real biological neurons! For example, it assumes that the state of a synapse can be represented by a single (scalar) parameter W_{ji}. It fact, it may take a set (or vector) of parameters. The model also assumes that the synaptic response at time t depends only on the presynaptic input at the same instant. In fact, it may very well depend on the inputs at previous times as well[1]. Thus the functions F_{ji} should really be *functionals* of $x(t)$ and $W_{ji}(t)$.

It remains to be seen whether or not the mathematical neuron captures enough of the essence of the biological neuron to accomplish the powerful information processing that the latter is capable of. Biology, physics, and chemistry can perform quite effortlessly functions that require enormously complicated mathematics to describe. Thus it is important for us to understand that when we say that neural networks consist of large numbers of *relatively simple processors*, we do not necessarily mean that the mathematical description of a neuron or synapse is simple. Rather, they are simple in the sense that they tend to perform single, fixed functions. They may also be simple in that a physical process can perform the function with ease. That is one of the reasons why we believe that implementation technology is the key element in making effective use of neural networks to solve real problems. Digital simulations of neural networks are unlikely to produce results of practical value.

We will now mention some of the simplifications that are often adopted. First of all, it is generally assumed that G_j and F_{ji} are the same functions G and F for all neurons and synapses, respectively. Second, G is assumed to depend only on the sum of its inputs from the synapses. Thus we have

$$G_j(F_{j1}, \ldots, F_{ji}, \ldots, F_{jn}) = G\left(\sum_i F(W_{ji}, x_i)\right) \tag{1}$$

The function G is usually taken to be a form of step function. One form is the rigorous step function, which has a sharp discontinuity at some threshold value and constant values on either side (typically 0 and 1, or -1 and +1). Another form is the sigmoid, which makes the same kind of transition but smoothly and continuously. The MNOS/CCD network we will describe later uses a function with a sharp step between values of -1 and +1. The setting of the threshold is generally handled by assuming a threshold of zero for the function and connecting one synapse to a fixed external input (x_0) with a value of 1. The synaptic weight parameter (W_{j0}) corresponding to that input effectively shifts the threshold.

A few simple functional forms are often assumed for F. The most common are the following:

$$\begin{aligned} F(W,x) &= W \cdot x & (2) \\ F(W,x) &= (W-x)^2 & (3) \\ F(W,x) &= |W-x| & (4) \end{aligned}$$

The form in Eq. (2) is often assumed because it is very tractable mathematically using matrix algebra. This form is also relatively easy to implement in electronics using, for example, resistors or MOSFETs in their linear regime. It is the one we used in the MNOS/CCD network we will describe later.

With the form in Eq. (3), the neuron effectively computes the Euclidean distance in a multidimensional feature space between a pattern represented by the set $\{x_i\}$ and a pattern represented by the set $\{W_{ji}\}$. The neuron can be thought of as measuring that distance and putting out a signal that is a nonlinear function of it. The network may then select the stored pattern vector $\vec{W_j}$ that is closest to the input vector $\vec{x}$. The quadratic function is nice mathematically but makes this synapse more difficult to implement in electronics. The form in Eq. (4) gives rise to a computation of a Hamming distance instead of a Euclidean distance. It is mathematically the most difficult function of the three to handle, since it is not continuously differentiable, but it is simpler to implement.

[1]Learning, as discussed later, may incorporate some, but probably not all, of this history effect.

2.4 Network Architectures

So far we have been talking about neurons, the building block out of which neural networks are constructed. As complex as those supposedly simple objects have turned out to be, the really interesting behavior of neural networks arises when those unit cells are connected in networks. Fig. 3 illustrates three basic types of interconnect patterns.

Fig. 3(a) shows an example of what is called a feedforward network. The neurons are grouped into layers, three in this case. Neurons in a given layer receive inputs from neurons in the layer immediately below and send their outputs to neurons in the layer immediately above. The lowest layer of neurons generally represents the input signals applied to the network. When output signals from a higher layer are returned as input signals to a lower layer, as shown in Fig. 3(b), the network is called a feedback network. This architecture is the one we implemented in the MNOS/CCD neural network that we will describe later in this paper. Finally, Fig. 3(c) shows a network with lateral connections within a layer. The "lateral inhibition" network, in which an active neuron in the layer tries to inhibit its neighbors, has this architecture.

The feedforward interconnection architectures illustrated in Figs. 3(a) and 3(b) are what is called "fully connected." Each neuron in one layer receives inputs from *all* neurons in the layer below. The network in Fig. 3(c) illustrates sparse interconnection, in this case nearest-neighbor interconnection. Neural networks, of course, are not limited to these simple patterns. They can embody combinations of them, and the connections can skip layers.

2.5 Learning

The ability to learn is one of the most important characteristics of neural networks. It is through learning that they perform the inductive, statistical, correlational analysis of the input patterns to which they are exposed. In many hardware implementations, however, learning has not been incorporated as an integral function of the circuit but has been left to an adjunct digital computer. We have felt that it is very important to incorporate learning directly onto the chip, and the MNOS/CCD circuit we will describe in this paper was, we believe, the first neural network chip that was designed for and demonstrated on-chip learning.

First, learning on the chip may be important because learning may be very computationally intensive and thus may require parallel operation as much as recall does. Second, in the case of analog networks, one of the functions of learning may be to compensate for imperfections and defects in the circuitry. In this case, the chip elements must be part of the loop while learning is taking place, as is the case in biological networks.

In biological neural networks a variety of mechanisms could be responsible for learning. For example, new neurons, axons, and/or dendrites could grow and form new connections. For obvious reasons, this kind of learning mechanism is not likely to be applicable to artificial neural networks. Mathematics would have a hard time describing this process, and technologists would have an even harder time implementing it.

Another learning mechanism is based on changes introduced in the synaptic weight parameters W_{ji} in accordance with a learning rule or algorithm. This is the mechanism used in neural network models and hardware implementations.

One form of learning, called supervised learning, takes place with the assistance of a teacher. In this case the network can be told how its output compares to a desired or correct output. Unsupervised learning, which takes place without such information from a teacher, can be used to perform clustering — grouping patterns into classes that are similar — or memorization and interpolation, so that current inputs that are similar to patterns seen in the past can produce appropriately similar outputs.

Adaptation of the synaptic weights W_{ji} may involve information from various sources. It may be entirely local, depending only on the signals available at that synapse, namely x_i and G_j. Such a learning model makes sense biologically and was in the model we implemented.

It is also possible to provide global information, such as a signal representing the overall degree of accuracy of the neural network's response. Such a signal would be useful in a reward/punishment learning system, where a global signal would say either "good boy" or "bad boy" to all the synapses. They would then use this signal together with their local information to decide how to change their weights. It is not clear how biology would implement this mechanism (perhaps changes in the ambient chemical bath), but it is quite easy to implement in electronics.

Finally, there can be what might be called semi-local learning in which error signals developed elsewhere (such as at the ultimate output from the network) are passed back through the network using the same connections used to compute the forward response. In this case, nonlocal information arrives at a synapse, but additional connection structures are not required. The popular "backward error propagation" model uses this kind of learning.

3 Technology Components

In this section we describe briefly the two technologies that are combined in our implementation of neural networks. The first of these is charge-coupled devices (CCDs); the second is metal-nitride-oxide-semiconductor (MNOS) technology.

3.1 Charge-Coupled Devices

As we noted earlier, the usual function performed by the neural soma on the postsynaptic signals that arrive via dendrites is summation followed by a nonlinear operation on the sum. There are two physical phenomena in electronics that can be used to perform the summation rapidly using extremely compact circuitry: current summation and charge summation.

The most common electronic neural network implementations employ synapses with voltage inputs and current outputs. The currents from all the synapses on a given neuron flow onto a single wire, which by Kirchhoff's law carries a current equal to the sum of the individual currents. Ohmic resistors or MOSFETs operated in their linear regime are often used to implement an approximately linear multiplicative synaptic function (see Eq. (2)).

In our technology, the synapses also have voltage inputs, but the outputs are in the form of packets of charge. As with the networks that use currents, the charge packets from all of the synapses are transferred onto a common conductor acting as a capacitor. By the law of conservation of charge, the total charge on the conductor is the sum of the individual charge packets.

The structures that meter out and manipulate the charge packets are called charge-coupled devices. They can perform a variety of synaptic computational functions. In our network they perform binary/analog multiplication. They can also quite readily perform subtraction as needed for the synaptic functions shown in Eqs. 3 and 4. We will describe the fundamentals of CCD operation now.

3.1.1 CCD Structure

Fig. 4 shows the physical structure of a CCD. Depending on whether you are an electrical engineer or a physicist, you may regard the CCD alternatively as either a MOSFET with many gates or as a string of adjacent MOS capacitors.

Structurally, the CCD consists of a semiconductor substrate, in our case p-type silicon, on which a dielectric layer is grown and/or deposited. In our case, the dielectric layer was a sandwich with a lower layer of SiO_2 and an upper layer of N_3O_4. In most places, the oxide and nitride thicknesses were each several tens of nanometers. In special areas, however, the normal, thick oxide layer was replaced by a tunnel oxide less than 3 nm thick to form an MNOS structure.

On top of the dielectric layer, conducting electrodes (gates) are deposited and patterned. Finally, at the beginning and end of the device, openings are made through the dielectric and $n+$ regions are formed to act as sources and drains for charge.

3.1.2 Electrostatic Relationships

The CCD is operated by applying time-varying voltages to the gates in such a way that packets of minority carriers (electrons in our case) in the silicon are transported from the region under one gate to the region under an adjacent gate. To understand this operation, one must know how the voltage in the silicon under a gate is related to the voltage applied to the gate. We will not present a full derivation of the electrostatic equations for a CCD but will rely on qualitative observations.

When a positive voltage is applied to a gate, free positive carriers (holes) in the silicon are pushed away from the gate, leaving a region in the silicon that is depleted of carriers. At low gate voltages, this depletion region is thin, and little voltage is dropped across it. Most of the voltage applied to the gate is dropped across the dielectric layer, while the voltage at the surface of the silicon (which we call the surface potential) stays near ground.

As the gate voltage increases, the depletion layer becomes deeper and supports a voltage drop that is a larger and larger fraction of the applied gate voltage. At this point the surface potential begins to follow the gate voltage, and less additional electric field builds up across the dielectric. Fig. 5 shows how the potential at the silicon/oxide interface and the field in the dielectric vary with the gate voltage. The curves shown there ignore effects from quantum mechanics and trapped charges in the dielectric or at the silicon/dielectric interface. Inclusion of those effects generally leads to a shift in the curve along the gate-voltage axis.

So far we have also assumed that there are no free electrons at the surface of the silicon. If a packet of electrons does collect at the silicon surface, its effect on the potential in the silicon is quite precisely equivalent to reducing the voltage applied to the gate by the voltage that that amount of charge would develop if applied to a capacitor formed by the dielectric layer. In the case of an MNOS dielectric, charge trapped at the oxide-nitride interface has the same effect: electrons reduce the apparent gate voltage; holes increase it. After enough reflection (aided, perhaps, by actually solving the electrostatics equations), these results become obvious, and we will simply state them here.

Since the surface potential is brought closer to ground by the presence of a negative charge packet, the voltage drop across the dielectric, and thus the electric field there, must increase. This is one of the effects used to control the writing of charge in MNOS/CCD structures.

3.1.3 Visualizing CCD Operation

The operation of a CCD can be visualized using an analogy in which charge packets are represented by water and the electric potential by a gravitational potential. A high electric potential corresponds to low terrain (a deep well), into which water will tend to flow. The surface potential under the sequence of gates in the CCD is modeled by a topographical landscape. Highly doped source and drain regions are like deep reservoirs, whose water level corresponds to the voltage present at their ohmic contacts, through which the level can be set or measured directly.

Charge always flows from higher to lower levels. As the voltages applied to the various gates and diffusions in a CCD are raised and lowered, charge packets of precisely controlled size can be formed and made to move as desired. Since trapped charges in the dielectric act in effect like bias shifts in the gate voltages, MNOS devices can be used to control the operation of a CCD. We will see a specific example of this later (Fig. 8) when we analyze the MNOS/CCD neural network.

3.2 MNOS Nonvolatile Analog Storage

We will now describe briefly the technique developed at Lincoln Laboratory to store analog information in MNOS nonvolatile devices (1). A similar technique can be used with floating gate structures, but we will describe only the MNOS implementations in this paper.

3.2.1 MNOS Structure

The basic structure of an MNOS device is that of a metal-insulator-silicon or MIS capacitor. The essential difference is that the insulating dielectric is a sandwich consisting of a relatively thick layer of silicon nitride over a very thin layer of silicon oxide, a layer so thin that macroscopic quantum mechanical tunneling currents can be developed between the silicon and traps at the oxide/nitride interface with relatively low voltages, such as tens of volts, across the capacitor.

In the conventional operation of MNOS devices using p-type silicon, the silicon surface is held either in accumulation (negative gate voltages) or in full inversion (positive gate voltages). Accumulation occurs naturally when a negative gate voltage is applied; inversion is typically allowed to occur rapidly by providing a nearby $n+$ diffusion as a virtually unlimited source of electrons.

3.2.2 MNOS Operation

When a high negative voltage is applied to the gate, a high field develops across the dielectric that may cause (1) holes to tunnel from the silicon into interface traps and (2) electrons to tunnel from traps to the silicon. Both effects cause a positive shift in trapped charge in the interface traps, which in turn makes the gate voltage appear for subsequent operations to have a more positive bias than it would have had before. Similarly, when a high positive voltage is applied to the gate, carriers tunnel in the opposite direction, the total trapped charge shifts in a negative direction, and the gate voltage appears for subsequent operations to have a less positive bias that it would have had before.

For the Lincoln Laboratory writing technique, the silicon under the MNOS structure is operated as a CCD. With negative gate voltages, the silicon surface will be accumulated as described above, and the same processes will occur, leading to what is called the erased state. When positive voltages are applied, however, the situation is quite different.

As pointed out in the CCD discussion earlier (Section 3.1.2), when a high positive gate voltage is applied with no charge packet present, most of the voltage drop occurs across the depletion layer, and the electric field in the oxide will be relatively small, possibly even below the tunneling threshold. The presence of a charge packet will, as noted earlier, increase the field across the oxide. If the charge packet is large enough, the electric field will reach the tunneling threshold and a current will flow across the oxide barrier. No matter how high a voltage is applied to the gate, however, the total number of electrons that can tunnel from the silicon into interface traps is limited to the number in the charge packet. Although the details are complex, the experimentally demonstrated result is that the shift in stored charge is proportional to the size of the charge packet. As a result, a CCD can be used to control accurately the writing of analog values into MNOS memory devices.

The combination of (1) CCD-controlled analog writing to MNOS nonvolatile storage and (2) MNOS controlled charge transfer in CCDs provides just the right ingredients for the design of a neural network.

4 MNOS/CCD Neural Network Chip

We now turn our attention to the MNOS/CCD neural network that we fabricated to test our technology concepts. We will first describe the Hopfield network model chosen for the implementation. Then we will describe the design of the MNOS/CCD synapse. Charge-transfer diagrams will illustrate the operation of a simplified version of the synapse; the more complex design actually used to implement the complete synaptic function will be described briefly. Finally, test results will be presented.

4.1 The Hopfield Model and IC Architecture

The design of our chip grew out of a visit at Lincoln Laboratory by John Hopfield, who has been responsible for much of the recent renewed interest in neural networks, especially among physicists and electrical engineers (2). Hopfield's associative memory network fit our technology well and appeared to offer valuable information processing potential. Although subsequent studies convinced us that this particular neural network model did not offer any advantages over alternative conventional information processing approaches (3), it did serve well as a technology development vehicle.

The Hopfield network is a fully connected feedback network of the form shown in Fig. 3(b). There are N input signals connected to N output neurons through an $N \times N$ matrix of synapses. The outputs of the N neurons are fed back as the inputs to the network. This network architecture translates very efficiently into a synaptic array integrated circuit with the architecture shown in Fig. 6. Our test chip contains only the synaptic array and neural input summation circuitry. To facilitate testing, the neural processing functions G and the feedback are implemented external to the chip.

The Hopfield model appears in a variety of forms. For our implementation the neuron function G was a sharp step between values of -1 (below threshold) and +1 (above threshold), and the synapse function was the one shown in Eq. (2). Since the synapse inputs have values of ± 1, each synapse contributes either $+W$ or $-W$ to the neuron's input.

The Hopfield model uses a local learning rule with a teacher to tell it explicitly which patterns to learn. For a set k of input vectors x^k to be learned, Hopfield's equation for the weights is

$$W_{ji} = \sum_k x_j^k \cdot x_i^k \tag{5}$$

This can be expressed in an incremental learning form by considering the change in weights when the k-th pattern is added to the information stored in the network from the previous $k-1$ patterns. The synaptic weight changes are given by the expression

$$\Delta W_{ji} = x_j^k \cdot x_i^k \tag{6}$$

For the step function neural response with values of ± 1, the change in weight is +1 if the input to a synapse and the output desired from that synapse's neuron are the same (either both +1 or both -1). Conversely, the weight change is -1 if the input and output are different. Thus, as a logic function, the synapse performs an exclusive-or operation during learning.

4.2 The MNOS/CCD Synapse

Fig. 7 shows the plan view of a simplified MNOS/CCD synapse for partially implementing the Hopfield network. We will explain the operation of this simpler synapse before describing the more complex circuit required for a complete implementation.

Each synapse consists of a three-gate CCD. The middle gate has an MNOS structure and stores the synaptic weight parameter. The output drain of the CCD (D) is connected to a charge-summing bus serving all the synapses feeding a particular output neuron. The input axonal signal is applied to the first gate, where it acts as a binary control signal. The other two gates and the CCD source are connected to control and bias lines.

Fig. 8 shows the potentials and charge flow during operation of the synapse when the network is performing associative recall. In the upper diagram (time A), the output gate (OG) has been biased off (low gate voltage), the synapse weight gate (W) has been biased on (high voltage), and the CCD source (S) has been biased off (high voltage). The CCD drain is driven to a high voltage and then isolated from external signals (floated).

The next operation (times B and C) is to apply a negative-going pulse to the source. When the source voltage is lowered (time B), charge will flow across the axon gate (A) — if it is active — and flood the region under the weight gate (W). If the axon gate is inactive (low voltage, high barrier), then no charge will flow across it, and the region under the weight gate will remain empty. After the source voltage has returned to normal (time C), a carefully metered charge packet will have formed under gate W. The amount of charge will depend on the difference between the effective biases on the axon gate and the weight gate. The value of the latter depends on the amount of charge stored in the nitride traps.

The final step (time D) of the network recall operation involves turning on the output gate and forcing the charge under the weight gate to flow into the output drain, where it combines with the charge packets from all the other synapses connected to the same neuron.

For learning, operation proceeds in a similar manner except that the charge packets under the weight gates instead of being transferred to the neuron diffusion are transferred into nitride traps by applying a high writing voltage to the MNOS gate there. With the simplified structure shown here, it is not possible to form the required charge packets to implement the learning rule. In addition, this simplified synapse cannot handle the bipolar values required for the Hopfield model with neural outputs of ± 1.

In the actual integrated circuit, the fully balanced, differential synapse shown in Fig. 9 was used. This design incorporates two neural dendrite diffusions (D and $\overline{D}$) and two axonal input lines (A and $\overline{A}$). Axon line A has a higher voltage when the input is active (+1) and a lower voltage when the input is inactive (-1). With axon line $\overline{A}$ it is the reverse: high for -1 and low for +1. The neuron forms separate summations of the positive signal components on dendrite D and the negative components on dendrite $\overline{D}$. The net signal is determined by taking the difference between the D and $\overline{D}$ signals.

The synapse has two weight gate regions, W and $\overline{W}$, with the difference between them representing the net weight. In addition, there are two non-MNOS regions called holding wells (H and $\overline{H}$)) that are used during learning, as discussed below. During readout of the network, the bias on the holding gates is made low (high barriers), while the bias on the weight gates is raised so that wells to receive charge are formed there. Both dendrite diffusions are then pulsed as shown in Fig. 8, times B and C. This ensures that both weight gate regions W and $\overline{W}$ will be filled with charge, since the potential barrier under one or the other of gates A and $\overline{A}$ will be low. Once the charge metering operation is complete, the dendrite diffusions are both allowed to float in their high-bias state as discussed for time A in Fig. 8. They now serve as charge detectors.

For the final readout step, the bias on the weight gates is reduced, forcing the charge to flow out of the regions under those gates. The charge will flow across the axon gate with the lower barrier. If the input is +1, axon $\overline{A}$ will block charge flow. The charge packet under gate W will flow to dendrite D, while the charge packet under gate $\overline{W}$ will flow to dendrite $\overline{D}$. The charge difference measured across the pair of dendrite diffusions for an input signal of +1 will thus be

$$Q_{+1} = W - \overline{W} \tag{7}$$

For an input of -1, axon A will block charge flow, and the two packets of charge will flow across the $\overline{A}$ gates to the opposite dendrites. The charge difference for an input of -1 will thus be

$$Q_{-1} = \overline{W} - W = -Q_{+1} \tag{8}$$

This implements the desired Hopfield synapse function of Eq. (2). The balanced design, besides allowing bipolar output values, makes the circuit insensitive to DC bias offsets and other even-order error terms.

The weight-gate regions cannot be used to form the charge packets for learning, because the size of a charge packet formed under such a gate would depend on the information already stored there from previous learning operations. To get around this problem, holding wells with standard, non-MNOS gates are used to form charge packets during learning. The sequence of steps is similar to that described for readout. The first difference is that the weight gates are biased to a low voltage while the holding gates are biased to an active voltage. The second difference is that only one dendrite is subjected to a negative-going pulse. If the desired neural output for the pattern to be learned is +1, then dendrite $\overline{D}$ is given a pulse; if the desired state is -1, then dendrite D is pulsed.

During readout, both weight-gate regions were filled with charge packets. For learning, only one of the holding regions will receive charge. Region $\overline{H}$ will form a packet if the input to the synapse and the desired output from the neuron are the same. If they are both +1, then gate A will be active, dendrite $\overline{D}$ will be pulsed, and charge will enter holding region $\overline{H}$ from below in Fig. 9. If they are both -1, then gate $\overline{A}$ will be active, dendrite D will be pulsed, and charge will enter region $\overline{H}$ from above. Similarly, if the desired input and output signals are different, a charge packet will form in holding well H.

After the charge packet has been formed in the appropriate holding region, the bias on the two weight gates is raised to a high level for writing while the bias on the holding gates is reduced. The weight gate whose associated holding well contains a charge packet will receive electrons, and the stored charge in its nitride traps will shift in a negative direction, reducing the effective bias on the gate during subsequent readout cycles.

4.3 Test Results

The synaptic matrix in the test circuit was small (9×9), and an associative memory network would be expected to store no more than two states. In our testing experiments we wanted to demonstrate two features: the ability to learn and recall an initial state, and the ability to incrementally learn a second state and to recall either of the two learned states.

In the first experiment, the synaptic memory was erased by applying a high negative bias to all the weight gates. Then the first pattern to be learned was applied to the network and stored into the MNOS devices as just described. After that, the network was operated in the readout mode and presented with patterns that were either identical to the learned pattern or different in 1, 2, or 3 bit positions. Fig. 10(a) shows the experimental results in comparison with mathematical results for the Hopfield model. The agreement is almost perfect.

For the second experiment, the network was left in the state that resulted from the first experiment. A second pattern to be learned was then applied and written into the memory incrementally. The network was then operated in the readout mode and probed with patterns that differed from one or the other of the learned patterns in from 0 to 3 bit positions. The results are shown in Fig. 10(b). The network was clearly able to learn both patterns, though the agreement with theory is no longer as good. The discrepancy results mostly from a preference of the network to recognize a test pattern as being the second of the learned patterns. Charge retention losses from the first pattern may have been the reason for this.

5 Summary and Conclusions

Neural networks based on charge-coupled devices for computation and MNOS devices for non-volatile analog storage of synaptic parameters offer a number of advantages over alternative approaches. The synapses and neural input structures allow extremely dense network circuits to be constructed. This follows in part from the fact that the analog synaptic weights are stored in single physical devices and in part from the fact that the computations, both for recall and learning, are performed using physical mechanisms. Addition of signals from the multitude of synapses feeding a single neuron, for example, is performed by the law of conservation of charge.

Representation of neural excitation in the dendrites in the form of charge packets offers specific advantages over other analog technologies. One is low power consumption. CCD operation is essentially dynamic. There is no standby dissipation; energy is dissipated only when charge packets fall from higher levels (low voltage) to lower levels (high voltage). Thus the circuits exhibit CMOS-like characteristics even with NMOS technology.

CCD circuits also scale well in contrast to neural network circuits that represent excitation in the form of currents. Neural networks require extremely high effective resistances in order to keep total currents at a reasonable level, but as transistors become smaller their currents tend to stay the same or to increase. This is good for high speed RAMs but bad for neural networks. In charge-coupled circuits, the quantities of charge scale down automatically to maintain induced voltage changes precisely commensurate with the voltages used to operate the circuits. Thus, there is no circuit difficulty in adapting the circuitry to finer design rules. Another advantage is that the charge-controlled writing into MNOS offers direct control over the amount of charge stored in the nitride traps.

Finally, although we made no use of it in our network circuit, the optical sensitivity of CCDs can be used in implementations of neural networks for vision preprocessing (artificial retinas).

In general, digital circuitry offers higher accuracy than analog circuitry; however, neural networks are generally believed to be (and in a few cases have actually been demonstrated to be) relatively tolerant of device inaccuracies. What neural networks may not tolerate is reduced resolution, since learning algorithms will sometimes not converge unless very small changes can be made in the weights. Analog circuits have virtually unlimited resolution.

The CCD/MNOS writing method we described here is limited to unipolar weight changes, since the CCD channel can support only electrons. We worked around this limitation by using a pair of devices in a balanced circuit, but this approach places constraints on dynamic range. Some neural network models require weight adaptation in only one direction. Alternatively, other implementation approaches may allow writing in both directions.

To conclude, we set out to build an electronic neural network that would, in addition to performing recall, also be capable of self-directed learning, that is, learning using computations implemented within the network circuitry. We succeeded in demonstrating an associative memory network that used charge-coupled computations for both recall and learning, that offered very compact, nonvolatile, electrically programmable and erasable analog synapses, and that achieved on-chip incremental learning.

This work was supported by the Department of the Air Force.

REFERENCES

(1) R. S. Withers, R. W. Ralston, and E. Stern, "Nonvolatile Analog Memory in MNOS Capacitors," *IEEE Elec. Dev. Let.*, vol. EDL-1, Mar. 1980

(2) J. J. Hopfield, "Neural Networks and Physical Systems with Emergent Collective Computational Abilities," *Proc. Natl. Acad. Sci. USA*, vol. 79, Apr. 1982

(3) P. M Grant and J. P. Sage, "A Comparison of Neural Network and Matched Filter Processing for Detecting Lines in Images," *AIP Conf. Proc.*, vol. 151, 1986

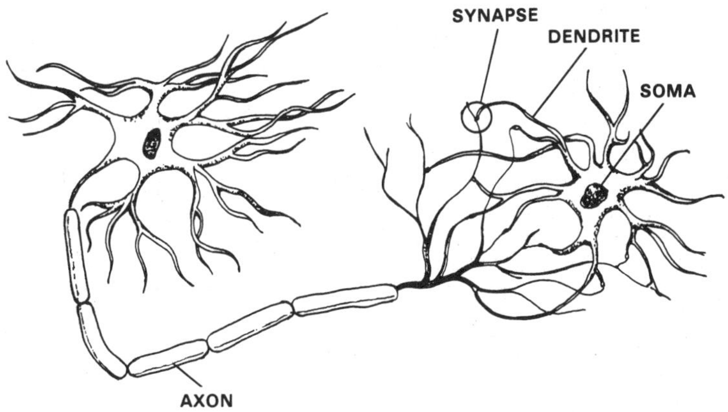

Figure 1: Artist's conception of a typical biological neuron illustrating the principal structures and interconnections.

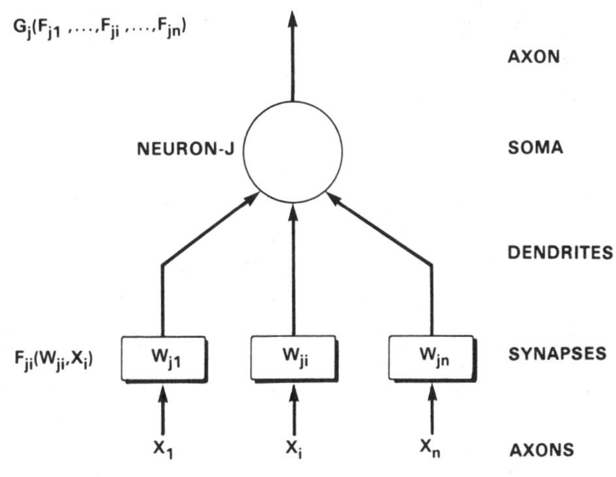

Figure 2: A mathematical model of a neuron, showing the functional relationships and the correspondence to biological structures.

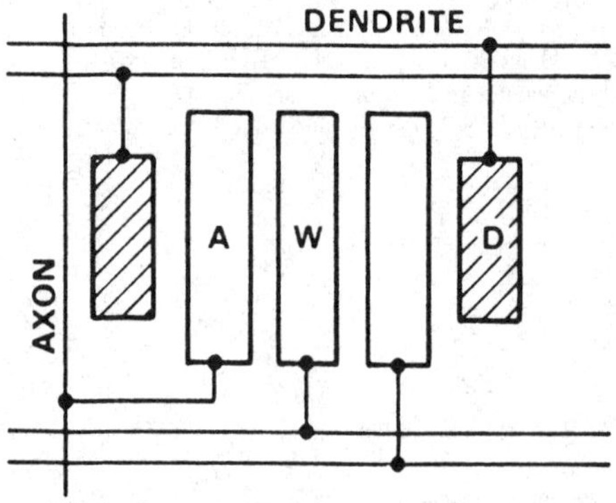

Figure 7: A simplified synapse using a three-gate CCD for performing the functions required in a Hopfield network. The axon input controls the first gate. The second gate has an MNOS structure and stores the synaptic weight. The neuron receives the charge packets from the output diffusion. The input diffusion and the third gate are used for control.

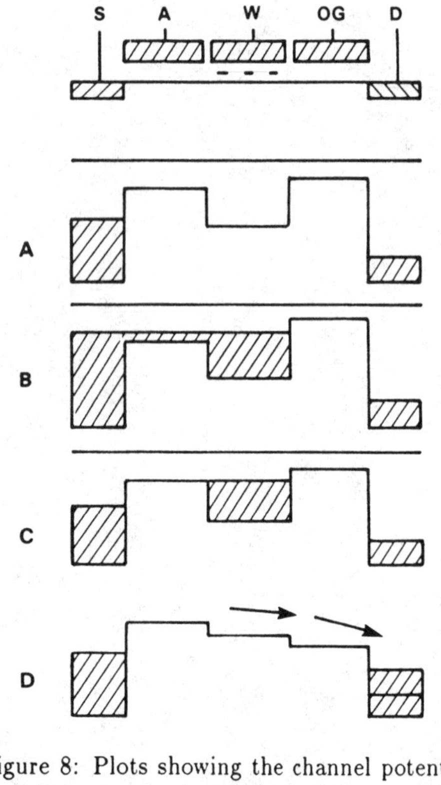

Figure 8: Plots showing the channel potentials and charge packet locations during operation of the simplified Hopfield synapse.

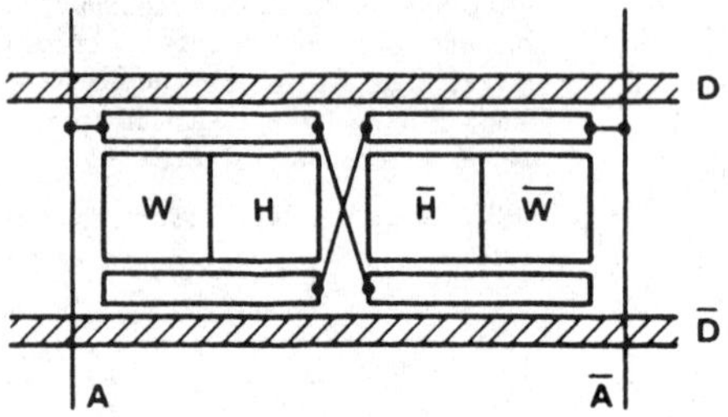

Figure 9: Structure of the more complex synapse used to achieve balanced, bipolar operation in our network. Axons, synapses, and dendrites all occur in push/pull pairs.

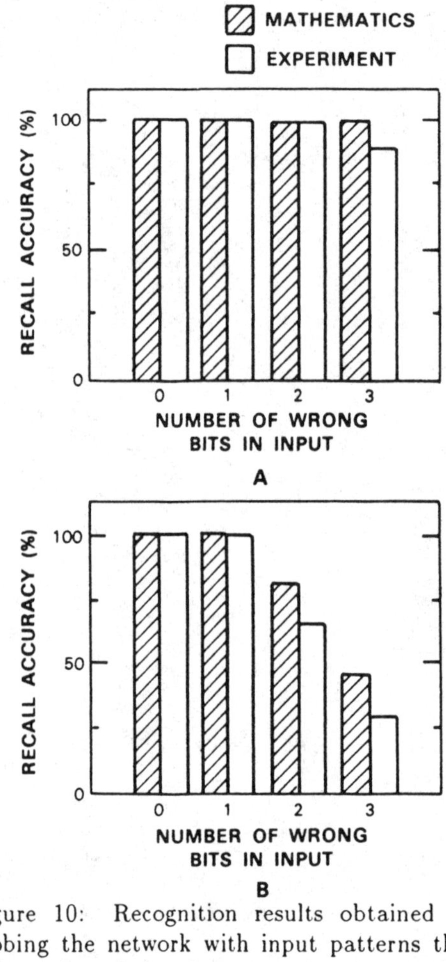

Figure 10: Recognition results obtained by probing the network with input patterns that differed from learned patterns in 0, 1, 2, or 3 of the 9 features representing a pattern. (A) shows the results after a single pattern had been learned; (B) shows the results after a second pattern had been learned incrementally.

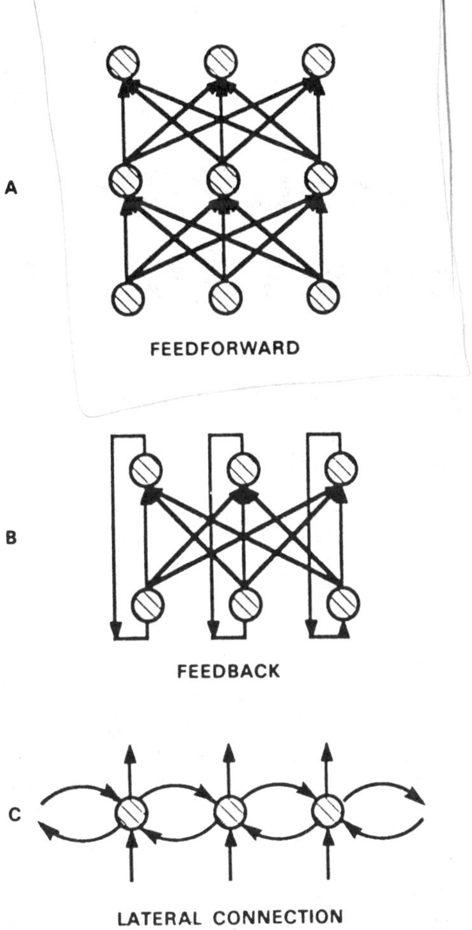

Figure 3: Three examples of network architectures. Form (A) is called feedforward; form (B) adds feedback connections; form (C) involves lateral interconnections.

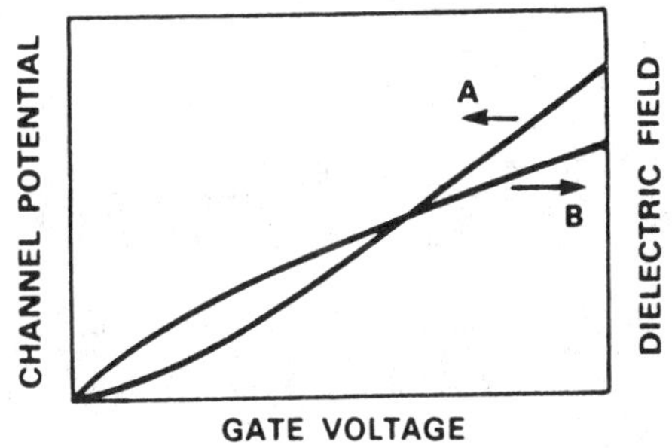

Figure 5: Plot of the dependence on the voltage applied to the gate, of (A) the channel potential ϕ_{ch} at the silicon-dielectric interface and (B) the electric field E_{ox} across the tunnel oxide.

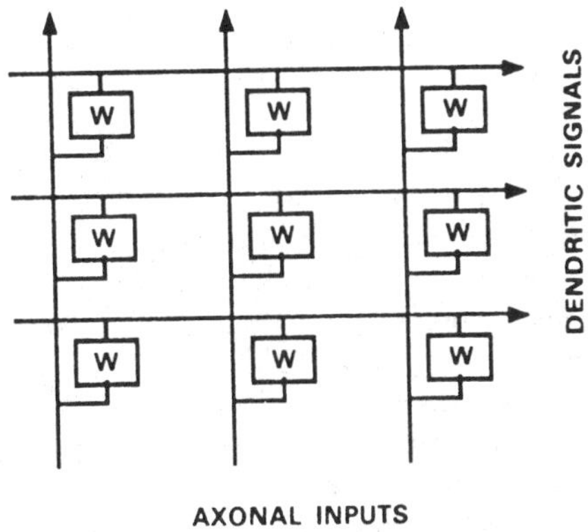

Figure 6: The translation of the network architecture of Fig. 3(b) into an integrated circuit architecture.

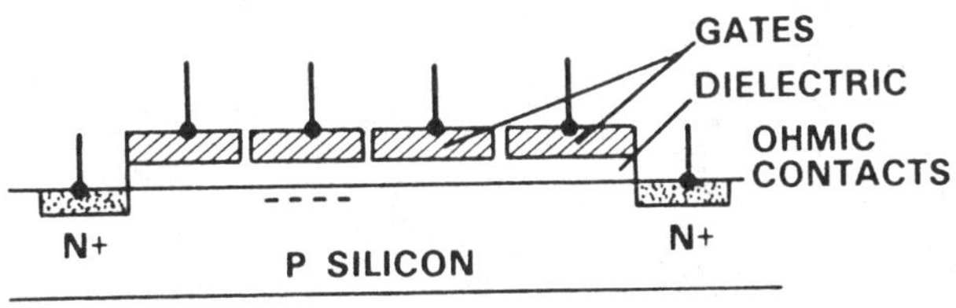

Figure 4: Schematic of the structure of a charge-coupled device. Diffusions at the beginning and end serve as sources and sinks for charge packets, whose movement through the device is controlled by voltages applied to a series of gates which are separated from the silicon by a dielectric layer.

VLSI Implementation of a Neural Network Model

Hans P. Graf, Lawrence D. Jackel, and Wayne E. Hubbard
AT&T Bell Laboratories

Models of neural networks are receiving widespread attention as potential new architectures for computing systems. The models we consider here consist of highly interconnected networks of simple computing elements. A computation is performed collectively by the whole network with the activity distributed over all the computing elements. This collective operation results in a high degree of parallel computation and gives the network the potential to solve complex problems quickly. Neural network models have demonstrated functions such as associative memory, adaptive learning from examples, and combinatorial optimization.

To date, the research concerning neural network models has focused mainly on theoretical studies and computer simulations. However, the real promise for applications of the models lies in specialized hardware, in particular specialized microelectronic circuits. Simulations of large networks on serial computers are painfully slow, and only with customized hardware can we hope to realize neural network models with speeds fast enough for applications.

Digital accelerators to simulate neural networks are now commercially available, but they are still orders of magnitude slower than what we can achieve by directly fabricating a network with hardware. Several researchers have built models with discrete electronic components. These implementations help us study properties such as the dynamics of these circuits, but they are too bulky for real applications.

To obtain the full benefit of neural network algorithms, we need special-purpose hardware. An experimental CMOS VLSI circuit was tested as an associative memory and as a pattern classifier.

The most promising approach for implementing electronic neural nets is to fabricate special-purpose very-large-scale-integration chips. With today's integration density, a large number of simple processors can be packed on a single chip together with the necessary interconnections to make a collective computing network. Several groups have initiated experiments with VLSI implementations and demonstrated a few functioning circuits.[1-3]

Attempts are under way to build neural network models with optics.[4] The high interconnectivity of the networks makes optics attractive because interconnections can be made optically in three dimensions. The circuit on a microchip is bound to the two dimensions of the chip's surface. However, optical computing technology is still in its infancy and realizations suitable for applications probably lie further in the future.

We describe a complementary metal oxide semiconductor (CMOS) very large scale integrated (VLSI) circuit implementing a connectionist neural network model that consists of an array of 54 simple processors fully interconnected with a programmable connection matrix. This experimental design tests the behavior of a large network of processors integrated on a chip. We can operate the circuit in several different configurations by programming the interconnections between the processors. We made tests with the circuit working as an associative memory and as a pattern classifier. The results were so encouraging that we interfaced the chip to

EH2029-3/90/0000/0034$01.00

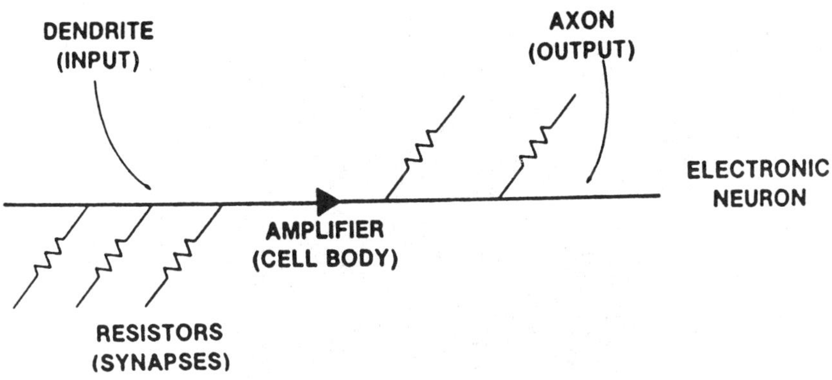

Figure 1. An electronic "neuron."

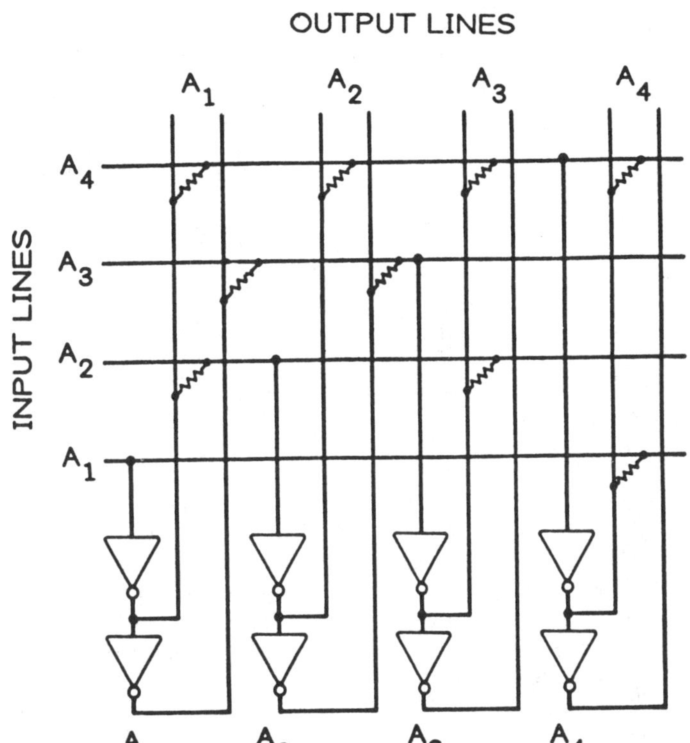

Figure 2. Schematic of the implemented circuit. At each crosspoint of an input and an output line, a resistive connection can be set. All the connections are programmable. The configuration of resistors shown here is just one example. Two inverters are connected in series and work as one amplifier unit. To have the inverted and the noninverted output going into the connection matrix makes it easy to control excitatory and inhibitory connections.

a minicomputer and now use it as a coprocessor in pattern recognition experiments. This mode of operation allows us to test the chip's behavior in a real application and study how pattern recognition algorithms can be mapped into such a network.

Connectionist model

Biological neural networks inspired the models we are implementing in electronics, but we are not attempting to imitate real neurons. Clearly, the models used grossly simplify the biological networks. But even these relatively simple networks have complex dynamics and show interesting collective computing properties. It is this collective computation that we try to exploit by building such networks.

The type of circuit described here is often referred to as a *connectionist model.* In a connectionist model, an individual "neuron" does very little computation, typically just a thresholding of its input signal. The kind of computation performed by the whole network depends on the interconnections among the neurons. Figure 1 shows a possible electronic circuit for such a simple neuron. An amplifier models the cell body, wires replace the input structure (dendrite) and the output structure (axon), and resistors model the synaptic connections between neurons. The amplifier's output voltage replaces the firing rate of a real neuron.

Each of the resistors connects the input line of the amplifier to the output line of another amplifier. Therefore, the state of an amplifier is determined by the states of all the other amplifiers. When the amplifier measures the current flowing into the input line, we can express this as

$$\begin{aligned} Vout_j &= f(\sum_i I_i) \\ &= f(\sum_i (Vout_i - Vin_j) T_{ij}) \qquad (1) \end{aligned}$$

where *Vin, Vout* are the input and output voltages of an amplifier; I_i is the current flowing through one resistor; T_{ij} is the conductance of the resistor connecting amplifier i with amplifier j; and $f()$ is the transfer function of the amplifier.

Equation 1 shows how the states of the amplifiers, represented by $Vout_j$, determine how much current flows into the input line and therefore determine the state of this amplifier. The output voltage of the amplifier is then given by its transfer characteristics. Its output connects to the input of many other amplifiers and influences their states. A network of highly interconnected amplifiers forms in this way. It is very difficult to describe the dynamics of such a system for an arbitrary distribution of the resistive connections, but many special cases can be controlled well and exploited for collective computation. Such networks have been demonstrated as functional associative memory and as optimizers.[5,6]

The implemented circuit well suits work as an associative memory or as a pattern classifier. To have the network perform these functions does not require precise control of the gain of the amplifiers or the ability to fine tune the resistive connections. This makes it possible to design interconnections and amplifiers using only a small area, so many of these components can be integrated on a single chip.

The function described by Equation 1 could be implemented in digital hardware. But this would require a complex multiplier-adder circuit at the input of each neuron, resulting in a large circuit even for a modest number of neurons. The implementation described here uses a mixture of analog and digital CMOS VLSI technology.

Using analog computation, we can achieve a multiplication with a single resistor, and the summing of currents is accomplished "for free" on the input wire of the amplifier. However, designing large integrated analog circuits is a difficult task. There is a strong tendency in signal processing today to avoid analog computation and do everything digitally. Yet the high interconnectivity and relatively low precision needed for the signals in a neural net are well tailored for an analog approach, and the gain in computing power of the network should outweigh the extra design effort.

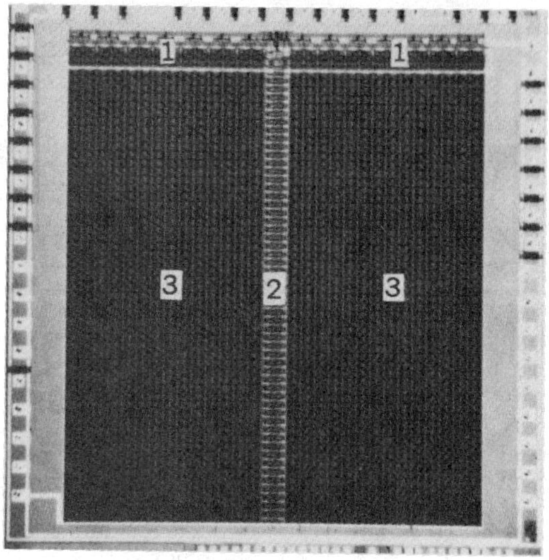

Figure 3. Photomicrograph of the chip. The modules are: 1 = amplifiers, control logic, bit decoder, input bus, and output bus; 2 = decoder to address rows in the interconnection matrix; 3 = interconnection matrix.

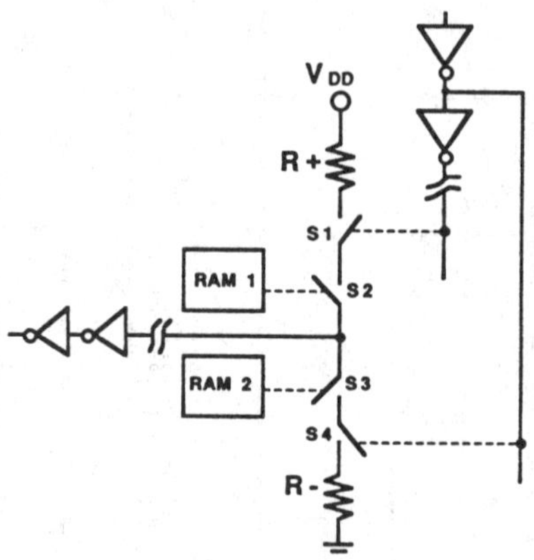

Figure 4. One of the coupling elements connecting the output of an amplifier to the input of another amplifier. S_1 and S_4 are closed when the output of the amplifier controlling them is high (noninverted output high). If a "1" is stored in RAM 1, S_2 is closed and the connection is excitatory. If a "1" is stored in RAM 2, S_3 is closed and the connection is inhibitory. If both RAM cells store a "0," no current flows through this interconnection regardless of the state of the controlling amplifier.

The circuit

Figure 2 shows a schematic of the implemented circuit. It consists of an array of 54 amplifiers with their inputs and outputs interconnected through a matrix of resistive coupling elements. All of the coupling elements are programmable—a resistive connection can be turned on or off.

Figure 3 shows a photomicrograph of the circuit. Fabricated in CMOS technology with 2.5-micrometer design rules, it contains roughly 75,000 transistors in an area measuring 6.7×6.7 millimeters. By far the largest active area of the chip, almost 90 percent, is used for the programmable coupling network.

In this design the circuit shown in Figure 4 replaces the resistors of Figure 2. The output lines of the amplifiers do not feed current into the input lines; instead they control the switches S_1 and S_4. This method reduces the amplifier load to just the capacitance of the output line. For each connection between two amplifiers, two memory cells control switches S_2 and S_3. The content of these memory cells determines the type of connection. One of three connections can be selected: an excitatory (S_2 enabled), an inhibitory (S_3

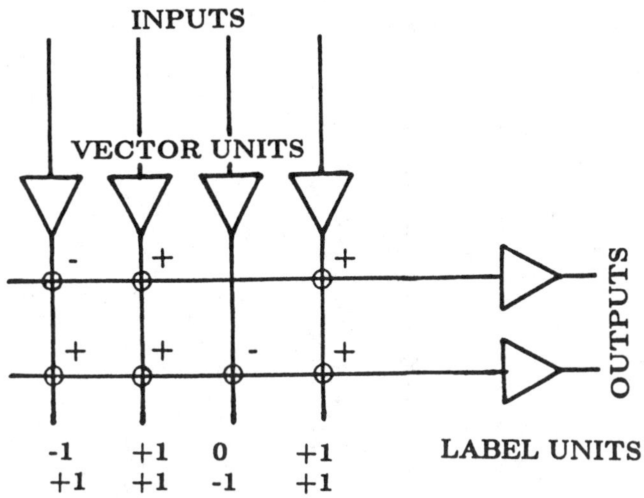

Figure 5. Programming of the interconnections for the pattern classifier circuit. The "+" and the "−" mark excitatory and inhibitory connections, respectively. Below the schematic the stored vectors are shown.

enabled), or an open (both disabled) state. The network contains a total of 2916 such coupling elements. Notice that when an amplifier output is low, the connection turns off completely and no current flows in either direction.

The voltage of an input line of an amplifier is determined by the sum of the currents flowing into the node. This voltage adjusts to a value where the total current is zero. Since the input impedance of the amplifiers is very high, this leads to

$$\sum_{i=0}^{i=N} I_{ij} = \sum_{i=0}^{i=N} \frac{\Delta V_{ij}}{R_{ij}} = 0 \qquad (2)$$

where I_{ij} is the current flowing through a resistor of the coupling element controlled by amplifier i; ΔV_{ij} is the voltage difference across a resistor, $(Vin_j - V_{DD}, Vin_j - V_{SS})$; and R_{ij} is the resistor, (R_+, R_-).

Thus, the voltage Vin_j is an analog measure of the sum of the contributions of all the amplifiers connected to input line j. The amplifiers used have a high gain and work essentially as threshold elements, with the switching threshold about halfway between the ground and the supply voltage. Analog computation is used only within the connection matrix; input and output data and all the control signals are digital.

Data input and output are transferred through a register where one memory cell is connected to each amplifier. The input data are first loaded into this register. From there they can be loaded into the memory cells of the connection matrix, or used to initialize the circuit. Initialization of the circuit is done by charging the network with the voltage levels corresponding to the components of the input vector. The amplifiers are turned off during this initialization cycle. For the computation, the amplifiers are turned on and the network evolves to a stable state without any external control or synchronization between the amplifiers. After the circuit has reached a stable state, the output voltage of each amplifier is stored in the register, which can then be read out.

Programming the chip

The circuit's architecture facilitates mapping several different configurations into the network simply by programming the connections between the amplifiers. Figure 5 shows the arrangement of the interconnections for a configuration used to do pattern classification. The amplifiers are divided into two groups: the label units and the vector units. A number of vectors are stored in the circuit, each one along the input line of one label unit. The components of the stored vectors can have the values +1, −1, or 0. An excitatory connection is set for a +1 and an inhibitory connection for a −1.

The input vector is presented on the inputs of the vector units. Its components can have the values +1 or 0. Wherever a +1 in the input vector is set, current can be injected or drawn from the input line of a label unit depending on the type of the connection. As described by Equation 2, the condition for a stable state is that the total current flowing into an input line equals 0. If the input voltage is above the threshold of the amplifier, this label unit turns on; otherwise, it remains off. Whether a label turns on or not is described by Equation 3:

$$\sum_{i=0}^{i=N} \frac{v_i \mu_i}{R_i} = \begin{cases} >0: & Vout = high \\ <0: & Vout = low \end{cases} \qquad (3)$$

where v_i denotes components of the input vector, $(+1, 0)$; μ_i denotes components of the stored vectors, $(-1, 0, +1)$; and R_i is the resistance of the connections, (R_-, R_+).

The input vector is compared in parallel with all the stored vectors and an inner product between the input vector and the stored vectors is evaluated. All the stored vectors closely resembling the input vector turn on their label units.* A +1 in the input vector at the position of a +1 in the stored vector gives a positive contribution to the sum, while a −1 in the stored vector in this position gives a negative contribution. R_+ is about six times larger than R_-. Therefore, a mismatch (a +1 in the input in the position of −1 in the stored vector) counts six times as much as a match. This ratio of R_+ to R_- has no great significance; it simply reflects the ratio of the resistance of the p-channel and the n-channel transistors of the CMOS circuit. For the applications described later, it is convenient to have the inhibition stronger than the excitation, but we could obtain the same effect by using multiple connections.

By using a few amplifiers as bias units, we can shift the threshold of a label unit. We can program the connections between the bias units and the label units to set different thresholds for each stored vector. The right-hand side of Equation 3 is then replaced by the bias value.

*The classification properties of this circuit correspond to those of a single-layer perceptron; it can discriminate between linearly separable patterns. Since we are dealing with binary vectors, the configuration space consists of the corners of an n-dimensional hypercube. Decision regions of any shape can be built in this space as the sum of linearly separable regions.

The number of stored vectors and their lengths are limited by the number of amplifiers in the circuit. Each component of the input vector uses one amplifier, and each label unit needs one. Therefore, the number of bits in a vector plus the number of stored vectors must be smaller than 54. Usually, a few amplifiers are used for biases, reducing this number to approximately 50.

This arrangement uses only the connections between the outputs of the vector units and the inputs of the label units, while the largest part of all the connections in the matrix remains idle. We can achieve a more efficient use of the circuit by using the register cells as the vector units. The arrangement described uses these cells only as intermediate storage for the input vector, but they can also charge the matrix to its initial condition. All the amplifiers then work as label units. Up to 54 vectors, each 54 bits long, can be stored in the network and are compared in parallel to the input vector. To read out the result, the register cells must switch quickly from writing the input vector to reading the result without feeding the result back into the connection matrix. This requires a precisely timed pulse controlling the length of time the amplifiers are turned on. This mode of operation is used for feature extraction from images (see the section "Examples of applications").

Adding inhibitory connections between the label units and connecting the outputs of the label units to the inputs of the vector units can yield an associative memory. This arrangement is shown schematically in Figure 6. In this circuit, vectors with components +1 and 0 are stored. In addition to the connections along the input lines of the label units described above, there are inhibitory connections between all the label units. Each label unit inhibits all the other label units, but not itself. For the connections between the label outputs and the vector inputs, the same vector is placed along the output line of a label unit stored along its input line. For a +1 in the vector, an excitatory connection is set, and for a 0, an inhibitory connection is set.

The circuit is initialized with all input lines of the label units discharged to ground. The input vector is given on the input lines of the vector units. Wherever a +1 in the input vector and in a stored vector occupy the same position, current is injected into the input line of a label unit. The speed at which an input line of a label unit changes state depends on the inner product of the input vector and a stored vector. That is,

$$\frac{dV_{in}}{dt} = \frac{1}{CR_+}(V_{DD} - V_{in}) \sum_{i=1}^{N} v_i \mu_i \qquad (4)$$

where V_{in} is the voltage of the input line; C is the capacitance of the input node of a label; R_+ is the resistance of the excitatory connection; v_i denotes the components of the input vector, (0, +1); and μ_i denotes the components of the stored vector, (0, +1).

The stored vector that has the largest inner product with the input vector will turn on its label unit first. As one label unit turns on, it inhibits all the other label units. If this inhibition is strong enough, no other label unit will turn on.

As mentioned above, an inhibition is six times stronger than an excitation. This limits the allowed mutual overlap (number of common 1's) of two stored vectors to five bits; biases are used to circumvent this limitation. The label unit that comes on first generates the vector stored along its output wire at the inputs of the vector units. In this way, in a stable state one label unit is on and the vector connected to that label appears at the outputs of the vector units.

This circuit performs a minimum distance classification. The input vector is compared with all the stored vectors in parallel, and the circuit determines which of them most closely matches the input vector (common 1's are counted).

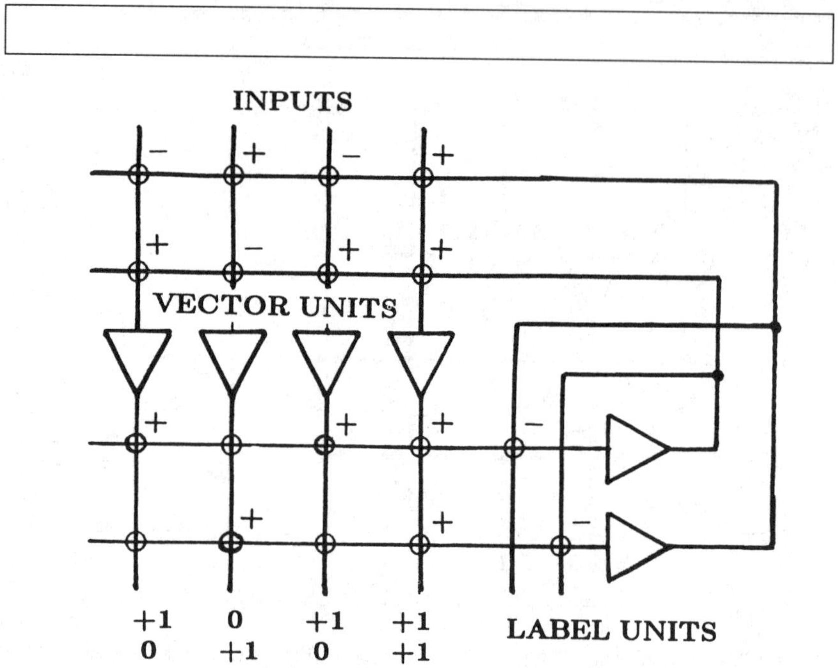

Figure 6. The interconnections set for an associative memory circuit.

Extensive tests with 10 stable states, each 40 bits long, programmed into the associative memory circuit showed that the circuit converges to a stable state in 50 to 600 nanoseconds.[2] Associative recall performed reliably, and we observed only the stable states programmed into the circuit; we saw no spurious stable states. The convergence time depends on how closely the input vector resembles the stored states. Additional tests run with up to 20 stable states, each 30 bits long, programmed into this circuit obtained similar results.

In this circuit the stored data are represented locally in the interconnection matrix. This means that a stored bit can be localized at one or two of the interconnections. In contrast, other circuits based on neural network models use a distributed representation of the data (e.g., the outer product of a stored vector determines the distribution of the connections).

The great interest in associative memory circuits implemented with neural network models has resulted in the description of several programming methods.[5,7] Experiments conducted with this type of associative memory soon made clear the far

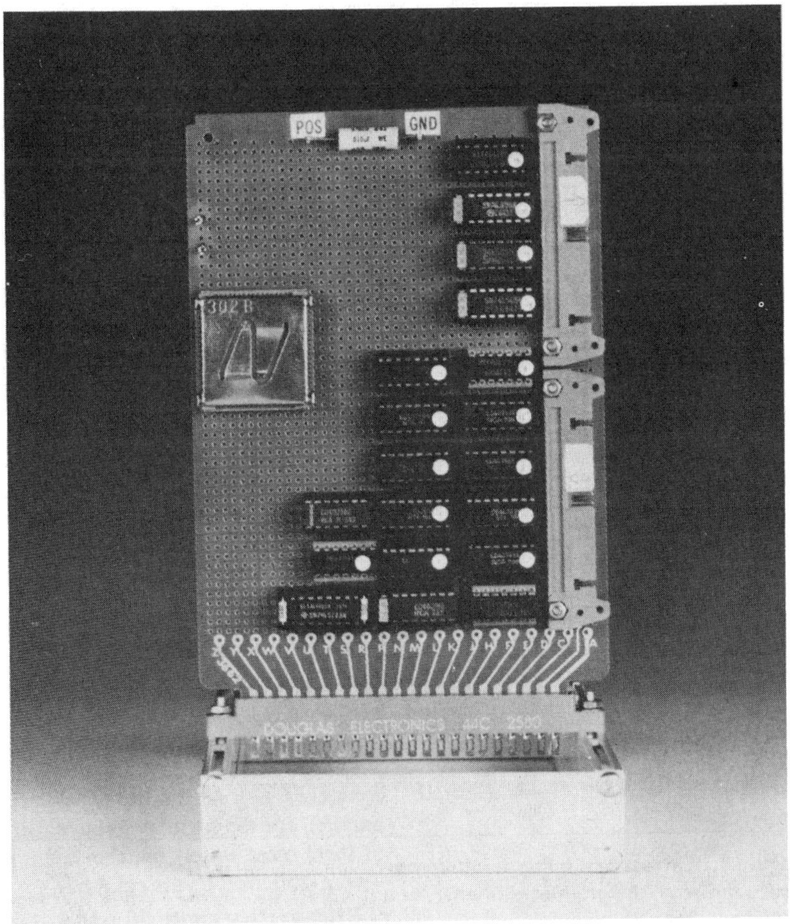

Figure 7. The interface connecting the chip to a minicomputer. The network chip is on the left side of the board. The other chips control the data exchange with the computer.

superior results given by local representation of data. With distributed representation of data, the different stored vectors influence each other because they share the same interconnections. This leads to unwanted spurious stable states and to erroneous recalls of vectors that do not correspond to the nearest neighbor.

These problems do not exist in the circuit we describe here. We observed reliable recall of the nearest neighbor and no unwanted stable states. Moreover, the storage density is considerably higher with this circuit. With a distributed representation of the data, it would hardly be possible to get 20 arbitrary stable states in this circuit. But the arrangement described here still does not use the interconnections of the chip efficiently. None of the connections among the vector units are used. In the case of 10 stored vectors, this means that less than one third of all the connections are used.

With the present chip we do not see a way to further increase storage efficiency. However, a design optimized for this new associative memory circuit can achieve 100 percent storage density.[2] This means that one RAM cell stores one bit. In contrast, associative memory circuits with distributed representation of data typically require five or more RAM cells to store one bit. High storage efficiency is crucial for an electronic implementation. Other researchers have recently proposed circuits similar to the associative memory we have described.[8,9]

We can configure the circuit to move through a sequence of vectors by placing a vector along the output line of a label that differs from the vector along its input line. Mixing connections of two vectors can stabilize the circuit at a vector and make it sensitive to the next vector in the sequence only. When the input lies within a set range of this vector, the circuit will move to the next stable state. Otherwise, it just stays in its present state. Other versions of programming techniques allow for omissions and branches in a parsed sequence of vectors.[10]

Examples of applications

In order to evaluate the behavior of the circuit in an application, we used it in a character recognition experiment. An interface connected the chip to a minicomputer to handle the transfers of the large amounts of data characteristic of image processing requests.

Figure 7 shows the board with the network chip and some additional off-the-shelf integrated circuits to control data flow. Data transfers can be made directly from the minicomputer's memory to the chip at a rate between one and two megabytes per second. This rate is limited by the interface and the minicomputer and not by the chip. One complete processing cycle, which includes loading the input vector, accomplishing a computation with the circuit, and reading back the result into the computer, requires approximately 25 clock cycles or 25 to 50 microseconds. Most of the time is required for reading the data in and out. The processing in the circuit requires only one clock cycle.

The whole process of recognizing a character proceeds as follows: A handwritten character is read with a camera, digitized, and then normalized in size to fill a 128 × 128-pixel frame. The image is then coarse-blocked into a 16 × 16-pixel binary image. After this, the character is *skeletonized*—the width of the lines is reduced to one pixel—and the skeletonized picture is searched for a number of geometrical features. The positions of these features are compared to a training set and a best match with one of these training characters is determined. Of this whole process, the line thinning and the feature extraction have been mapped onto the chip; the minicomputer accomplishes the remaining operations.

Figure 8 shows an example of a result of the line thinning operation. The chip is used in the configuration of Figure 5 for this task. Stored in the circuit are 20 different vectors, each representing a 5 × 5-pixel area. The input vector to the chip is a 5 × 5-pixel region of the character image, which we will refer to as a *card*. Based on which label units are on after a run, a decision is made whether or not to delete the center pixel of this card from the image. For the next run the card is shifted by one row or column of pixels on the image; this new card is used as the input vector. In this way the whole picture is scanned. For each pixel position, a processing cycle is accomplished with the appropriate card as the input vector. For each pixel in the image, a decision has to be made whether that pixel makes the line fat or whether its presence is crucial to keeping intact the connectivity of the character.

Figure 9 shows an example of a vector stored in the circuit to make one such decision. If the label connected to this vector turns on, then the center pixel is part of a diagonal line or a corner and that line is at least two pixels wide. In this situation, the pixel can be deleted without destroying the connectivity of the character. The 20 vectors stored on the chip analyze the neighborhood of each pixel for all the configurations that allow its deletion. All the computation needed to decide whether a pixel can be deleted is done in one clock cycle. A total line-thinning operation requires about three scans across the whole character, depending on the width of the lines because only boundary pixels are deleted.

Line thinning is an important step in machine vision, not only in character recognition, but also in tasks like fingerprint analysis and inspection of manufactured parts. Many algorithms have been developed to handle this problem.[11] The algorithm implemented with the network circuit does not differ fundamentally from other pixel-based algorithms. The stored vectors facilitate making the same type of tests as those formulated in the other algorithms with a set of Boolean functions. Most other algorithms base their decision on a 3 × 3 area around the pixel under test, since the test of larger areas becomes very time consuming. However, with the network it is not a problem to analyze the larger 5 × 5 pixel area, since it still takes only one clock cycle. Using a larger area makes the algorithm more robust, and it supports integrating some smoothing to enhance the thinning operation.

To accomplish the extraction of geometrical features, 40 vectors are stored in the

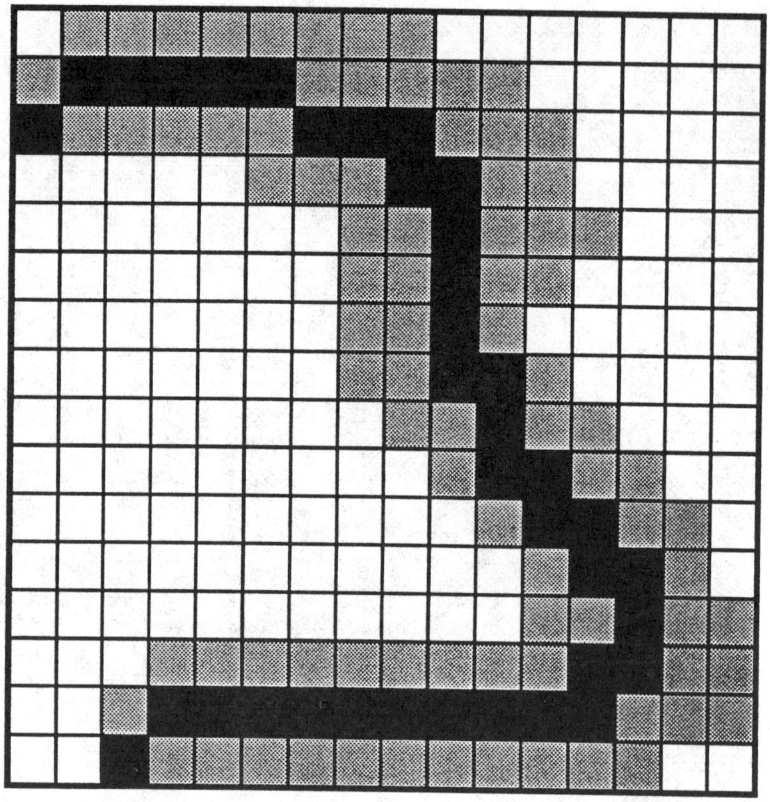

Figure 8. The result of a line-thinning operation on a handwritten "3." The gray area represents the original character, and the black area is the portion that remains after three thinning scans.

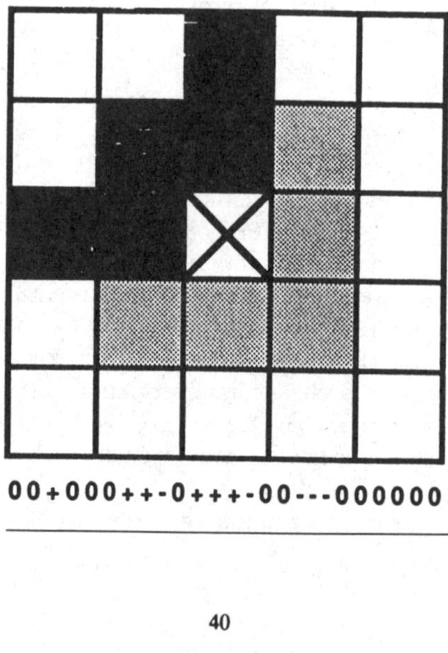

00+000++-0+++-00---000000

Figure 9. One of the kernels stored in the chip for the line-thinning operation. If the label connected to this vector turns on, the center pixel is erased in the image. The black pixels are coded as excitatory connections (+) and the gray pixels as inhibitory connections (−). The bias is set to −4. The label turns on whenever five black pixels in the image correspond to the black pixels in this kernel and no black pixel in the image is at a position of a gray pixel in the kernel. Then, the center pixel is a part of the boundary of a thick diagonal line or a corner and can be deleted.

circuit. Each one looks for a feature like a straight line, an endpoint of a line, a corner, crossing lines, or an arc. Whenever one of these features is present in the image, the label of this feature-vector turns on.

The image is scanned sequentially, as described for the line-thinning operation. For every pixel position, a 7×7 pixel neighborhood is searched in parallel for the 40 different features. Such a scan results in 40 feature maps that indicate where particular features occur. To compress this large amount of data, the resolution of the feature maps is then reduced from 16×16 to 3×3 positions. These feature maps are compared with reference characters and the best match is chosen. Currently, the minicomputer accomplishes this last matching operation, but a way to map this final operation onto the network circuit is under development.

The successful recognition rate for hand-written digits is approximately 90 percent. We assume that we can improve this rate considerably by using finer resolution for the character images as well as the feature maps. We now use only local geometrical features of a maximum size of 7×7 pixels. We can expect better results when large features such as long strokes or large circles are generated first from these local features. However, the main purpose of this experiment was to test the circuit's performance and to gain experience programming different algorithms into the network. We have not yet pushed the analysis to find the highest recognition rate.

Character recognition based on feature extraction is more robust against distortions than simple template-matching algorithms that compare the pixel positions of the whole character to reference data. Feature extraction is one of the most versatile functions of low-level machine vision and can be applied to many problems.

Discussion

We have tested the circuit with several programmed algorithms and conclude that a network like this one is reliable and robust enough for applications. We designed this circuit to study the behavior of a large analog network and did not specialize it for any particular application. Since input and output of data limit the processing, we must optimize the I/O structure in new designs for particular applications.

The analog portion of the circuit represents a very powerful processor. With 50 stored vectors, each 50 bits long, the chip completes a processing cycle in less than one microsecond. This means that the circuit evaluates 50 inner products between two 50-bit vectors per microsecond. On a standard microprocessor this computation would require more than one hundred instructions.

A new chip being fabricated was designed specifically for image processing. The input vector is shifted in a shift register along the inputs of the amplifiers. In this way a new input vector is ready for a computing cycle at each clock cycle when a card of 8×12 pixels is scanned over an image. It is possible to store 46 vectors, each 96 bits long, and simulations indicate that a complete program cycle can be accomplished in approximately 100 nanoseconds.

This circuit will evaluate several hundred million inner products between two 96-bit vectors per second. For example, the circuit can do the line-thinning operation described above at a rate of a few hundred microseconds per character compared to the few hundred milliseconds per character a standard computer takes.[10] (With character sizes of 32×32 pixels, each scan requires 1024 cycles if the whole area is scanned; about three scans are required.)

This new design is fabricated with the same conservative 2.5 micrometer CMOS process. Switching to smaller design rules will allow packing considerably more circuitry on a single chip. Also, since this network is implemented with a standard digital fabrication process, it can be combined easily with other memory and processor modules on the same chip to enhance its versatility.

A system concept with a layered structure is also under development. In this scheme a layer of network processors is followed by a memory module, with several of these units stacked in series. In an application like character recognition, the different tasks such as line thinning or feature extraction are then done in different processor layers. Each layer of processors inputs the data from the memory module below it and outputs its results in the memory module above it.

The data flows mainly in one direction, from the raw data at the input of the lowest layer to the output layer that does the pattern identification. However, communication is also provided in the opposite direction, so that results from a higher layer can determine the operation performed in a lower level. This feature facilitates scanning certain areas in the image with a different resolution, or scanning the image for different features when the results in the higher levels are ambiguous. We need additional research on the mapping of different algorithms into the network, and how to format the data optimally to feed from one network into the next with minimal intermediate reformatting.

The network described provides a flexible tool because it can evaluate Boolean expressions and arithmetic equations. Methods of statistical as well as structural pattern recognition can be mapped into the chip. Ideas from the artificial intelligence community on bit-mapped classifiers[12] suggest that expert systems could be made from this network. With all these elements at hand, this network looks promising for building powerful recognition systems. □

Hans Peter Graf is a member of the technical staff at AT&T Bell Laboratories. He is doing research on collective computing systems and has designed several CMOS chips implementing connectionist neural network models. He has also been involved in the development of microfabrication processes of resistive connections with submicron dimensions for neural network circuits.

Graf received the diploma in physics in 1976 and the PhD in 1981 from the Swiss Federal Institute of Technology in Zurich, Switzerland.

Lawrence D. Jackel has been at AT&T Bell Laboratories since 1975 and is now head of the Device Structures Research Department. His current research interests include the physics, fabrication, and application of devices with nanometer scale features and electronic neural networks.

Jackel received the BA degree in physics from Brandeis University in 1969 and the PhD degree from Cornell University in 1976. His thesis research was in the physics and applications of superconducting weak links.

Wayne E. Hubbard is a member of the technical staff at AT&T Bell Laboratories, where he has been involved in such diverse projects as optical recording, vapor phase epitaxial growth systems, and currently, neural networks.

Hubbard began his career in electronics and computer science in 1969 at RCA, then served six years with the US Navy Tactical Data Systems. From 1976 until joining Bell Labs in 1982, he worked for Digital Equipment Corp. as a district support engineer.

Readers may write to the authors at AT&T Bell Laboratories, Room 4G320, Holmdel, NJ 07733.

Acknowledgments

We acknowledge many helpful discussions with Henry Baird, John Denker, Richard Howard, and Sara Solla. We designed the chips with the MULGA design tools, and acknowledge the support of Brian Ackland and Robert Clark in using these tools.

References

1. M.A. Sivilotti, M.R. Emerling, and C.A. Mead, "VLSI Architectures for Implementation of Neural Networks," *Proc. Conf. Neural Networks for Computing*, J.S. Denker, ed., 1986, American Institute of Physics Conf. Proc. 151, pp. 408-413.
2. H.P. Graf and P.G.N. deVegvar, "A CMOS Implementation of a Neural Network Model," *Advanced Research in VLSI, Proc. Stanford Conf. 1987*, P. Losleben, ed., MIT Press, Cambridge, Mass., 1987, pp. 351-367.
3. J.P. Sage, K. Thompson, and R.S. Withers, "An Artificial Neural Network Integrated Circuit Based on MNOS/CCD Principles," *Proc. Conf. Neural Networks for Computing*, 1986, J.S. Denker, ed., American Institute of Physics Conf. Proc. 151, pp. 381-385.
4. Y.S. Abu-Mostafa and D. Psaltis, "Optical Neural Computers," *Scientific American*, March 1987, pp. 88-95.
5. J.J Hopfield, "Neurons with Graded Response Have Collective Computational Properties Like Those of Two State Neurons," *Proc. Academy of Science USA*, Vol. 81, 1984, pp. 3088-3092.
6. D.W. Tank and J.J. Hopfield, "Simple 'Neural' Optimization Networks: An A/D Converter, Signal Decision Circuit, and Linear Programming Circuit," *IEEE Trans. Circuits and Systems*, Vol. CAS-33, 1986, pp.533-541.
7. J.S. Denker, "Neural Network Models of Learning and Adaptation," *Physica D*, Vol. 22D, 1986, pp. 216-232.
8. J. Moody, "Perspectives on Associative Memories," *Proc. IEEE First Int'l Conf. Neural Networks*, M. Caudill and C. Butler, eds., IEEE, 1987.
9. R.P. Lippmann, "An Introduction to Computing with Neural Nets," *IEEE Acoustics, Speech, and Signal Processing*, Vol. 4, 1987, pp. 4-22.
10. P.G.N. deVegvar and H.P. Graf, "Studies of Associative Memory and Sequence Analyzer Circuits on a Programmable Neural Network Chip," to be published. Contact Graf for preprint copies.
11. N.J. Naccache and R. Shingal, "SPTA: A Proposed Algorithm for Thinning Binary Patterns," *IEEE Trans. Systems, Man, and Cybernetics*, Vol. SMC14, 1984, pp. 409-418.
12. P.W. Frey, "A Bit-Mapped Classifier," *Byte*, Nov. 1986, pp. 161-172.

A Programmable Analog Neural Network Chip

DANIEL B. SCHWARTZ, RICHARD E. HOWARD, MEMBER, IEEE, AND WAYNE E. HUBBARD

Abstract —The parallelism inherent in neural network algorithms is thrown away when they are implemented on digital hardware, resulting in learning that is slow even after careful optimization. A more natural approach is to build real networks with analog VLSI—retaining the parallelism of the algorithm and allowing for some degree of fault tolerance since the circuit may "learn" to compensate for defects. We have fabricated experimental versions of such networks by using MOS capacitors for analog storage of the weights. The incremental weight changes needed for learning are obtained by moving charge between a pair of MOS capacitors on the channel of a transistor connecting them, mimicking a CCD. A 2.5-μm CMOS version has better than 10 bits of dynamic range while using only a 140×350-μm^2 area to store each weight. A 1.25-μm chip based upon the same cell is capable of peak learning rates of at least 2×10^9 weight changes per second with a 3.5×6.0-mm^2 die size.

I. Adaptive Networks

MUCH OF THE recent excitement about neural network models of computation has been driven by the prospect of new architectures for fine grained parallel computation using analog VLSI. In 1979, Moore predicted that the rate of increase in VLSI complexity would ultimately be limited by product definition; a decade later, the fundamental question of what to do with a million transistors besides making memory and processors is still an open one [1]. Neural network models of learning and adaptation play a special role in this light, offering the hint of complex systems that, like RAM, can be built up from regular arrays of simple primitives, but with the increasingly expensive testing and programming replaced by some form of automatic learning [2]. Many modern telecommunication systems such as modems and echo cancelers could not function without "neural networks" like the adaptive transverse filters used to cancel distortion and reduce noise. The output of such filters is the dot product of some stored weights ω_i with a time series formed by sampling the input signal. Most transverse filters are digital even though analog implementation would have a clear advantage in cost and speed if an analog storage technology to represent the weights ω_i were available. Adaptive systems are especially good targets for analog VLSI because the adaptive process can compensate for the inaccuracy of individual devices as easily as for the variability of the signal. Some of the properties needed by a storage technology for analog VLSI adaptive systems are as follows.

- The minimum available weight change Δw must be small. The simplest adaptive algorithms optimize the weights by minimizing the output error with a steepest descent search in weight space [3]. Iterative improvement algorithms such as steepest descent are based on the heuristic assumption of "better" weights being found in the neighborhood of "good" ones—a heuristic that fails when the granularity of the weights is not fine enough. In the worst case, the resolution required just to represent a function can grow exponentially in the dimension of the input space.
- The weights must be able to represent both positive and negative values and the changes must be easily reversible. Frequently, the weights may cycle up and down while the adaptive process is converging and millions of incremental changes during a single training session is not unreasonable. If the weights cannot easily follow all of these changes, then the learning must be done off chip.
- The parallelism of the network can be exploited to the fullest only if the mechanism controlling weight changes is simple enough to be reproduced at each weight. Ideally, the change is determined by some easily computed combination of information local to each weight and signals global to the entire system. This type of locality, which is as much a property of the algorithm as of the hardware, is necessary to keep the wiring cost associated with learning small.
- Weight decay, $\omega' = \alpha\omega$ with $\alpha < 1$, is useful although not essential. Global decay of all the weights can be used to extend their dynamic range by rescaling when the average magnitude becomes too large. Decay of randomly chosen weights can be used both to control their magnitude [5] and to help gradient searches escape from local minima.

To implement an analog storage cell with MOS VLSI, the most obvious choices are between floating-gate devices, multiplying digital-to-analog converters (MDAC's), with

Manuscript received September 2, 1988; revised December 14, 1988.
D. B. Schwartz was with AT&T Bell Laboratories, Holmdel, NJ 07733. He is now with GTE Laboratories, Inc., Waltham, MA 02254.
R. E. Howard and W. E. Hubbard are with AT&T Bell Laboratories, Holmdel, NJ 07733.
IEEE Log Number 8926479.

Reprinted from *IEEE Journal of Solid State Circuits*, Vol. 24, No. 3, April 1989, pages 688-697.

conventional digital storage and dynamic analog storage on an MOS capacitor. The attractiveness of nonvolatile storage on floating-gate devices is reduced by the difficulty in making small weight changes [6], the limitation to a finite number of WRITE cycles, and the inaccessibility of the technology. In EEPROM's the complex WRITE circuitry can be shared by thousands of bits since only a few bits are written at a time. An analog floating-gate storage cell requires still more elaborate WRITE circuitry than a digital one owing to the difficulty of controlling small changes. Analog/digital hybrids such as MDAC's are an attractive solution with the virtues of ease of design and simulation but limited to 4 to 5 bits of dynamic range by device matching. Circuits with 4-bit weights of this type have been made, but the complexity achieved has been small [7].

We will show the utility of dynamic storage on an MOS capacitor when some compromises are made in terms of layout area and the environmental requirements of the circuits. Our experiments show that careful designs can reduce leakage to a level low enough that analog refresh by backing up the network with conventional analog/digital conversion techniques and digital memory is practical if desired. Even without refresh, analog MOS storage with local learning represents a powerful tool for experimenting with complex adaptive systems if the chips are cooled or the system is constantly adapting.

Representation of both positive and negative weights can be obtained by storing the weights ω_i differently on a pair of capacitors in which case

$$\omega \propto V_+ - V_-.$$

Differential storage can be used to obtain some degree of rejection of leakage and can guarantee that leakage will reduce the magnitude of the weight as compared with a scheme where the weights are defined with respect to a fixed level, in which case as a weight decays it can change signs. A constant common-mode voltage also eases the design constraints on the differential input multiplier used to read out the weights. An elegant way to manipulate the weights is to transfer charge from one capacitor to the other, keeping constant the total charge on the system and eliminating the common-mode voltage as an extra variable to keep track of.

II. Weight Changes

Small packets of charge can easily be transferred from one capacitor to the other by exploiting charge injection, a phenomenon carefully avoided by designers of switched-capacitor circuits as a source of sampling error [8]–[12]. An example of a storage cell with the simplest configuration for a charge transfer system is shown in Fig. 1. A pair of MOS capacitors is connected by a string of narrow MOS transistors, a long one to transfer charge and two

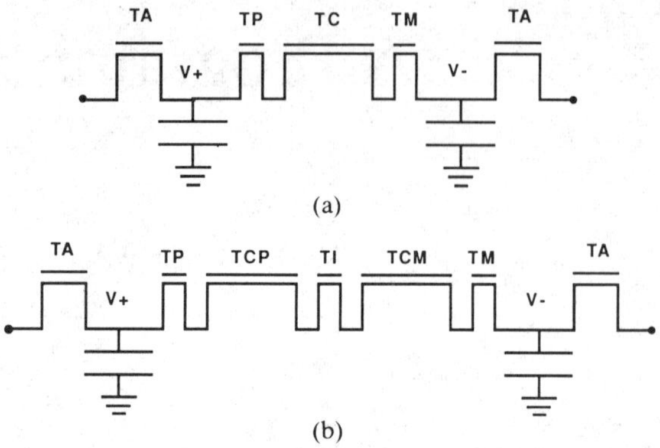

Fig. 1. (a) The simplest storage cell, with provisions only for single-size increment/decrement operations and no weight decay. (b) A more sophisticated cell with facilities for weight decay. By suitable manipulation of the clock signals, the two charge transfer transitors can be used to obtain different sizes of weight changes. Both circuits are initialized by turning on the access transistors *TA* and charging the capacitors up to a convenient voltage, typically $V_{DD}/2$.

minimum length ones to isolate the charge transfer transistor from the storage nodes. For the sake of discussion, we can treat the isolation transistors as ideal switches and concentrate on the charge transfer transistor which we here assume to be an n-channel device. To increase the weight (see Fig. 1), the charge transfer transistor (*TC*) and isolation transistor attached to the positive storage node (*TP*) are turned on. When the system has reached electrostatic equilibrium the charge transfer transistor *TC* is disconnected from the plus storage node by turning off *TP* and connected to the minus storage node by turning on *TM*. If the charge transfer transistor *TC* is slowly turned off, the mobile charge in its channel will diffuse into the minus node, lowering its voltage. The process can easily be described within a charge sheet model [13], where the inversion charge is assumed to reside in a layer of zero thickness at the oxide–silicon interface. In equilibrium, the mobile or inversion charge is given by

$$qN_{inv} = C_{ox}\left(V_G - V_{FB} - \psi_s - \left(\frac{a}{\beta}\right)\sqrt{\beta\psi_s - 1}\right) \quad (1)$$

where V_G is the gate voltage, V_{FB} is the flat-band voltage, ψ_s is the potential at the silicon surface, $\beta = q/kT$, $a = \sqrt{2}\,\kappa_{Si}t_{ox}/\kappa_{ox}L_B$, L_B is the bulk Debye length $[\kappa_{Si}\epsilon_0/\beta_q N_A]^{1/2}$, and N_A is the bulk acceptor density in the channel. The surface potential ψ_s can be obtained by using Newton–Ralphson to solve [14]

$$\beta(V_G - V_{FB} - \psi_s) = a\left[e^{\beta(2\phi_f + \psi_s - V_S)} + (\beta\psi_s - 1)\right]^{1/2} \quad (2)$$

where the Fermi level $\phi_f = (1/\beta)\ln(n_i/N_A)$, n_i is the intrinsic carrier density, and V_S is the substrate-to-source voltage of the charge transfer transistor. In Fig. 2, a calculated curve for the injected charge as a function of the source voltage is shown. Physically, the nonlinearity associated with the last term in (2) rises from the variation of the size of the depleted region underneath the channel with source-to-substrate voltage. For $V_S \ll V_G - V_T$, the charge

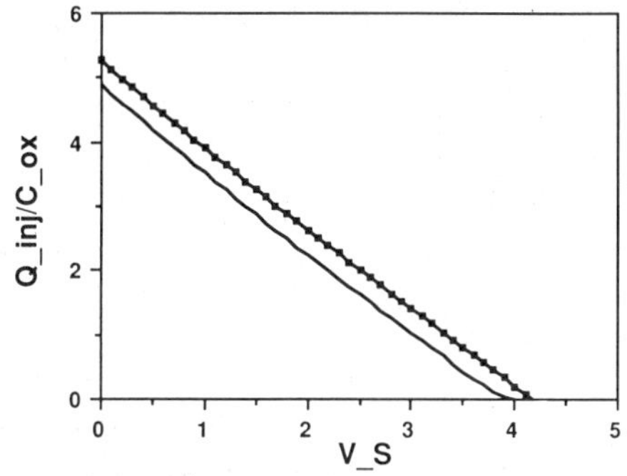

Fig. 2. The charge Q_{inj} moved in a single transfer. The process parameters are for the 2.5-μm CMOS used to fabricate one of the circuits discussed in the text, with $N_A = 2.68 \times 10^{16}$ cm^{-3}, $a = 5.8$, $t_{ox} = 335$ Å, $V_{FB} = -0.789$, and $T = 300$ K. The solid curve is calculated with the charge sheet model and the dotted curve from (3).

on the transfer transistor is roughly linear in the source voltage.

The charge sheet model for the amount of inversion charge on the transfer transistor is awkward for simulating the properties of a system containing many charge transfer elements. When the channel is heavily inverted the inversion charge is commonly approximated by

$$qN_{inv} = C_{ox}(V_G - V_{TE})$$

where

$$V_{TE} = V_{FB} + |2\phi_f| + \gamma\sqrt{V_S + 2|\phi_f|}$$

is the usual expression for the threshold including body effect where $\gamma = a/\sqrt{\beta}$. An even rougher model can be obtained by linearizing the body-effect term [9]

$$\Delta Q = C_{eff}(V_G - V_T - \eta V_S)$$

where C_{eff} contains both the gate oxide capacitance and the effects of parasitic capacitance and $\eta = \gamma / 2\sqrt{|2\phi_f|}$. Within the linearized approximation, the change in voltage on a storage node with capacitance C_{store} after n transfers is

$$V_n = V_0 + \frac{1}{\eta}(V_G - V_T - \eta V_0)(1 - \exp(-\alpha n)) \qquad (3)$$

with $\alpha = C_{eff}/C_{\text{store}}$ and where V_0 is the initial voltage on the storage node. Due to the dependence of the size of the transfer on the stored voltage, when the transfer direction is reversed the increment size changes unless the stored voltages on the capacitors are equal. This can be partially compensated for by using complementary pairs of p-channel and n-channel charge transfer transistors, similarly in spirit to a transmission gate. A weight decay operation can be introduced by using the more complex string of charge transfer transistors shown in Fig. 1(b). A weight decay (see Fig. 3) is initiated by turning off the transistor in the middle of the string (TI) and turning on all the other transistors. When the two sides of the charge transfer string have equilibrated with their respective storage nodes, the connections to the storage nodes (TM and TP) are turned off and the two charge transfer transistors (TCP and TCM) are allowed to exchange charge by turning on the transistor TI which separates them. When two equal charge packets have been obtained, TI is turned off again and the charge packets held by TCP and TCM are injected back into the storage capacitors. The resulting change in the stored weight is

$$\Delta V^{\text{decay}} = -\frac{C_{eff}}{C_{ox}}(V_+ - V_-)$$

which corresponds to multiplying the weight by a constant $\alpha < 1$ as desired. Besides allowing for weight decay, the more complex charge string shown in Fig. 1(b) can also be used to obtain different size weight changes by using different clock sequences (Fig. 3).

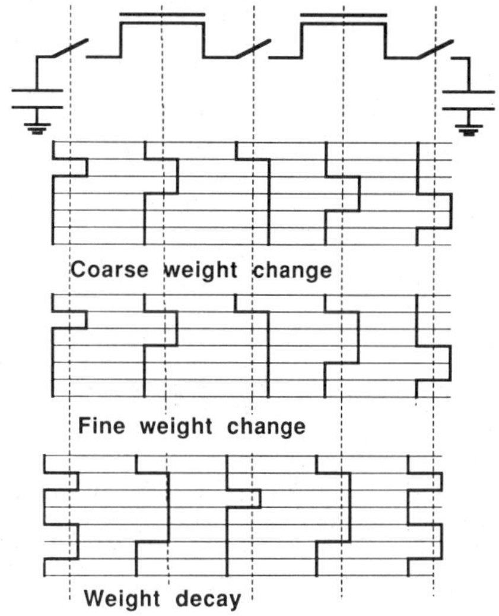

Fig. 3. The clock sequences required to obtain different size weight changes and weight decay. For clarity, the minimum-length transistors which separate the charge transfer transistors are here represented by normally open switches.

The phenomenon we are relying on to manipulate weights is familiar to CCD designers, although the implementation is not. We can execute our designs in single-polysilicon digital CMOS because the low transfer efficiency associated with the parasitic capacitance to the substrate from the diffusion connecting the transistors in the charge transfer string is not a problem for our circuits. In a CCD circuit where a charge packet must survive many transfers without distortion, the charge transfer efficiency must be very close to one. In our circuits, as long as the total amount of charge on the system remains constant and amplifiers used to read out the weights have decent common-mode rejection, the temporary loss of some charge to a parasitic capacitor is unimportant. To obtain reasonable charge transfer efficiency, we use long, narrow transistors, which increase the ratio of oxide capacitance to parasitic capacitance.

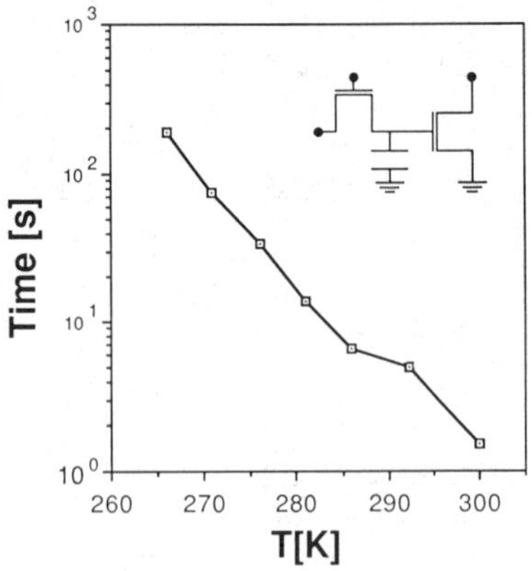

Fig. 4. Experimental measurements of the time for the storage capacitor in the circuit shown in the inset to lose 1 percent of its charge. The circuit was fabricated in 1.25-μm CMOS with a 500-μm^2 MOS accumulation mode capacitor and a 3×3-μm^2 access transistor. The data shown represent a worst-case value where the source of the access transistor is held at ground.

III. Charge Storage

Minimizing the effects of leakage from the storage capacitors requires a detailed understanding of the underlying device physics. The dominant mechanisms for decay of the voltage stored on the capacitor in the circuit shown in the inset of Fig. 4 are as follows.

1) Leakage into the substrate by the reverse-biased p-n junction forming the drain of the access transistor. In Si diodes at room temperature the leakage is dominated by the recombination currents from centers in the depleted regions of the junction, especially near the edges in small junctions. Recombination currents scale with temperature as $\exp(-eV_g/2kT)$ and can be minimized by using small contacts at any node where charge is stored.

2) Subthreshold conduction by the access transistor, scaling with temperature as $\exp(-eV_g/kT)$. By using long, narrow access transistors, subthreshold leakage can be reduced to the level of junction leakage at some cost in area.

3) Nonthermal processes like minority carriers injected into the substrate [15] and photons emitted by energetic carriers can cause excessive leakage as well as long-term degradation of active devices. Hot-carrier effects are well understood [16] and can be avoided by placing circuits that drive large capacitances at high speed away from storage nodes and by guarding the storage nodes.

As an example, for the test circuit used in the measurements shown in Fig. 4, which had a 3×3-μm^2 access transistor and a 3×3-μm^2 drain contact, the subthreshold current almost canceled the reverse-bias diode current when the access transistor was turned off and its source held at V_{DD}.

In classic DRAM designs the gate of the storage transistor is held at constant voltage and information is stored as charge packets in the channel. We store charge in polysilicon capacitors whose bottom plates are tubs held in accumulation; the resulting leakage is independent of the area of the capacitor. Leakage is controlled by layout to allow the circuits to be tested and used for some applications at room temperature. If further increase in hold time is desired, the circuits can be cooled. As shown in Fig. 4, cooling to $-8°C$ increases the hold time by a factor of over 100. At 77 K, as obtained from cooling with LN_2, the leakage rate of the same circuit was immeasurable.

Above and beyond the effects of leakage, it is important that as little charge as possible is lost to the substrate during weight transfer. Some unavoidable pumping of charge into the substrate is expected from traps at the silicon–oxide interface. When an electron is captured by a trap in the channel, it is no longer mobile and will remain in the trap after the channel goes into depletion when the transistor is turned off. If the trap emits the electron when the channel is in depletion, that electron will be lost to the substrate. Neglecting the possibility of being captured by a trap, the time for an electron to diffuse across the channel is given by the channel transit time:

$$\tau_0 = L^2/\mu_0(V_g - V_T)$$

where L is the channel length, V_T is the threshold of the transistor, and μ_0 is the mobility of electrons in the channel. Detailed calculations show negligible charge will be pumped into the substrate when the gate of the charge transfer transistor is ramped over $10\tau_0$ or longer. When the charge transfer gate is ramped down too quickly, the ends of the channel pinch off before the electrons in the middle of the channel have enough time to diffuse out, allowing the channel to become more negative than the substrate and hence for electrons to escape as a substrate current [10].

IV. Experimental Evaluation

Test chips have been fabricated in both 1.25- and 2.5-μm CMOS, using the AT&T twin-tub technology [18]. To evaluate the properties of an individual cell, especially the charge transfer mechanism, an isolated test structure consisting of five storage cells was built on one section of the 2.5-μm chip. The storage cells were differentially read out by two quadrant transconductance amplifiers whose input–output characteristics are shown in Fig. 5. By using the bias current of the amplifiers as an input, the amplifiers were used as two quadrant multipliers. Since many neural network models call for a sigmoidal nonlinearity, no attempt was made to linearize the operation of the multiplier. The output currents of the five multipliers were summed by a single output wire and the voltages on each of the ten capacitors were buffered by voltage followers to allow for detailed examination of the inner workings of the cell (Fig. 6). After trading off between hold time, resolution, and area we decided upon 20-μm-long charge transfer transistors and 2000-μm^2 storage capacitors with the 2.5-μm process based upon the minimum channel width of 2.5 μm. For a 20-μm channel and a 2.5-V gate-to-source voltage the channel transit time τ_0 is approximately 5 ns and charge transfer clock frequencies exceeding 10 MHz

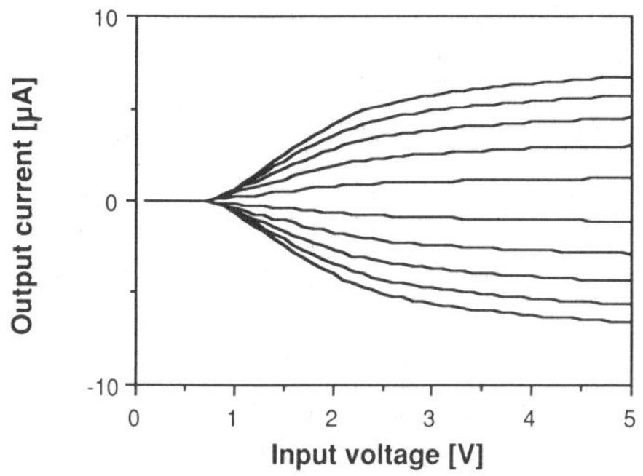

Fig. 5. A family of transfer characteristics for one of the transconductance multipliers for several different values of stored weight. The different branches of the curves are each separated by ten large charge transfers. No attempt was made to linearize the input/output characteristic since many neural network models call for nonlinearities.

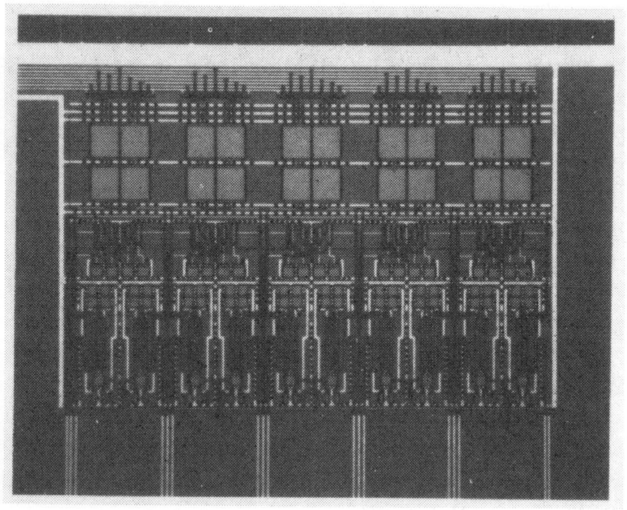

Fig. 6. Die photograph of a test circuit. The charge transfer transistors, the capacitors, and the multiplier are on top and occupy a $140 \times 350\text{-}\mu\text{m}^2$ area. The lower half of the die contains voltage followers used to buffer the capacitor voltages.

are possible without measurable charge pumping. The 2.5-μm-wide access transistors were 12 μm long, leading to leakage rates from the individual capacitors of about 1 percent of the stored value in 100 s, limited by surface leakage in our unpassivated test structures. Even with uncapped wafers, the leakage was small enough to allow all the tests described here to be made without special provisions for environmental control of either temperature or humidity.

As mentioned earlier, the more complex set of charge transfer transistors needed to introduce weight decay can also be used to obtain several different size of charge transfers. The different clock sequences required to obtain fine and coarse weight changes as well as weight decay are shown in Fig. 3. Some typical results for the voltages on a pair of capacitors under the application of 2000 small increments are shown in Fig. 7. As expected, the sum of the two voltages is a constant and the difference can be accurately fit with (3) using only the effective capacitance as a fitting parameter. The worst-case resolution with small weight changes near zero is 10 bits, which is remarkable in view of the area required to obtain equivalent resolution from a traditional DAC. In Fig. 8 we use large charge

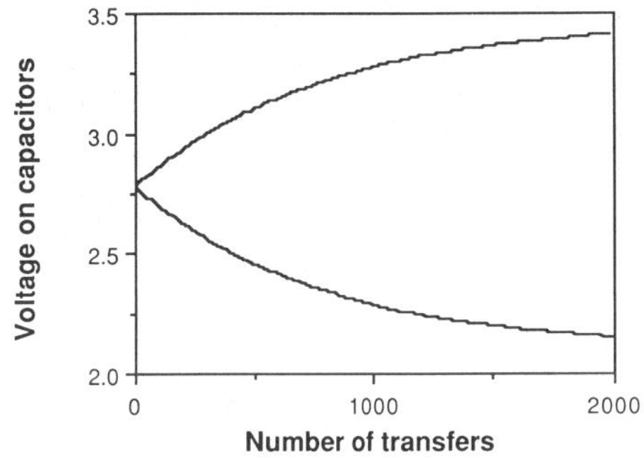

Fig. 7. The voltages on a pair of capacitors in a cell plotted against the number of small charge transfers applied. The granularity of the plot is due to the voltmeter used for the measurement, not that of the charge transfers.

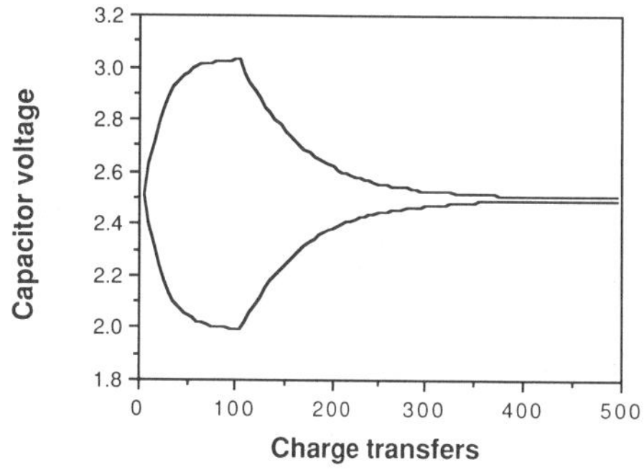

Fig. 8. The voltage on the two storage capacitors when the weight is initially set to saturation using large increments and then reduced back towards zero using weight decay.

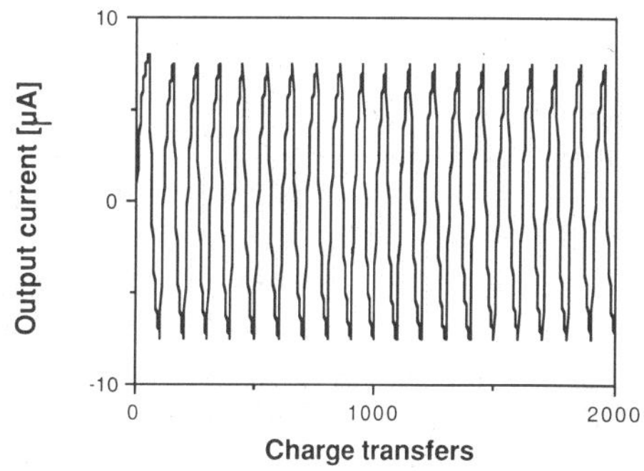

Fig. 9. The output of the multiplier when a weight is repeatedly incremented and decremented. As in the previous figures, the common-mode voltage is constant during the measurement to within the accuracy of the voltmeter.

transfers to quickly increment the weight up to its maximum value and then reduce it back to zero with weight decays. Again, the sum of the voltages on the capacitors remains constant, even though the weight was driven into saturation. Finally, to graphically show the reversibility of the weights, in Fig. 9 we use large charge transfers to increase and decrement a weight, changing directions every 100 transfers to demonstrate the absence of charge pumping. The shape and amplitude of this waveform are frequency independent for clock frequencies of up to 10 MHz.

The long-term goal of this work is to develop analog VLSI chips that are complete "learning machines," capable of modifying their own weights when provided with input data and some feedback based on the output of the

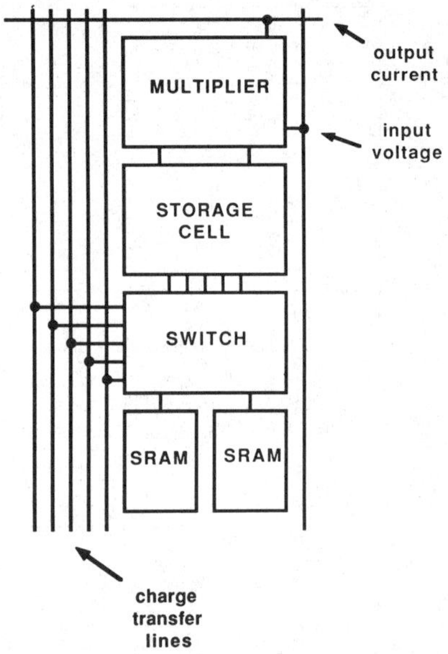

Fig. 10. Block diagram of the cell. The switch block contains a pair of 2×2 crossbar switches to facilitate weight decay and variable size charge transfers.

network. However, except the classical work on adaptive linear filters, the study of learning algorithms is in a state of flux and most existing learning algorithms have been optimized for serial digital hardware with floating-point arithmetic. Rather than cast an inappropriate algorithm in silicon, we have designed our first test chips to be used as adaptive systems with an external controller, allowing us to develop algorithms that are appropriate for the medium once we understand its properties. As with digital hardware, the most powerful algorithm will be the one that best matches the strengths and weaknesses of the hardware. The networks are organized as rectangular matrix multipliers with voltage inputs and current outputs with 46 inputs and 24 outputs in a 96-pin package for the 1.25-μm chip. Since none of the analog input/output lines of the chip is multiplexed, larger and more complicated networks can be built by cascading several chips.

To the digital controller, the chip looks like a 1104×2 static RAM with some extra clock inputs to drive the charge transfers. The charge transfer clock signals are distributed globally and are connected to the individual strings of charge transfer transistors through a pair of 2×2 crossbar switches controlled by two bits of static RAM local to each cell (Fig. 10). The use of a pair of crossbar switches is necessitated by the facilities for weight decay; if the simpler charge transfer string shown in Fig. 1(a) were used then only a single switch would be needed. When both of a cell's RAM's are zeroed, the global charge transfer lines are not connected to the charge transfer transistors. The global lines are connected to the individual strings of charge transfer transistors either normally or in reverse depending upon which RAM cell contains a ONE. By reversing the order of the signals on the charge transfer lines, a weight change can also be reversed. Neglecting the dependence of the size of the charge transfer upon stored weight, the RAM's represent a weight change vector $\Delta\vec{\omega}_{ij}$ with components $\Delta\omega_{ij} \in [-1,0,1]$. Once a weight change vector has been written serially to the RAM's, the weight changes along that vector are made in parallel by manipulating the charge transfer lines. This architecture is also a powerful way to implement programmable networks of fixed weights since our estimates show that a complete matrix of 10-bit fixed weights can be written to the chip in a few milliseconds if an efficient decomposition of the desired weight vector into global charge transfers is made. In view of the speed with which the chip can evaluate the output of a network, an overhead of less than a percent for a refresh operation is acceptable in many applications.

V. Conclusions

We have implemented a generic chip to facilitate studying adaptive networks by building them in analog VLSI. By exploiting the well-known properties of charge storage and charge injection in a novel way we have achieved a high enough level of complexity ($>10^3$ weights and 10 bits of analog depth) to be interesting, in spite of the limitation of a modest 6.00×3.5-mm^2 die size required by a multi-project fabrication run. If the cell were optimized to represent fixed weight networks by eliminating weight decay and bidirectional weight changes, the density could easily be increased by a factor of 2 with no loss in resolution. Once a weight change vector has been written to the RAM cells, charge transfers can be clocked at a rate of 2 MHz, corresponding to peak learning rates of 2×10^9 weight changes/second and exceeding the throughput of "neutral network accelerators" by two orders of magnitude.

Acknowledgment

A large group of people assisted the authors in taking this work from concept to silicon, a few of whom we single out for mention here. The IDA design tools used for the layouts were provided and supported by D. D. Hill and D. D. Shugard at Murray Hill and the 1.25-μm process was supported by D. Wroge and R. Ashton. The first author wishes to acknowledge helpful discussions with H. P. Graf, S. Mackie, and G. Taylor, with special thanks to R. G. Schwartz.

References

[1] G. Moore, "VLSI: Some fundamental challenges," *IEEE Spectrum*, vol. 16, no. 4, p. 30, 1979.

[2] J. Denker *et al.*, "Large automatic learning, rule extraction, and generalization," *Complex Systems*, vol. 1, p. 877, 1987.

[3] B. Widrow and S. D. Stearns, *Adaptive Signal Processing*. Englewood Cliffs, NJ: Prentice-Hall, 1985.

[4] M. Minski and S. Papert, *Perceptrons*. Cambridge, MA: M.I.T. Press, 1969.

[5] D. H. Ackley, G. E. Hinton, and T. J. Sejnowski, "A learning algorithm for Boltzman machines," *Cognitive Science*, vol. 9, p. 147, 1985.

[6] V. Hu, A. Kramer, and P. K. Ko, "EEPROMs as analog storage devices for neural nets," *Neural Networks*, Suppl., vol. 1, p. 385, 1988.

[7] J. Raffel, J. Mann, R. Berger, A. Soares, and S. Gilbert, "A generic architecture for wafer-scale neuromorphic systems," in *Proc. IEEE 1st Int. Conf. Neural Networks*, vol. III, 1987, p. 501.
[8] W. B. Wilson, H. Z. Massoud, E. J. Swanson, R. T. George, and R. B. Fair, "Measurement and modeling of charge feedthrough in n-channel MOS analog switches," *IEEE J. Solid-State Circuits*, vol. SC-20, no. 6, pp. 1206–1213, 1985.
[9] G. Wegmann, E. A. Vittoz, and F. Rahali, "Charge injection in analog MOS switches," *IEEE J. Solid-State Circuits*, vol. SC-22, no. 6, pp. 1091–1097, 1987.
[10] J. A. Kuo, R. W. Dutton, and B. A. Wooley, "MOS pass transistor turn-off transient analysis," *IEEE Trans. Electron Devices*, vol. ED-33, no. 10, pp. 1545–1555, 1986.
[11] J. R. Kuo, R. W. Dutton, and B. A. Wooley, "Turn-off transients in circular geometry MOS pass transistors," *IEEE J. Solid-State Circuits*, vol. SC-21, no. 5, pp. 837–844, 1986.
[12] J.-H. Shieh, M. Patil, and B. J. Sheu, "Measurement and analysis of charge injection in MOS analog switches," *IEEE J. Solid-State Circuits*, vol. SC-22, no. 2, pp. 277–281, 1987.
[13] J. R. Brews, "A charge-sheet model of the MOSFET," *Solid-State Electron.*, vol. 21, pp. 345–355, 1978.
[14] J. R. Brews, "Subthreshold behavior of uniformly and nonuniformly doped long-channel MOSFET," *IEEE Trans. Electron Devices*, vol. ED-26, no. 6, pp. 1282–1291, 1979.
[15] B. Eitan, D. Frohman-Bentchkowsy, and J. Shappir, "Holding time degradation in dynamic MOS RAM by injection-induced electron currents," *IEEE Trans. Electron Devices*, vol. ED-28, no. 12, pp. 1515–1519, 1981.
[16] T. H. Ning *et al.*, "1-μm MOSFET VLSI technology: Part IV—Hot electron design constraints," *IEEE Trans. Electron Devices*, vol. ED-26, no. 4, pp. 346–353, 1979.
[17] P. A. Chatterjee, G. W. Taylor, R. L. Easley, H.-S. Fu, and A. F. Tasch, Jr., "A survey of high-density dynamic RAM cell concepts," *IEEE Trans. Electron Devices*, vol. ED-26, no. 6, pp. 827–839, 1979.
[18] J. Argraz-Guerena *et al.*, "Twin tub III—A third generation CMOS," in *IEDM Tech. Dig.*, 1984, pp. 63–66.

Richard E. Howard (M'81) received the B.S. degree in physics from the California Institute of Technology, Pasadena, and the Ph.D. degree in applied physics from Stanford University, Stanford, CA, where he studied the transport properties of refractory superconducting films and layered composites made using e-beam evaporation. He also developed microfabrication techniques for making superconducting electronic devices using these films.

He joined AT&T Bell Laboratories in 1978 where he is now the head of the Microelectronics Research Department. His research has been concentrated in the areas of microfabrication and the physics of submicrometer devices. This work has been centered around high-resolution ($\ll 0.1$ μm) electron-beam lithography and related technologies including multilevel resists and plasma etching. Device studies have included quantum properties of small-area (0.1×0.1 μm) Josephson junctions, silicon MOSFET's as small as 0.02 μm, and high-density electronic neural networks. He has also applied these microfabrication techniques to other fields including optical storage and fiber optics.

Dr. Howard is a member of the American Physical Society, the American Vacuum Society, and the Materials Research Society.

Daniel B. Schwartz received the Ph.D. degree in physics from the State University of New York at Stony Brook in 1985. His research concerned tunneling in heavily damped macroscopic systems and he also worked extensively on the physics and technology of Josephson junctions.

He was a postdoctoral Member of the Technical Staff at AT&T Bell Laboratories in Holmdel, NJ, working on algorithms for, and VLSI implementations of, electronic neural networks. He is now at GTE Laboratories, Inc., Waltham MA.

Wayne E. Hubbard is a Member of the Technical Staff at AT&T Bell Laboratories, Holmdel, NJ, where he has been involved in such diverse projects as optical recording, vapor-phase epitaxial growth systems, and currently, neural networks. He began his career in electronics and computers in 1969 at RCA, then served six years with the U.S. Navy Tactical Data Systems. From 1976 until joining Bell Labs in 1982, he worked for Digital Equipment Corporation as the District Support Engineer.

Reprinted from *The Proceedings of the International Annual Conference on Neural Networks*, 1989, pages II-191--II-196.

An Electrically Trainable Artificial Neural Network (ETANN) with 10240 "Floating Gate" Synapses

Mark Holler, Simon Tam, Hernan Castro, Ronald Benson*
Intel Corporation, Technology Development
Novel Device Group
2250 Mission College Blvd. SC9-34
Santa Clara, Ca. 95052-8125
Ph. 916-351-2704

ABSTRACT

Use of "floating gate" non-volatile memory technology for analog storage of connection strengths or "weights" has previously been proposed and demonstrated. This paper reports the analog storage and multiply characteristics of a new floating gate synapse and further discusses the architecture of a neural network which uses this synapse cell. In the architecture described 8192 synapses are used to fully interconnect 64 neurons and to connect the 64 neurons to each of 64 inputs. Each synapse in the network multiplies a signed analog voltage by a stored weight and generates a differential current proportional to the product. Differential currents are summed on a pair of bit-lines, transferred through a sigmoid function and appear at the neuron output as an analog voltage. Input and output levels are compatible for ease in cascade connecting these devices into multi-layer networks. Processing is done in parallel with an anticipated delay from input to output of approximately 1us. Weights are changed individually similar to the technique used to write data into EEPROM's. The pulse width and height of a weight change pulse must be calculated externally. Synapse cell size is 2009 sq. microns using a 1u CMOS EEPROM technology.

INTRODUCTION

Implementation of modifiable artificial neural connections or synapses using "Floating gate" non-volatile memory technology [1], has been proposed by Alspector, et al [2]. Alspector proposed the use of an analog charge on a floating gate to replace digital flip-flops used to store a connection strength or weight. The purpose of substitution being to reduce the size of the synapse. Since this time several specific floating gate synapse circuits have been revealed [3,4,5]. Electrical results have been reported for one of these cells [3]. This paper describes a new floating gate synapse cell which operates differentially to avoid the problems associated with power supply and temperature changes which occur between the time a network is trained and the time it processes information. Differential operation affords several other benefits such as full four quadrant multiply function and improved linearity of the multiply.

The cell described places a variety of constraints on the architecture of the network in which it is used. The architecture of an Electrically Trainable Analog Neural Network (ETANN) which uses the synapse described will be discussed to elaborate on some of the issues encountered in using a fully differential, analog, non-volatile synapse. General issues pertaining to VLSI implementation of neural networks are also discussed. Some key aspects of the architecture are: emphasis on speed via parallelism, both feed forward and feedback connections on chip, analog voltage input and output, a large pin count package, and the option to operate in a fast static mode or in a clocked mode useful with multiplexed external buses.

Learning calculations have been left off chip to allow flexibility in applying the network and to avoid the complexity and cost penalties associated with implementing learning on chip. Writing weights into the ETANN will be referred to as training rather than learning as it implies passive involvement of the ETANN. Several additions have been made to the architecture to speed up training and minimize the connection overhead required by external learning and control of training. Addresses are provided which allow the external processor to select individual weights for modification in the same way that a byte of data is addressed in an EEPROM.

SYNAPSE CELL

The synapse cell circuit, shown in Figure 1, is an NMOS version of a Gilbert-Multiplier [6]. A pair of EEPROM cells are incorporated in which a differential voltage representing the weight may be stored or adjusted.

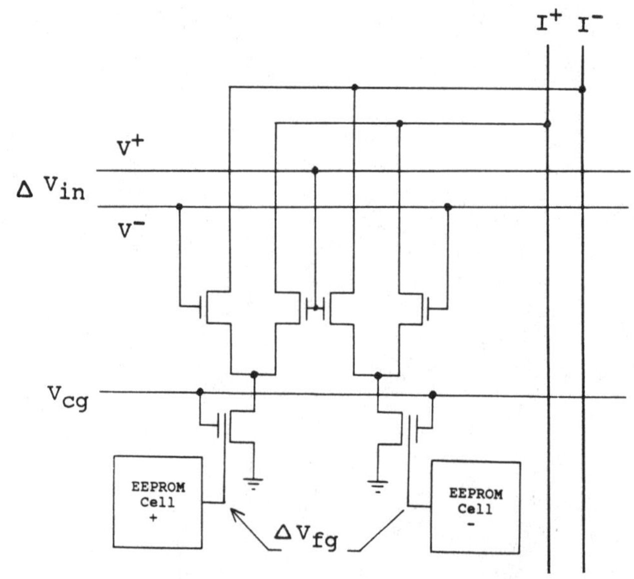

Figure 1. Differential "floating gate" synapse schematic diagram.

Electrons are added to or removed from the floating gates in the EEPROM cells by Fowler-Nordheim tunneling of electrons between the floating gates and the diffusions. A desired differential floating gate voltage can be attained by monitoring the conductances of the respective EEPROM MOSFETs. In particular, the respective floating gate voltages may be expressed as:

$$V_{fg} = \frac{C_{pp}}{C_{tot}} * V_{cg} + \frac{Q_{fg}}{C_{tot}}$$

where C_{pp} is the capacitance between the floating gate and the top gate (control gate) and C_{tot} is the total floating gate capacitance. V_{cg} is a static control gate voltage used for biasing and Q_{fg} is the charge stored on the floating gate. Assuming that all the transistors in the MOS multiplier stayed in saturation, we have the differential output current as:

$$\Delta I_{out} = I^+ - I^-$$

$$\Delta I_{out} = \Delta V_{in} * \Delta V_{fg} \qquad \Delta V_{fg} = \frac{\Delta Q_{fg}}{C_{tot}}$$

where ΔV_{in} is the differential input voltage and ΔQ_{fg} is the differential charge stored between the two EEPROMs' floating gates.

A photo-micrograph of the synapse circuit is shown in Figure 2. Figure 3 shows the output characteristics of the synapse with symmetrical differential weights. The differential input voltage plotted along the x-axis is defined to be:

$$\Delta V_{in} = V^+ - V^-$$

In this particular illustration V^+ was varied from 1V to 5V while V^- was fixed at 3V. The differential weight was varied symmetrically between approximately -.8V and +.8V. Since the average of V^+ and V^- increased as V^+ was varied from 1V to 5V, we observed that the output current ΔI_{out} is higher in the positive ΔV_{in} regime (right half plane) than the negative ΔV_{in} regime.

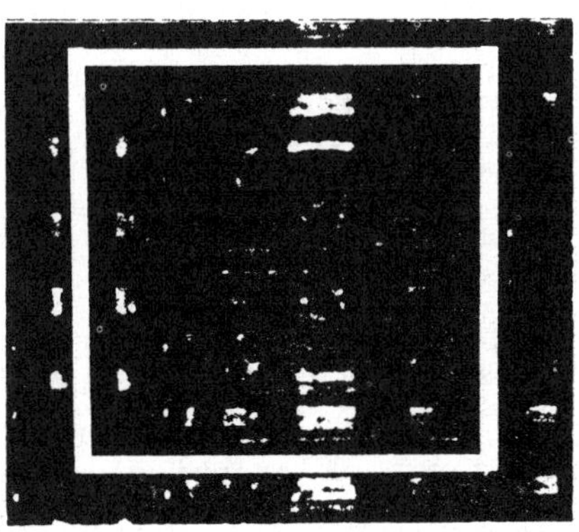

Figure 2. Floating gate synapse cell. Cell size 41.6u x 48.3u.

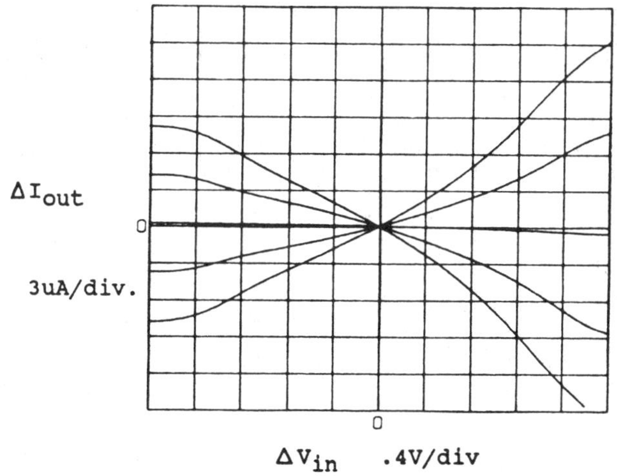

Figure 3. Characteristics of the synapse multiplier for five different values of weight. EEPROM cells written symmetrically.

Figure 4 shows the output characteristics of EEPROM based synapse when the conductance of one of the EEPROM devices was varied through the Fowler-Nordheim tunneling process with the "reference" EEPROM device remaining unchanged. The "weight" EEPROM's threshold was varied from approximately 1.95V below to +1.65V above the "neutral" threshold of the reference EEPROM. These characteristics present how the differential current representing the product changes when the charge on only one floating gate is adjusted.

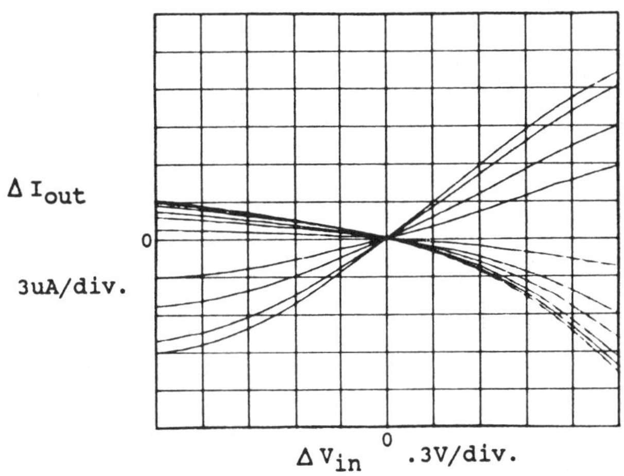

Figure 4. Characteristics of the synapse multiplier for varying values of the weight. One EEPROM cell written.

In previous work [3] it was demonstrated that the voltage on a floating gate could be adjusted with .4% resolution (8 bits) using channel hot-electron programming. The physical limit on the smallest increment which can be made is the voltage shift due to adding a single electron. For the cell discussed in this paper the smallest increment will not be limited by the discreteness of the charge of a single electron but, rather by the ability of the neuron circuits to detect a change. 250 million electrons have to be stored on one of the floating gates to cause a 2V shift in the threshold of the transistor. If single electron increments could be sensed this cell would be capable of storing 30 bits of information.

No data is presented here which shows that single electrons can be added or removed. This is due to measurement limitations not a physical limitation of Fowler-Nordheim tunneling. Fowler-Nordheim tunneling is exponentially dependent upon the voltage applied making it possible to slow the rate of tunneling down indefinitely. Some finite probability of tunneling remains even under normal operating biases. Scaling of floating gate synapse cells will not likely be limited by the discreteness of the electron charge for some time to come.

To show adequate weight change resolution for this cell the threshold of one of the EEPROM devices in a synapse has been plotted as a function of the number of 20us pulses applied. 180 pulses were applied to shift the threshold by 4 V. See Figure 5. The average threshold change per pulse was 22 mV or .6% which corresponds to more than 7 bit weight setting resolution. Higher weight setting resolution is possible.

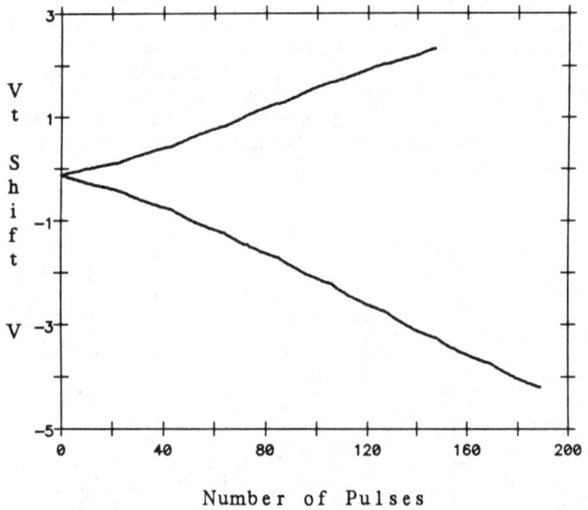

Figure 5. EEPROM threshold vs. the number of 20us pulses applied. Weight change pulse voltage increased by .5 V every 21 pulses.

WEIGHT RETENTION

How well the value of a weight is retained is an important characteristic of any synapse because it limits the amount of information which can be stored in the synapse. For example if a weight changes in time by 10% of full range then no more than 10 different states of the weight can be distinguished from one another. The number of distinct states the weight can have is directly related to its information capacity.

To characterize how much undesirable change in the weights will occur over the life of a device several synapses were baked at 250C to accelerate the charge relaxation phenomenon that is known to occur in floating gate memory devices. Figure 6 shows the percentage change in the weight as a function of

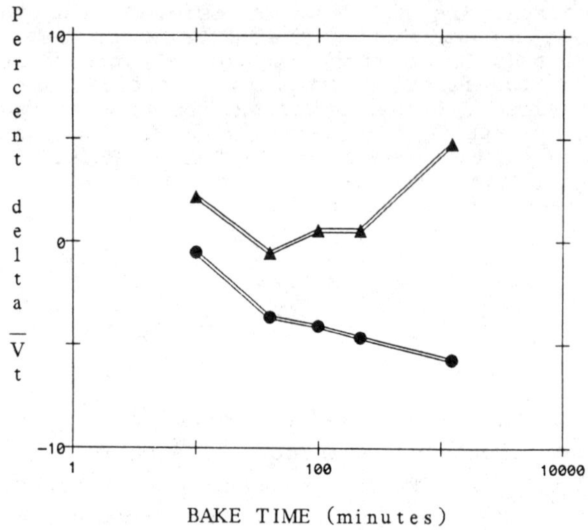

Figure 6. Percent change in EEPROM threshold vs. bake time at 250C. Upper curve - erased cell, Lower curve - programmed cell.

time in the 250C bake. Since no activation energy has yet been determined for the synapse cell it cannot be said with certainty that any point on this graph is a precise equivalent to the desired lifetime of the device. However, using a 1.1eV activation energy derived from a similar floating gate technology [7] a time on the order of 3200 minutes at 250C is equivalent to a 15 year lifetime for a floating gate device at 125C. Extrapolating out to this time in Figure 5 it is indicated that the weight will change approximately 6-7% which would allow long term storage of one of 14-17 distinct states. Sixteen distinct states corresponds to 4 bits of resolution.

In applications where the network is retrained frequently the high weight setting resolution of the cell can be utilized. In applications where the network is trained only once and used for a long period of time 4-bit resolution appears to be the limit. However, it may be possible to accelerate the relaxation process and retrain the network or pre-compensate for the relaxation phenomenon and bake the network to improve resolution.

NETWORK ARCHITECTURE

Learning vs. Speed

Two of the desirable characteristics of neural networks are their ability to learn and their potential for high speed processing when truly parallel architectures are implemented. The architecture which will be discussed is optimized for processing speed. Learning capability is provided but, only in a rudimentary sense.

For maximum processing speed as much parallelism as possible was attempted, multiplexing was avoided. The limiting factor in the amount of parallelism which could be achieved was the pin count of practical integrated circuit packages. A large pin count pin grid array package was selected for this reason.

Analog input and output were selected to

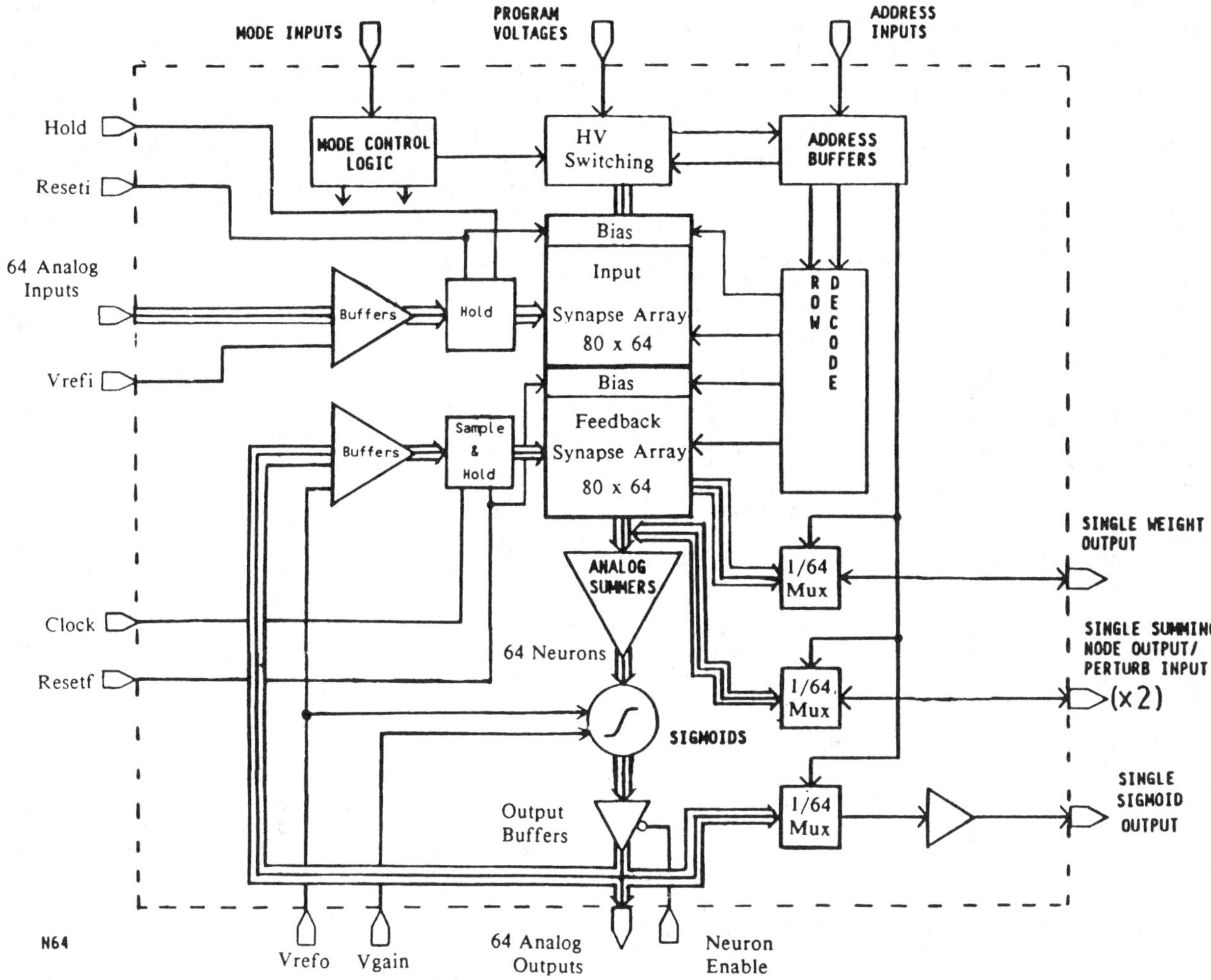

Figure 7. ETANN Block diagram

maximize information throughput on the limited number of pins.

An external intelligent supervisor must calculate the weight changes and must calculate the voltages to be applied to each synapse to modify the weight. Weights are addressed and are changed one at a time. The learning rate will likely not be any faster than an average simulation. However, one benefit of this approach is that the network can be trained equally well by a training controller using Hebbian learning, back-propagation, unsupervised learning, Madaline or nearly any other learning algorithm. It was necessary to add circuitry to be able to perturb the neuron inputs as is necessary in Madaline learning.

Architecture with Feedback

A block diagram of the architecture of the ETANN is shown in Figure 7. The chip has 64 inputs, and 64 neurons fully interconnected by 4096 synapses. Neuron outputs are available at 64 output pins.

A 64 signal feedback path from the outputs to a separate synapse array of 4096 synapses was provided. It allows implemention of Hopfield networks [8] and networks capable of processing and producing sequences of patterns [9]. The die size did not increase signicantly with the addition of the feedback synapse array since the die size is limited primarily by the perimeter required for the large number of bonding pads. See Figure 9.

Feedback is gated by a clock controlling the sample and hold buffers in much the same way that feedback is gated by a clock in synchronous digital circuits. "Free-running" Oscillations are prevented regardless of the values given to the weights in the feedback synapse array. A repeating sequence of patterns can still be generated at the neuron outputs but the rate of repetition is controlled by the clock.

The sample and hold buffer is also useful for storing data input via the output pins. A signal is provided which can disable the neuron output buffers, allowing data to be input to the chip via the output pins. In this mode of operation input pattern vectors with 128 components may be processed.

The ETANN has a single layer of neurons for maximum flexibility in design of multi-layer networks at board level. However, multiplexing the use of the neurons is allowed which makes two layer operation of a single ETANN possible. Two layer operation is discussed below.

Extra rows of synapses are provided with fixed positive input to allow setting a bias for each neuron. A block of 16 rows of biasing synapses are enabled when the input connections are enabled and a separate block of 16 rows is enabled when the feedback connections are enabled. A total of 2048 synapses are dedicated to setting biases.

Two Layer Operation

Two layer operation is accomplished by first disabling the feedback synapse array and applying 64 input signals to the ETANN.

After sufficient time is allowed for the outputs to settle the outputs are clocked into the sample and hold buffer in the feedback path. Next the input synapse array is disabled which allows the stored previous state of the outputs to be processed without interference. The feedback synapse array is used as a second layer of connections. The neuron amplifiers which are a significant portion of the die area are used twice in two layer processing.

Differential circuitry was used throughout the analog signal path for power supply and temperature immunity as well as speed of operation.

Scaled CMOS technology is used for its packing density, performance and it's ability to power down to very low power levels.

INPUT/OUTPUT

Analog input and output was chosen over digital to maximize the information carrying capacity of the interconnect. Single ended inputs rather than differential inputs were also chosen to conserve pins. Each input is converted to a differential signal in the first stage of the input buffer which is a differential amplifier. The other input to the differential amplifier is a reference voltage supplied by the user. This reference voltage can have any value from 0 to 1.7V. Voltages above the reference are positive quantities while voltages below the reference are negative quantities for purposes of the multiply which occurs in the synapse. If the reference voltage is set to zero the inputs can only take on positive values. And the synapse is used as a 2-quadrant multiplier rather than a 4-quadrant multiplier. If the reference voltage is set to 1.5V the inputs become TTL compatible.

The use of a differential synapse to reduce the sensitivity to voltage and temperature variations yielded a synapse with full 4-quadrant multiply capability. Both the inputs and the stored weights can be positive or negative and the synapse will produce the correct signs for the products in all cases. The inputs may take on inhibitory characteristics and if connected to an inhibitory connection (a synapse storing a negative weight) will cause excitation of the subsequent neuron. Although this type of inhibitory input/inhibitory connection is generally thought not to exist in biological systems there is an indication in simulation results that it can speed up learning.

The neuron amplifiers sum the differential currents produced by the synapses and produce a differential voltage which is fed through an electronic emulation of a sigmoid function. The sigmoid function has variable gain controlled by the voltage applied to one external pin. Simulations of the sigmoidal transfer characteristics with various levels of gain are shown in Figure 8. The output inflection point is controlled by a reference voltage and can be matched with the input zero point by connecting the input and output references to the same voltage.

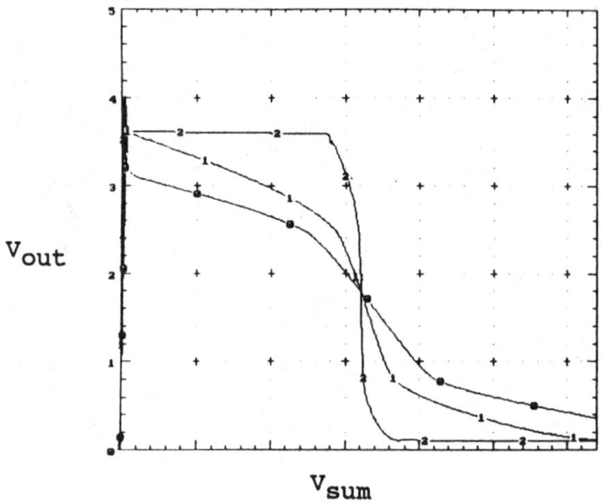

Figure 8. Simulated output characteristics as a function of the total sum of products V_{sum}. Characteristics for three different gain settings shown.

CHANGING WEIGHTS

Modifying weights is done much like programming an EEPROM except that the goal is to end up with a relatively precise amount of charge on the two floating gates in the cell rather than just more than some fixed value as in EEPROMs. To accomplish this an iterative process will likely have to be used. First the present state of the EEPROM cell floating gate is measured by using the multiplexer shown in the lower right hand corner of Figure 7. An address is applied to the 14 address lines to select one of the 10240 synapses. The external processor directing the training calculates the desired weight change based on the network's performance to the training pattern set and then calculates the appropriate pulse height based on the present state of the weight and the desired weight change. The weight can be measured again immediately and if further adjustment is required, another pulse of appropriate height can be applied. Each pulse will be in the range of 10us to 1ms in length and 12-20V in height. Because EEPROM cells are used the weights may be changed in either direction, thus, overshooting a desired value is not a problem.

An output multiplexer was provided to aid in reducing the number of connections the training processor will need to access information at the outputs. The neuron outputs can be read individually at a single output by applying an address to the 6 low order address pins and measuring the output voltage at the pin labeled single sigmoid output in Figure 7.

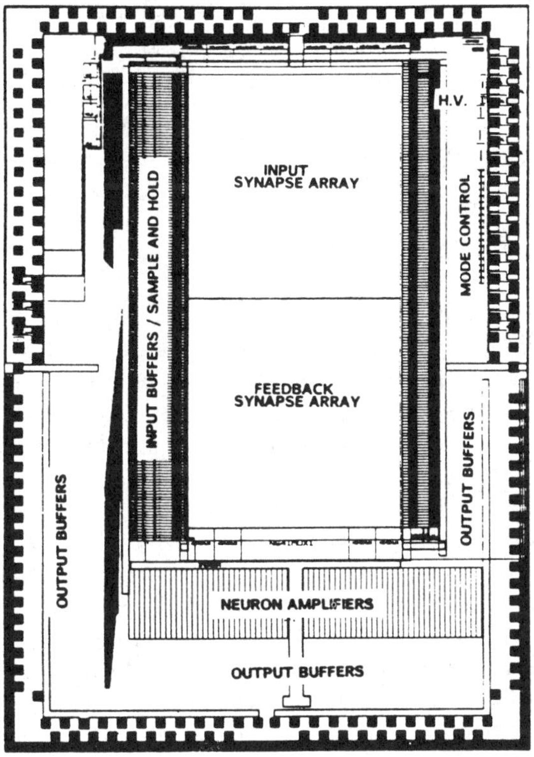

Figure 9. Chip plan of the ETANN discussed.

CONCLUSIONS

Analog weight storage and retention as well as 4-quadrant multiplication in a floating gate synapse cell have been demonstrated. An ETANN which uses 10240 of these cells has been designed and is anticipated to be capable of performing on the order of 10^{10} low precision multiplications per second relevant for pattern recognition tasks. This is several orders of magnitude more processing performance than Von Neumann computer based neural network simulations. Although learning speed had to be compromised significantly to accomplish this performance, this choice was made because it moves computing into a new realm of performance. Had the architecture been optimized for learning speed it is unlikely that the network would learn any faster than fast Von Neumann based computer simulations due to the relative slowness of the Fowler-Nordheim tunneling process and the difficulty of applying many different high voltages to the synapses in parallel. For this reason it seems apparent that floating gate silicon implementations of neural networks provide the most significant new capability by being optimized for speed.

ACKNOWLEDGEMENTS

The authors would like to thank Bruce McCormick and George Canepa for introducing us to neural networks and Dan Seligson for balancing our perspective by championing digital and difference calculating synapse approaches. Special thanks also to FAB 1 and the Flash Memory Group for fabricating the first synapses so quickly. This effort has been assisted by continued technical discussions with the Naval Weapons Center, China Lake in accordance with their need and request for VLSI ANN development or devices as specified in BAA# N60530-88-R-0427. *This material is based partially upon work supported under a National Science Foundation graduate fellowship. Ron Benson is a graduate fellow at the California Institute of Technology.

REFERENCES

[1] Frohman-Bentchkowsky, D., "Memory Behavior in a Floating-Gate Avalanche-Injection MOS (FAMOS) Structure", Applied Physics Letters, Volume 18, Number 8, April 1971.

[2] Alspector, J., et al, "A Neuromorphic VLSI Learning System", Proc. of the 1987 Stanford Conf., Advanced Research in VLSI, pp 313-349, 1987

[3] Tam, S., Holler, M.A., Canepa, G., "Neural Network Synaptic Connections Using Floating Gate Non-Volatile Elements", Neural Networks for Computing, AIP Conference Proceedings, Snowbird, Ut., 1988.

[4] Shoemaker, P., Lagnado, I., Shimabukuro, R., "Artificial Neural Network Implementation with Floating Gate MOS Devices", Hardware Implementation of Neuron Nets and Synapses, A Workshop sponsored by NSF and ONR, January 14,15, 1988. San Diego, Ca.

[5] Faggin, F., Lynch, G., Sukonick, J., "Brain Emulation Circuit with Reduced Confusion", U.S. Patent #4,773,024, Issued September 20, 1988.

[6] Soo, D., Meyer, R., "A Four-Quadrant NMOS Analog Multiplier", IEEE JSSC, Vol. SC-17, No. 6, Dec. 1982

[7] Verma, G., Mielke, N., "Reliability Performance of ETOX Based Flash Memories", Procceeding of the 1988 International Reliability Physics Symposium

[8] Hopfield J.J. & Tank D.W., "Computing with Neural Circuits: A Model", Science vol 233, P625, Aug. 86

[9] Kohonen, T. , Self-organization and Associative Memory, Springer-Verlag, 2nd edition, 1988, New York First edition 1984.

Asynchronous VLSI Neural Networks Using Pulse-Stream Arithmetic

ALAN F. MURRAY AND ANTHONY V. W. SMITH

Abstract —The relationship between neural networks and VLSI is explored. An introduction to neural networks relates the Hopfield model and the Delta learning rule to Grossberg's description of neural dynamics. A computational style is described that mimics that of a biological neural network, using pulse-stream signaling and analog summation. Digitally programmable weights allow learning networks to be constructed. Functional and structural forms of neural and synaptic functions are presented, along with simulation results. Finally a neural network implemented in 3-μm CMOS is presented with preliminary measurements.

I. Introduction

A NEURAL network is a massively parallel array of simple computational units (neurons) that models some of the functionality of the human nervous system and attempts to capture some of its computational strengths [1]–[3]. The abilities that a synthetic neural net might aspire to mimic include the ability to consider many solutions simultaneously, the ability to work with corrupted or incomplete data without explicit error correction, and a natural fault tolerance. This latter attribute, which arises from the parallelism and distributed knowledge representation, gives rise to graceful degradation as faults appear. This is attractive for VLSI.

Current research into computation by synthetic neural networks falls into essentially three broad categories. The first category is that of mathematical description and analysis of the dynamical and learning properties of neural nets, often working from biological or psychological exemplars (see, for example, [4]). The second, perhaps largest, research effort uses computer simulation, often based on array processor or other supercomputer architectures, to model and extend these mathematical descriptions and demonstrate their correctness (see, for example, [5]). The third group of research topics, into which this paper falls, aims to implement either particular neural functions, or classes of neural net, as LSI/VLSI hardware. A review of this work, at Edinburgh and elsewhere, appears in Section II of this paper.

At present, there is no application area for which neural networks are clearly the optimal solution, and it has been demonstrated that a more conventional solution is often better [6]. We do not believe, however, that this is the result of inherent weaknesses of neural networks. Knowledge of how neural networks should be designed, and how they should be programmed (or "taught") is rudimentary in comparison to knowledge of conventional computer architecture and programming techniques. This knowledge is advancing rapidly, however, and apparently small modifications of learning procedures in particular can enhance the computational power of a network considerably [5]. In addition, planar silicon technology is almost certainly not the ultimate medium in which neural networks will find their power fully realized. Three-dimensional biological materials are intrinsically better suited to the essentially three-dimensional form of a neural net, but their usefulness as understandable and predictable "circuit-building" media is a long way off. It is our view that to delay research into implementation of neural networks until analysis and simulation demonstrate their full power and a better technology emerges would be shortsighted. There is much to learn from LSI/VLSI implementation, and any hardware networks developed will be able to make rapid use of developments in network design and learning procedures to solve real problems.

In Section II of this paper we offer an engineer's perspective on neural computation, followed by an overview of LSI/VLSI neural research in Section III. In Section IV we describe our neural architecture and computation style, while Sections V and VI give circuit forms and results, respectively. Finally, we suggest future work and possible application areas for neural boards based on our chip set.

II. Synthetic Neural Networks: An Engineer's Perspective

The neural literature is rife with obfuscation of simple ideas by confusing jargon which often means something quite straightforward. This section places the formalism and principles of neural network research into engineering language, in order that the problems may be appreciated, and to form a basis for discussion of our own implementation style.

A. Descriptive

Fig. 1 shows, in schematic form, a network consisting of four neurons. In engineering language, a neuron is a state machine that is normally ON or OFF, although it may in

Manuscript received October 30, 1987; revised February 8, 1988.
The authors are with the Department of Electrical Engineering, University of Edinburgh, Edinburgh EH9 3JL, Scotland.
IEEE Log Number 8820724.

Reprinted from *IEEE Journal of Solid State Circuits*, Vol. 23, No. 3, June 1988, pages 688-697.

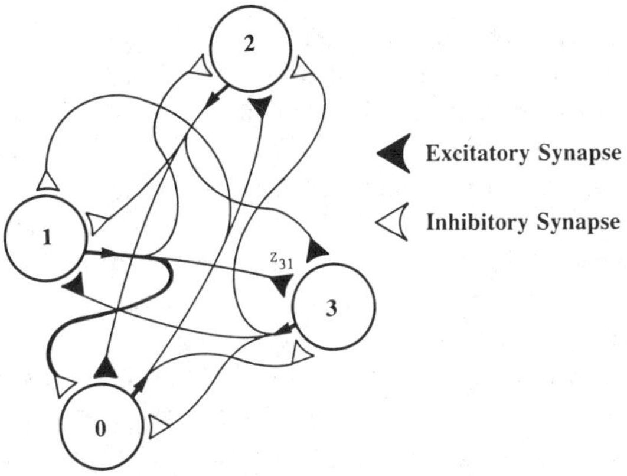

Fig. 1. A network of four neurons, denoted by circles.

general switch smoothly between these extremes, assuming intermediate states as it does so. In the nervous system, a neuron signals that it is ON by firing electrical pulses along its output or axon, and that it is OFF by ceasing to fire pulses. Each axon may fork to form connections, potentially to all other neurons in the network. These connections (inputs) are made through synapses, which are represented as triangular caps in Fig. 1. The function of the synapse is to gate the signal from the transmitting neuron such that it may be more or less excitatory or inhibitory to the receiving neuron; an excitatory input tends to turn a neuron ON, and an inhibitory input tends to turn it OFF. For instance, neuron 3 receives the output from neuron 1 as an input, gated by afactor z_{31}, that may be positive, negative, or zero. In Fig. 1, it is shown as a positive (excitatory) synapse. The synapses have therefore the effect of weighting the response of any neuron to its inputs from all the others, and the total weighted sum changes the level of activity of the neuron. Neural activity may also be increased by direct simulation of the neuron from sources outside the network (external inputs).

The network will therefore have an infinite number of possible states, corresponding to all combinations of the individual neural states (ON, OFF, or somewhere in between). The set of synaptic weights determines the stable states, and represents the learned information in the system. Learning is therefore a process by which the synaptic weights are changed to add to the network's store of knowledge. As a simple example, let us set the interconnect weights between neurons 0 and 2 and also those between neurons 1 and 3 as large and positive (excitatory). Also, let us set all other interconnect weights large and negative. The stable states will clearly be those with neurons 0 and 2 ON and neurons 1 and 3 OFF, and vice versa. If the network is forced into some other state, it will gravitate toward one or the other of these two preferred states. It is this dynamic behavior that is at the heart of neural computation.

B. Mathematical Description of a Neural Network

The discussion in this section is necessary to give an appreciation of how a neural network changes in time, and therefore how its computation proceeds. Only in this way can the full challenge for LSI/VLSI be appreciated, and the advantages of analog and digital implementation styles assessed. The ensuing discussion may seem unnecessarily detailed in an engineering context, but this article is aimed at the nonspecialist, who may not have encountered neural nets before, and it is necessary to explain the ground rules.

We will begin with a pair of equations initially proposed by Grossberg [1] that describe the dynamic behavior of a set of neurons and their synaptic weights. The equations are a combination of a phenomenological description of what is known to occur in the nervous system, extended by conjecture as to how it might work in detail. These equations carry a level of generality unmatched by any other description of synthetic neural networks, so they form a good starting point for a discussion of more restricted neural models. The equations have implications on the response of the network to external stimuli, and on the process of learning. To make contact with the enormous body of work done by Grossberg, much of which is ignored by the neural modeling community, we begin with his generalized form, and indicate how the general model it describes can be related to more simplified models.

These equations describe the time evolution of a set of n neurons whose states are represented as $\{S_i\}$ or $\{V_i\}$. These variables have the limits $0 \leqslant V_i \leqslant 1$ and $-1 \leqslant S_i \leqslant 1$. Grossberg's analysis uses a nonnegative V_i. There is, however, a one-to-one mapping between a description with $-1 \leqslant S_i \leqslant 1$ and one with $0 \leqslant V_i \leqslant 1$. The descriptions are therefore equivalent, and we may concentrate on the latter $(\{V_i \geqslant 0\})$ model for the present without loss of generality. The neural state V_i is related to the total neural activity stimulated by inputs to the neuron through an activation function F. The neural activity may be thought of as the level of excitation of the neuron, and the activation function as the way it reacts (by altering its state V_i) in response to a change in activation. Neural activity is represented by a number x_i that is not bounded in the same way as V_i, and whose magnitude is changed either by interactions from other neurons in the network via the synapses, or by direct stimulation from an external source. The neural output state V_i is related to the neural activity x_i by

$$V_i = F(x_i). \tag{1}$$

The activation function F ensures that V_i is 1 for x_i large and 0 for x_i small. The details of switching between these ON and OFF states are determined by the details of the activation function F. The function

$$V_i = \frac{1}{1 + \exp\left[\frac{(\tilde{x}_i - x_i)}{T}\right]} \tag{2}$$

is a widely accepted realistic "sigmoid" or "S-shaped" activation function, representing a smooth switch of neural state V_i from 0 to 1 (not firing to firing) as neuron activity

x_i increases through a threshold value $\tilde{x}_i$. T controls the sharpness of the transition. The dynamic behavior of a network of n neurons is then described by [1]

$$\frac{\partial x_i}{\partial t} = -A_i x_i + \sum_{j=0}^{j=n-1} z_{ij} V_j - \sum_{j=0}^{j=n-1} \tilde{z}_{ij} V_j + I_i(t) \quad (3)$$

and

$$\frac{\partial z_{ij}}{\partial t} = -B_{ij} z_{ij} + D_{ij} \tilde{V}_j u_q(x_i). \quad (4)$$

These two equations form a general description of the way a network's states $\{V_i\}$ (via $\{F(x_i)\}$) and synaptic interconnect weights $\{z_{ij}\}$ develop in time. Changes of state result from input stimuli $\{I_i(t)\}$ and interneural interactions z_{ij}, $\tilde{z}_{ij}$, and A_i, while the z_{ij} change as learning occurs. The rate of change of the synaptic weights must be much slower than that of the neural states, or confusion results. The function $u_i(x_j)$ represents a particular (threshold-linear) activation function, $u_q(x_i) = 0$ for $x_i \leqslant q$, and $u_q(x_i) = x_i$ for $x_i > q$. The variables in (3) and (4) are as follows.

x_i*—Neural Activity:* Quantifies the total level of activity in neuron i mediated by input stimuli and interneural interactions.

$z_{ij}(\tilde{z}_{ij})$*—Excitatory (Inhibitory) Synaptic Weighting Function:* Quantifies the weighting from neuron j to neuron i imposed by the relevant synapse. Learning changes this term. Grossberg splits the $\{z_{ij}\}$ into a path-dependent component and a true synaptic component, which is not necessary for this discussion.

A_i*—Self-Term:* This term represents the passive decay of neural activity in the absence of both synaptic input and direct external input. The solution to (3) is then

$$x_i(t) = x_i(0) \times e^{-A_i t}. \quad (5)$$

I_i*—Input to Neuron i:* The details of I_i are dependent on the network's function and environment. However, in principle, I_i can be made allowed to force a state on the network, or may be switched off completely, to allow the network to settle.

B_{ij}*—Forgetting Term:* Represents passive decay of synaptic weight if B_{ij} is a constant. Memory loss is modulated if B_{ij} is variable.

V_j*—Neural State:* Describes the state of neuron j.

$\tilde{V}_j$*—Neural "Learning Signal":* This variable describes the state of neuron j in the same way as V_j, although allowance is made for a different activation function relating $\tilde{V}_j$ to x_j (a different definition of neural state for learning purposes).

D_{ij}*—Learning Strength:* This allows learning to be modulated for each synaptic link.

The meaning of the terms in (2) and (3) may be related to the network in Fig. 1 as follows, using neuron 3 as an example ($i = 3$). The activity of neuron 3 decays in time owing to the self term $-A_3 x_3$. Its activity is increased by the inputs from the other neurons with excitatory synaptic connections (say neurons 1 and 2), and decreased by those from neurons with inhibitory connections (0). In addition, an external stimulus I_3 may be applied to affect the neuron's activity directly. Grossberg asserts that inhibitory connections are hard-wired and do not change during learning. This restriction is removed here, but the excitatory and inhibitory terms in (3) are kept separate to preserve the original form at this stage.

Continuing the example, (4) implies that synapse z_{31} constantly forgets a portion of itself, and learns new data by altering the synaptic weight z_{31} whenever both the learning signal from neuron 1 ($\tilde{V}_1$) and activity of neuron 3 (x_3) are both positive. The speed of learning is controlled by D_{ij}. Learning is therefore caused by correlations between the presynaptic input $\tilde{V}_1$ and the post-synaptic activity x_3. This is consistent with the accepted idea of learning from psychology, where repetition of an action (neuron 1 increasing neuron 3's activity) causes the action to be learned (by increasing neuron 1's influence on neuron 3 via z_{31}).

Our network style models the smoothly varying and asynchronous form of (3) directly, as does any fundamentally analog network implementation. However, simulation work cannot do this, and learning as yet always proceeds by incremental, discrete steps. Ideally, both the neural activities and states ($\{V_i\}$ and $\{x_i\}$) would change continuously, but understanding of learning mechanisms is such that examples of such unsupervised learning are rare (but see [7] for an example). The following three subsections give some examples of how (3) and (4) can be stepped in time to simulate smooth network dynamics and learning.

1. Hopfield and Other Simplified Models—Network Dynamics: Equation (3) may be written in a simpler form, if we merge the inhibitory and excitatory matrices (i.e., some of the z_{ij} are $\leqslant 0$) to give

$$\frac{\partial x_i}{\partial t} = -A_i x_i + \sum_{j=0}^{j=n-1} z_{ij} V_j(t) + I_i(t). \quad (6)$$

The time evolution of the state of the network may therefore be written as

$$x_i(t+\Delta t) \approx x_i(t) + \Delta t \times \frac{\partial x_i}{\partial t}. \quad (7)$$

This can be written, incorporating (6), as

$$x_i(t+\Delta t) \approx x_i(t) + \Delta t \left[-A_i x_i + \sum_{j=0}^{j=n-1} z_{ij} V_j(t) + I_i(t) \right] \quad (8)$$

for small Δt.

If Δt is taken to be a small constant increment in time, this equation can be stepped in time to simulate the dynamic behavior of the network. In particular, if we choose $\Delta t = A_i^{-1}$, and if $T_{ij} = z_{ij} A_i^{-1}$ and $\tilde{I}_i(t) = I_i(t) A_i^{-1}$

this becomes

$$x_i(t+\Delta t) = x_i(t) + \sum_{j=0}^{j=n-1} T_{ij}V_j(t) + \tilde{I}_i(t). \quad (9)$$

This expression for neural activity is exactly that given by Hopfield [2] for his neural model, with the restriction that $T_{ii}=0$ and $V_i=0$ or 1, with no intermediate values. It is worth remarking here that this represents a time step Δt that is far from small, as A_i is a weak passive decay, and A_i^{-1} is therefore large. Hopfield's network updating scheme is thus an extremely crude representation of time evolution described by (6). We have found that use of a much smaller Δt, and incremental update of the $\{V_i\}$ as is implied by (8) produces more elegant dynamic behavior, and much greater immunity from instability and oscillation. Hopfield also applies a step activation function, $h_q(x_i)=0$ for $x_i \leqslant q$, and $h_q(x_i)=1$ for $x_i > q$, to give a scheme for updating a set of neural states $\{V_i\}$ to give a new set $\{V_i'\}$:

$$V_i' = h_0\left(\sum_{j=0}^{j=n-1} T_{ij}V_j + \tilde{I}_i(t)\right). \quad (10)$$

2. Hopfield and Other Simplified Models — Learning: Creating a link between Grossberg's learning equation (4) and the simple storage prescription described by Hopfield [2] is also possible, although the conditions for equivalence are less trivial. If we expand (4) in the same way as we expanded (3) to give (8), we get an expression for iterating $T_{ij}=A_i^{-1}z_{ij}$ of the form:

$$T_{ij}(t+\Delta t) \approx T_{ij}(t) + \Delta t\left[-B_{ij}T_{ij}(t) + E_{ij}\tilde{V}_j(t)u_0(x_i(t))\right]. \quad (11)$$

To approach Hopfield's formula, we must first replace $u_0(x_i)$ by the step function $h_0(x_i)$ described in the previous section. As in (10), we must also choose $h_0(x_j)$ as the activation function relating $\{\tilde{V}_j(t)\}$ and $\{V_j(t)\}$ to the activities $\{x_j(t)\}$. Equation (11) then becomes

$$T_{ij}(t+\Delta t) \approx T_{ij}(t) + \Delta t\left[-B_{ij}T_{ij}(t) + E_{ij}V_i(t)V_j(t)\right]. \quad (12)$$

Hopfield's learning strategy, or "storage prescription" adjusts the synaptic weights $\{T_{ij}\}$ to store a set of N input vectors $\{V_i(n)\}$. In other words, the $\{V_i(n)\}$ become stable states of the network. For the network to "learn" the states through (12), it must be held in each of the states $\{V_i(n)\}$ for a fixed time Δt, while the synaptic weights evolve according to (12). If the synaptic weights are initially $\{T_{ij}(0)\}$, and are $\{T_{ij}(n)\}$ after exposure to the nth input vector, then (12) gives

$$T_{ij}(n) = T_{ij}(n-1) + \Delta t\left[-B_{ij}T_{ij}(n-1) + E_{ij}V_i(n-1)V_j(n-1)\right]. \quad (13)$$

If we define new constants of the network $\delta_{ij}=B_{ij}\Delta t$ and $\epsilon_{ij}=E_{ij}\Delta t$, this updating scheme gives a final form, once all N vectors $\{V_i(n)\}$ have been presented to the network:

$$T_{ij}(N) = (1-\delta_{ij})^N T_{ij}(0) + \sum_{n=1}^{n=N} V_i(n)V_j(n)\times\epsilon_{ij}(1-\delta_{ij})^{N-n}. \quad (14)$$

If we start with a set of null weights, $\{T_{ij}(0)=0\}$, and there is no forgetting term in the learning equation (i.e., $B_{ij}=0$ and therefore $\delta_{ij}=0$), then, for $\epsilon_{ij}=1$ ($E_{ij}^{-1}=\Delta t$), this gives

$$T_{ij}(N) = \sum_{n=1}^{n+N} V_i(n)V_j(n). \quad (15)$$

This is the Hopfield storage prescription, and again it must be said that this represents a large value for Δt, and therefore a coarse time stepping of (11).

3. Other Learning Recipes: There are many other learning algorithms. We show in this section how the delta rule [8], [9] can be related to the learning equation as expressed in (11) above. The delta rule imposes incremental learning whereby synaptic weights are altered in a series of steps until optimal storage is achieved. Between synaptic weight updates, the neural states are allowed to evolve in a controlled way to study the effects of the last weight change. This strategy amounts to allowing first (4) to dictate the weight changes, and subsequently (3) to dictate the state changes. This separation is necessary to allow simulation. In both cases, as for the Hopfield storage prescription, we must remove the "forgetting term" from (11) and replace $u_0(x_i)$ by V_i. The equation for a single synaptic update then becomes

$$T_{ij}(t+\Delta t) \approx T_{ij}(t) + \Delta t E_{ij}\tilde{V}_j(t)V_i(t). \quad (16)$$

Both the learning algorithms begin by forcing the values $\{V_i(n)\}$ of a particular vector to be stored on to the neurons in the network. The synaptic weights are then held constant while the $\{V_i\}$ are allowed to evolve for a time Δt. Therefore, $V_i(t)=V_i(n)$ and

$$V_i(t+\Delta t) = h_0\left(\sum_{j=0}^{j=n-1} T_{ij}V_j\right).$$

The desired response $\{V_i(n)\}$ is then compared with the actual response $\{V_i(t+\Delta t)\}$, and the result used to compute changes to the synaptic weights. The evolution of the next neural state is achieved by switching off the $\tilde{I}_i(t)$, and the network state develops according to (10). It is the subsequent change in the $\{T_{ij}\}$ at time $t+\Delta t$ via (16) that gives rise to learning.

For the delta rule, the learning signal is derived from the discrepancy between the actual and desired response of the network:

$$\tilde{V}_j(t+\Delta t) = V_j(t) - V_j(t+\Delta t) = V_j(n) - V_j(t+\Delta t). \quad (17)$$

The resultant increment to T_{ij} is then given by allowing T_{ij} to evolve for a time $\Delta t'$, with the neural states returned to their forced "desired" values, and the learning signal defined by (17):

$$\Delta T_{ij} = \Delta t' E_{ij}\left[V_j(n) - V_j(t+\Delta t)\right] \times V_i(n). \quad (18)$$

This is equivalent to the Delta rule.

4. Computational Requirements: Regardless of the updating scheme, and even if a direct implementation of (2) is attempted, the largest computational load is incurred by the weighted summation

$$\sum_{j=0}^{j=n-1} T_{ij}V_j.$$

Most effort in implementation of VLSI networks is concentrated on forming this sum, which contains (potentially) n^2 terms, and it is this calculation that can overwhelm conventional computers.

III. A Review of LSI/VLSI Neural Network Implementations

This catalog of activity is not exhaustive, as its purpose is to place the work reported in this article in the context of other attempts at implementation, rather than to be a definitive review. Neural network implementations fall into two broad categories—digital and analog—and we are active in both areas. We begin this review, therefore, by contrasting these two distinct approaches and highlighting their strengths and weaknesses.

A. Digital Neural Networks

The strengths of a digital approach are almost self-evident. They are:

- design techniques are advanced, automated, and well-understood;
- noise immunity is high;
- computational speed can be very high; and
- learning networks (i.e., those with programmable weights $\{T_{ij}\}$) can be implemented readily.

However, for neural networks, there are several unattractive features:

- digital circuits of this complexity must be synchronous, while real neural nets are asynchronous;
- all states, activities, etc. in a digital network are quantized; and
- digital multipliers, essential to the neural weighting function, occupy large silicon area.

B. Analog Neural Networks

The benefits of analog networks are more subtle:

- asynchronous behavior is automatic;
- smooth neural activation is automatic; and
- circuit elements can be small.

While on the debit side:

- noise immunity is low;
- arbitrarily high precision is not possible; and
- worst of all, no reliable analog, nonvolatile memory technology exists.

Digital technology has not been used extensively to build neural networks, although digital supercomputers have been used extensively in simulation work. Two distinct VLSI approaches are being taken. In the first, a high-speed multiplier is used in a multiplexed mode to calculate

$$\sum_{j=0}^{j=n-1} T_{ij}V_j$$

[10]. Combined with a microprocessor, supporting memory and a custom communications chip set, this forms an impressive neural hardware accelerator, capable of updating (for example) a network with 256 neurons, each with 1024 inputs, in 70 ms. A contrasting approach uses a larger number of bit-serial pipelined custom VLSI multipliers, with lower precision arithmetic, to implement a board capable of updating a similar network in under 2 ms [11].

Both approaches highlight a problem in VLSI neural implementations, in that the stored weights $\{T_{ij}\}$ have to be made available to the multiplication circuitry. In an architecture where a small number of multipliers is used, this means careful communications and fast memory access [10]. Where larger numbers of multipliers are present, local memory must be provided and loaded from standard RAM [11].

This problem also occurs in analog networks, although it is outweighed by the total lack of an analog memory capability. As a result, almost all analog VLSI implementations are nonprogrammable, and therefore have fixed functionality. Subthreshold MOS device characteristics have been used to mimic the nonlinearities of neural behavior, in implementing Hopfield style nets [12], associative memory [13], visual processing functions [14], and auditory processing [15]. Another major research group uses electron-beam programmable resistive interconnects to represent synaptic weights between more conventional operational-amplifier neurons [16], [17]. This work has also spawned an associative memory device using digital memory to store weights, and analog techniques to perform arithmetic [18]. The work reported in the latter portion of this paper, which has been previewed elsewhere [19], [20], uses a similar blend of digital and analog electronics, with greater precision in the interconnect weights. An interesting development is the use of charge-coupled device (CCD)/metal nitride oxide silicon (MNOS) technology to store analog weights, and thus keep the entire neural system analog, and yet programmable [21]. It is not yet clear how reliable, nonvolatile, and accurate the programmed weight memory will be, but this work indicates in our view the ultimate direction that must be taken to develop a true analog memory, even if unusual technology is necessary. Other architectural and computational styles have been proposed using variously charge-coupled device technology [22] and switched-capacitor techniques [23], but these have yet to be tested in silicon.

Most of the analog work is influenced, or at least inspired, by the work of Hopfield and Tank [24], who showed via simulation how neural functionality can be synthesized by networks of operational amplifiers, and demonstrated the technique via an elegant solution of the ubiquitous "traveling salesmen" problem.

IV. Neural Network Architecture and Computational Style

This section discusses the architecture, signaling strategy, and computational style used, without reference to detailed MOS circuitry.

A. Overall Architecture

Fig. 2 shows the architecture of a single network of n totally interconnected neurons. Neurons, represented by circles, signal their states $\{V_i\}$ upward into a matrix of synaptic operators. The state signals are connected to an n-bit horizontal bus running through this synaptic array, with a connection to one synaptic operator in every column. Each column consists, therefore, of n operators, denoted by squares, each adding a new contribution T_{ij} to the running total of activity for the neuron i at the foot of the column. This action is detailed for synapse T_{10} in the diagram. The function of the neuron is therefore to apply a sigmoidal function to this activity x_i to determine a neural state V_i. The synaptic function is to multiply a neural state V_p by a synaptic weight T_{ip} (stored in memory local to the synaptic operator), and add the result to a running total. To highlight this action, the path from neuron 1 to neuron 0 via T_{10} shown in black in Fig. 1 for the small network, is traced in Fig. 2.

This architecture has many attractions for implementation in two-dimensional silicon:

1) the large summation $\Sigma_{j=0}^{j=n-1} T_{ij}V_j$ is distributed in space;
2) the interconnect requirement (n inputs to each neuron) is distributed through a column, reducing the need for long-range wiring to an n-bit state bus;
3) the architecture is modular, and can be expanded or cascaded with ease; and
4) the architecture is regular.

B. Signaling Mechanism

We have given the name "pulse stream" to the signaling mechanism used by the neural circuitry. The process is analagous to that found in natural neural systems, where a neuron that is ON fires a regular train of voltage spikes (at a rate R_j^{max} pulses per second) on its output (or axon), while an OFF neuron does not. We use this signaling mechanism exactly, in that one of our synthetic neuron circuits receives a weighted summation from its input

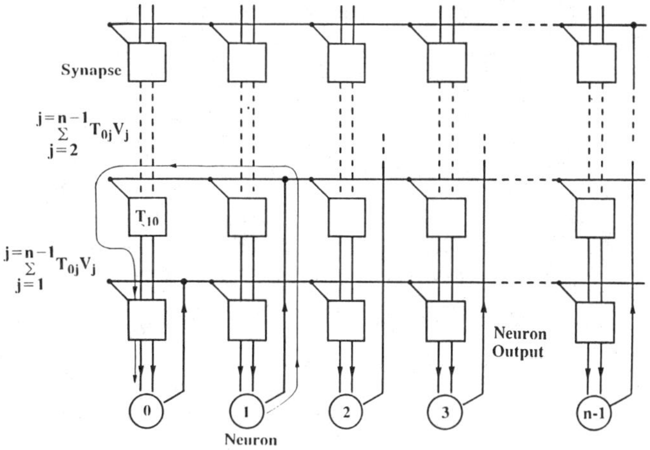

Fig. 2. Generic network architecture (schematic: ○ = neuron, □ = synaptic weighting operator). The interconnect path from neuron 1 to neuron 0 is highlighted.

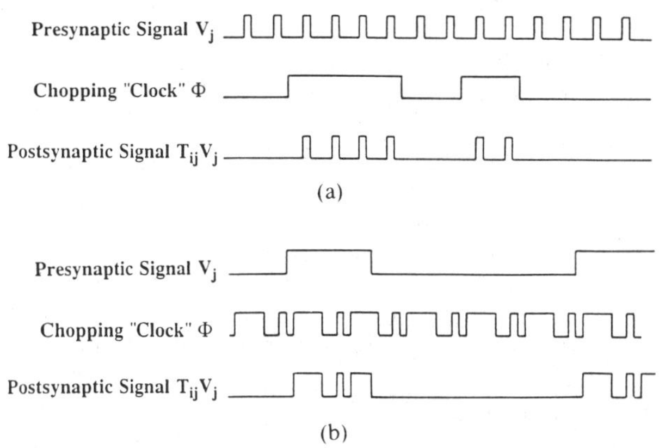

Fig. 3. Pulse-stream weighting: (a) with chopping signals slower than neural pulses, and (b) with chopping signals much faster than neural pulses.

synapses (in the column above in Fig. 2), and operates upon this activity to decide a state and a firing rate.

We also do arithmetic directly on these streams of pulses, by restricting the synaptic weights to $-1 \leqslant T_{ij} \leqslant 1$. The state of a neuron V_j is represented by a firing rate R_j, such that $R_j = 0$ for $V_j = 0$, and $R_j = R_j^{max}$ for $V_j = 1$. We may therefore multiply the state (and therefore perform the synaptic function) by (say) one half (from $V_j = 1$ to $V_j = 0.5$) by removing half of the presynaptic pulses. Similarly, we can multiply by 0.25 by removing three quarters of the pulses and so on. The product $T_{ij}V_j$ therefore becomes the original pulse stream representing V_j, gated by a signal that allows the appropriate fraction of pulses through.

Fig. 3 shows this with a neural state V_j. A "chopping" signal Φ is introduced that is asynchronous to all neural firing, and is logically "high" for exactly the correct fraction of time to allow the appropriate fraction T_{ij} of the presynaptic pulses through. In Fig. 3(a), the chopping clock has a frequency well below R_j^{max}, and appropriately sized bursts of complete neural pulses are allowed through. In Fig. 3(b), each neural pulse is chopped by a signal that is of higher frequency than R_j^{max}. It will be shown that either of these two methods will work.

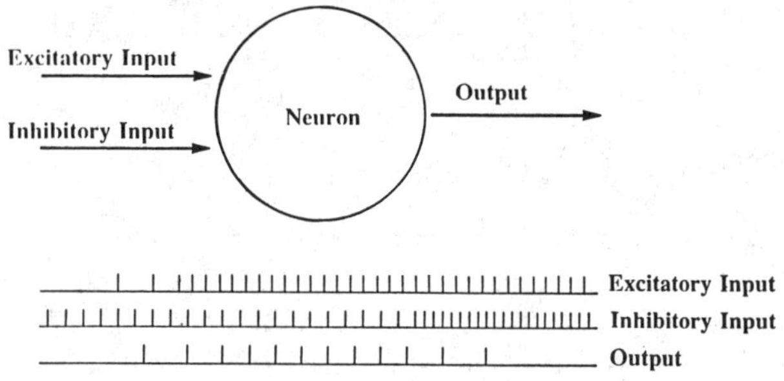

Fig. 4. Neural functional block (schematic).

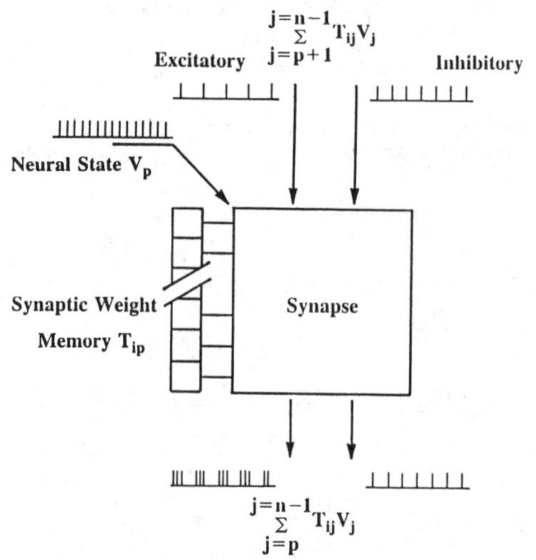

Fig. 5. Synaptic weight functional block (schematic).

C. Neuron Function

The neuron function is illustrated in Fig. 4. The neuron is shown as receiving excitatory and inhibitory inputs, and producing a state output. In the diagram, the neuron is initially OFF, with relatively weak inhibition reinforcing this state. The onset of stronger excitation turns the neuron ON, and it commences firing at its maximum rate $R^{\max}$, and is subsequently switched OFF by strong inhibition.

D. Synaptic Weighting Function

The synaptic function is also straightforward at the functional level. Fig. 5 shows a single synapse block. The (positive or negative) synaptic weight T_{ip} is stored in digital memory. To form the product $T_{ip}V_p$, the presynaptic neural state is gated according to the chopping signals derived from T_{ip}. The resultant product, $T_{ip}V_p$, is added to the running total propagating down either the excitatory or inhibitory activity channel, to add one term to the running total, as shown. One binary bit (the MSBit) of the stored T_{ij} determines whether the contribution is excitatory or inhibitory.

V. Neuron and Synapse Circuit Elements

In this section, the function blocks outlined in Section IV for neural and synaptic functions are expanded into MOS circuitry.

A. Neuron Circuit

Fig. 6 shows a pulse-stream neuron i. The output stage consists of a ring oscillator whose natural frequency is $R^{\max}$, driving a "pulse generator," to convert the oscillator square wave into a sequence of short pulses. Both the oscillator frequency and the pulse length are determined by time constants related to different transistor ON resistances and capacitor values.

The oscillator loop is broken by a NAND gate. The NAND gate acts as an inverter, completing the ring, if the neuron "activity," x_i, is 0 V, and causes the oscillator to fire if x_i is 0 V. The transition between these two states as x_i rises or falls is smooth, if rapid. The neural activity is represented by the voltage level on the capacitor on the NAND gate input. To determine this activity level, the streams of aggregated inhibitory and excitatory pulses are applied to an "integrator" circuit. A p-channel transistor dumps a small packet of charge on the integrating capacitor whenever an excitatory pulse reaches its gate, while an n-channel device removes packets of charge when inhibitory pulses arrive at its gate. In the diagram, the excitatory pulses are more frequency (i.e., the excitation exceeds the inhibition), and the neural activity rises as more charge is dumped than is removed. As a result, the neuron switches ON, and begins to fire.

B. Synaptic Weighting Circuit

Fig. 7 shows a pulse-stream synapse T_{ip}, with precision M bits. The M chopping signals Φ_0, $\Phi_1 - \Phi_M$ are introduced to match the binary bits $0-M$ of the synaptic weight, while the $M+1$'th bit determines the sign of the weight. Clock Φ_M is high for 50 percent of the time, clock Φ_{M-1} for 25 percent, clock Φ_{M-2} for 12.5 percent, etc. The NAND gates attached to the weight bits will therefore allow 50, 25, 12.5 percent (etc.) of the presynaptic pulses in V_p through, if the corresponding bits of T_{ip} are logically high. The chopping signals are asynchronous to the neuron firing signals and the network dynamics, but synchronized to one another. In fact, the sets of chopping signals to different synapses, rows or columns of synapses, or groups of synapses need not be synchronized provided the signals within such a set are synchronized to one another.

The chopping clock signals selected by the bits of T_{ip} are then ORed to form the total chopping clock, which gates the presynaptic neural signal V_p via an AND gate. The resultant product signal $T_{ip}V_p$ is subsequently ORed onto the appropriate output channel, according to the MSBit of T_{ip}.

As stated in Section IV, the chopping signals can be either much slower or much faster than the neural firing rate. Provided the aggregated pulse streams are integrated over a time constant much longer than either the chopping clock period or the firing rate period, it is the proportion of time during which the total input signal is high that matters. This will be the same in both cases, regardless of whether bursts of entire pulses or fragmented pulses are incident on the neuron inputs.

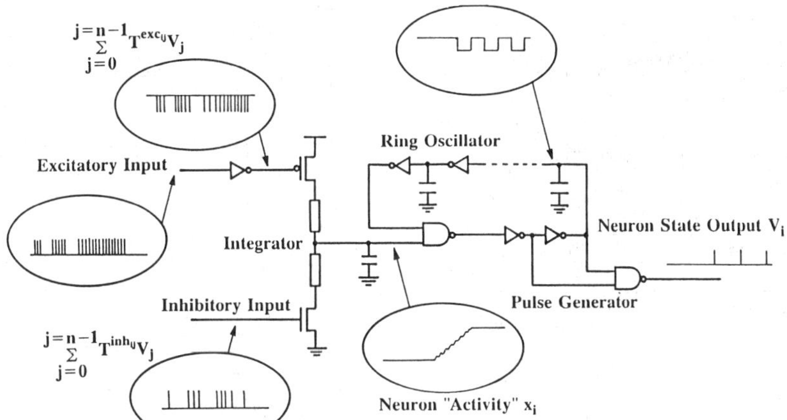

Fig. 6. Neural functional block (details).

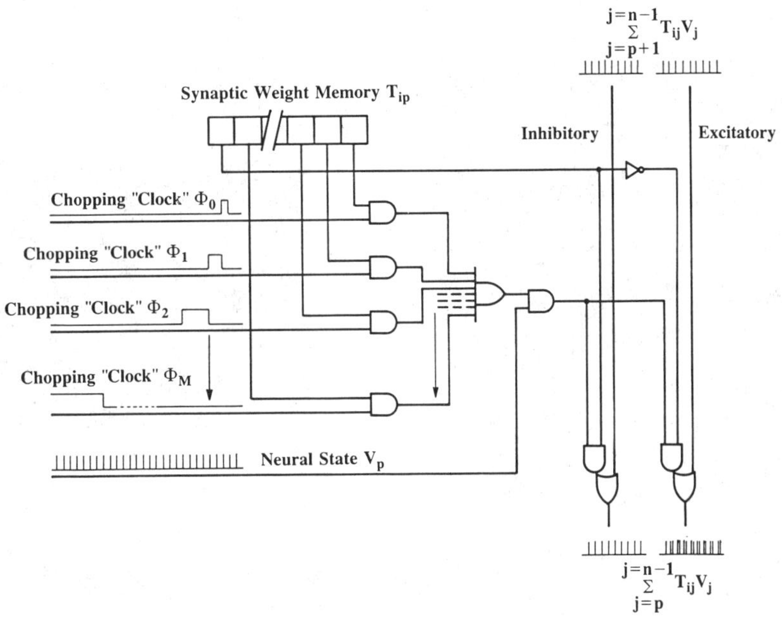

Fig. 7. Synaptic weight functional block (details).

VI. Results

This section gives a summary of the results (from both simulation and silicon). Simulation results are presented where actual oscilloscope traces are uninformative owing to long exposure times. At the time of writing this paper, the full neural board was under construction, and not therefore available. Full results will be published in due course.

A. Physical Layout

Fig. 8 shows an overall chip photograph, and Fig. 9 a detail, from the synaptic array. At present, the neural function is realized in SSI/MSI parts to allow maximum flexibility in the choice of capacitor values, and therefore time constants. The chip integrates 64 synapses (each as shown in Fig. 9), each occupying 200×400 μm^2, so the total chip area is 16 mm^2. It should be noted that the restriction on chip complexity in this application is fundamentally one of pin count, rather than of area. As Fig. 8 shows, some silicon area is wasted, because the standard frame used precludes the availability of extra pins to support further synapses.

Fig. 9 shows a block of 3×3 synapses. Observe at the center synapse that the lower section is a 5-bit shift register, which has a parallel output, and corresponds to the 5-bit T_{ij} memory element. The upper part is that of the controlling logic which gates the chopping clocks with the various bits of the shift register before directing to either of the inhibitory or excitatory output.

B. Simulation Results

Fig. 10 shows a device level (SPICE) simulation of the neural circuit in Fig. 6. The neural potential is the integrator output, representing x_i. A strong excitatory input causes the neuron to turn ON, during which time the neural potential can be seen to rise in steps (corresponding to

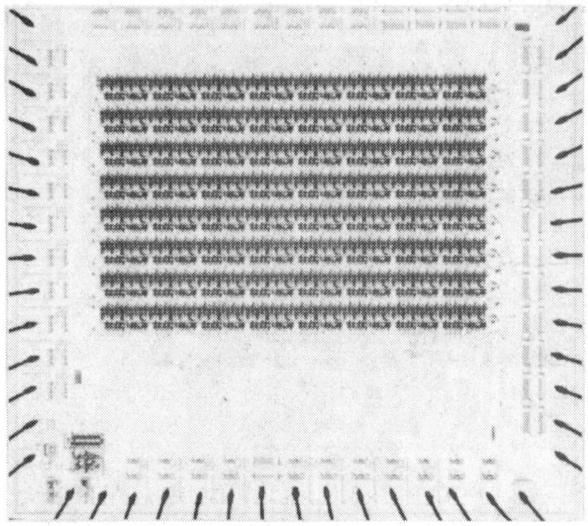

Fig. 8. Integrated circuit implementing an 8×8 synapse array.

Fig. 9. Synapse (chip photograph).

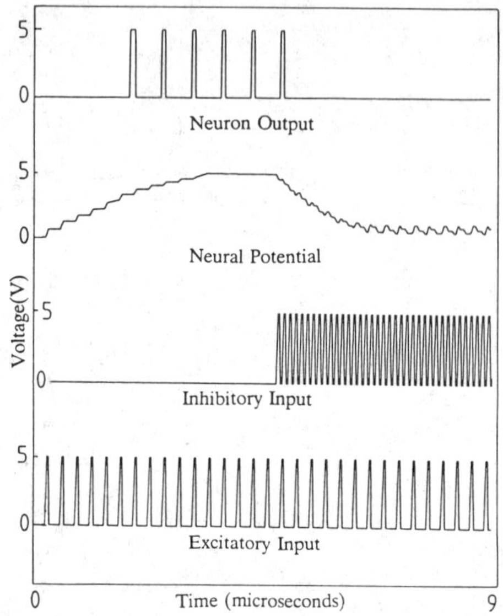

Fig. 10. Analog (SPICE) simulation of neural circuit. A neuron initially OFF is switched ON by an excitatory input, and subsequently switched OFF by stronger inhibition.

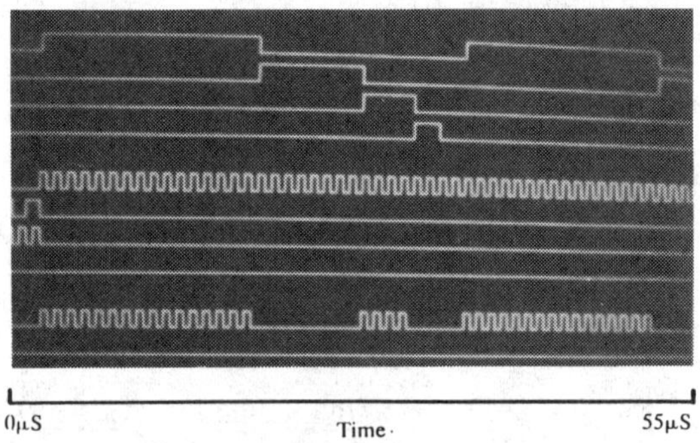

Fig. 11. Input and output waveforms for a synapse weight of +0.625.

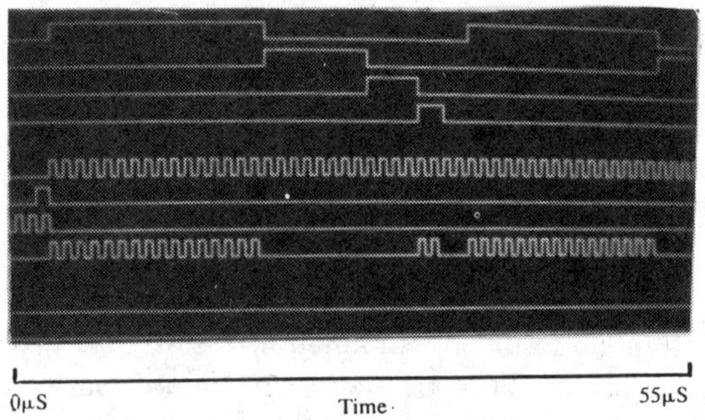

Fig. 12. Input and output waveforms for a synapse weight of −0.5625.

packets of charge being dumped on the integrator capacitor) until the ring oscillator begins to fire. Subsequently, a stronger inhibitory input removes charge packets from the capacitor at a higher rate, driving the neural potential down and switching off the ring oscillator. The "firing" pulses therefore cease.

C. Actual Results

Figs. 11 and 12 show traces from a synapse circuit. The upper four signals in the photograph are the chopping clocks $\Phi_0-\Phi_3$. The clock with the longest high period corresponds to the MSB, and the shortest to the LSB of T_{ij}. The fifth trace is the presynaptic input which is firing constantly. The sixth and seventh traces can be ignored as they relate to the loading of weights. The eighth and ninth traces are, respectively, the inhibitory and the excitatory outputs from the synapse (progressing down the summation column in Fig. 7). Fig. 11 corresponds to a weight T_{ij} of 0.625. All the selected pulses are directed onto the excitatory output line while the inhibitory line remains high, as there are, as yet, no inhibitory pulses propagating down this column. Fig. 12 corresponds to a weight of -0.5625. The pulses are let through on Φ_1 and Φ_4 but not on the Φ_2 and Φ_3. If Φ_1 represents 0.5 and Φ_4 represents 0.0625 then the weight is equal to $0.5+0.0625=0.5625$. Since the pulses are directed to the inhibitory line, the weight T_{ij} is -0.5625.

VII. Conclusions and Future Work

At present, work is in progress to assemble a neural board, interfaced to a host computer for loading weights and initiating computations. The board will comprise a small number of neurons initially ($\simeq 16$) to test the technique properly, and to acquire some experience in controlling the dynamics of this unusual circuit form. Subsequent to this trial period, we hope to assemble a more significant pulse-stream network computer, with enough neurons to perform real tasks.

The initial application area envisaged for our hardware is in automation of the Grossberg/Carpenter classifier network [7], although the "learning" portion of the network's behavior will still be time stepped.

References

[1] S. Grossberg, "Some physiological and biochemical consequences of psychological postulates," *Proc. Nat. Acad. Sci. U.S.*, vol. 60, pp. 758–765, 1968.

[2] J. J. Hopfield, "Neural networks and physical systems with emergent collective computational abilities," *Proc. Nat. Acad. Sci. U.S.*, vol. 79, pp. 2554–2558, Apr. 1982.

[3] R. P. Lippmann, "An introduction to computing with neural nets," *IEEE ASSP Magazine*, vol. 4, pp. 4–22, Apr. 1987.

[4] S. Grossberg, in *Studies of Mind and Brain*. Dordrecht, The Netherlands: Reidel, 1982.

[5] D. J. Wallace, "Memory and learning in a class of neural network models," in *Proc. Workshop Lattice Gauge Theory: A Challenge in Large Scale Computing*, Nov. 1985, pp. 313–331.

[6] P. M. Grant and J. P. Sage, "A comparison of neural network and matched filter processing for detecting lines in images," in *AIP Conf. Proc.*, vol. 151, *Neural Networks for Computing, Snowbird*, John S. Denker, Ed. New York: American Inst. of Physics, 1986, pp. 194–199.

[7] G. A. Carpenter and S. Grossberg, "A massively parallel architecture for a self-organising neural pattern recognition machine," *Computer Vision, Graphics and Image Processing*, vol. 37, pp. 54–116, 1987.

[8] R. S. Sutton and A. G. Barto, "Toward a modern theory of adaptive networks: Expectation and prediction," *Psychol. Rev.*, vol. 88, pp. 135–170, 1981.

[9] D. E. Rumelhart, G. E. Hinton, and R. J. Williams, "Learning internal representations by error propagation," *Parallel Distributed Processing: Explorations in the Microstructure of Cognition*, vol. 1, pp. 318–362, 1986.

[10] S. C. J. Garth, "A chipset for high speed simulation of neural network systems," presented at the IEEE Conf. Neural Networks, San Diego, CA, 1987.

[11] A. F. Murray, A. V. W. Smith, and Z. F. Butler, "Bit-serial neural networks," to be published in *Proc. IEEE Conf. Neural Information Processing Systems — Natural and Synthetic* (Denver, CO), 1987.

[12] M. A. Sivilotti, M. R. Emerling, and C. A. Mead, "VLSI architectures for implementation of neural networks," in *Proc. AIP Conf. Neural Networks for Computing, Snowbird*, 1986, pp. 408–413.

[13] M. Sivilotti, M. R. Emerling, and C. A. Mead, "A novel associative memory implemented using collective computation," in *Proc. Chapel Hill Conf. VLSI*, 1985, pp. 329–342.

[14] M. A. Sivilotti, M. A. Mahowald, and C. A. Mead, "Real-time visual computations using analog CMOS processing arrays," private communication, 1987.

[15] C. A. Mead, in *Analog VLSI and Neural Systems*, 1987, to be published.

[16] W. Hubbard *et al.*, "Electronic neural networks," in *Proc. AIP Conf. Neural Networks for Computing, Snowbird*, 1986, pp. 227–234.

[17] H. P. Graf *et al.*, "VLSI implementation of a neural network memory with several hundreds of neurons," in *Proc. AIP Conf. Neural Networks for Computing, Snowbird*, 1986, pp. 182–187.

[18] H. P. Graf and P. de Vegvar, "A CMOS associative memory chip based on neural networks," in *ISSCC Dig. Tech. Papers*, 1987, pp. 304–305.

[19] A. F. Murray and A. J. W. Smith, "Asynchronous arithmetic for VLSI neural systems," *Electron. Lett.*, vol. 23, no. 12, p. 642, June, 1987.

[20] A. F. Murray and A. V. W. Smith, "A novel computational and signalling method for VLSI neural networks," presented at the European Solid State Circuits Conf., 1987.

[21] J. P. Sage, K. Thompson, and R. S. Withers, "An artificial neural network integrated circuit based on MNOS/CCD principles," in *Proc. AIP Conf. Neural Networks for Computing, Snowbird*, 1986, pp. 381–385.

[22] A. Argranat and A. Yariv, "Semiparallel microelectronic implementation of neural network models using CCD technology," *Electron. Lett.*, vol. 23, no. 11, pp. 580–581, 1987.

[23] Y. P. Tsividis and D. Anastassiou, "Switched-capacitor neural networks," *Electron. Lett.*, vol. 23, no. 18, pp. 958–959, 1987.

[24] J. J. Hopfield and D. W. Tank, "Neural computation of decisions in optimisation problems," *Biol. Cybern.*, vol. 52, pp. 141–152, 1985.

Alan F. Murray was born in 1953 in Edinburgh, Scotland, where he also went to school. In 1975 he received the B.Sc. Hons (1st Class) degree in physics at the University of Edinburgh, and the Ph.D. degree in solid state physics in 1978.

Since then he worked for three years as a Research Physicist (two in Canada), and for three years as an Integrated Circuit Design Engineer. Since 1984 he has been a Lecturer in Electrical Engineering at Edinburgh University. He is interested in all aspects of integrated circuit (IC) design, and is active in VLSI modeling of neural networks. He has 42 publications, including an undergraduate textbook.

Anthony V. W. Smith received the B.Sc. degree in computer technology from Teesside Polytechnic, England, in 1985. He is presently completing the Ph.D. degree at Edinburgh University, Edinburgh, Scotland.

His present interests are in the implementation of, and applications for, neural networks.

Performance of a Stochastic Learning Microchip

Joshua Alspector, Bhusan Gupta,* and Robert B. Allen
Bellcore, Morristown, NJ 07960

We have fabricated a test chip in 2 micron CMOS that can perform supervised learning in a manner similar to the Boltzmann machine. Patterns can be presented to it at 100,000 per second. The chip learns to solve the XOR problem in a few milliseconds. We also have demonstrated the capability to do unsupervised competitive learning with it. The functions of the chip components are examined and the performance is assessed.

1. INTRODUCTION

In previous work,[1] [2] we have pointed out the importance of a local learning rule, feedback connections, and stochastic elements[3] for making learning models that are electronically implementable. We have fabricated a test chip in 2 micron CMOS technology that embodies these ideas and we report our evaluation of the microchip and our plans for improvements.

Knowledge is encoded in the test chip by presenting digital patterns to it that are examples of a desired input-output Boolean mapping. This knowledge is learned and stored entirely on chip in a digitally controlled synapse-like element in the form of connection strengths between neuron-like elements. The only portion of this learning system which is off chip is the VLSI test equipment used to present the patterns.

This learning system uses a modified Boltzmann machine algorithm[3] which, if simulated on a serial digital computer, takes enormous amounts of computer time. Our physical implementation is about 100,000 times faster. The test chip, if expanded to a board-level system of thousands of neurons, would be an appropriate architecture for solving artificial intelligence problems whose solutions are hard to specify using a conventional rule-based approach. Examples include speech and pattern recognition and encoding some types of expert knowledge.

2. CHIP COMPONENTS

Fig. 1 is a photograph of the silicon chip. It contains various test structures, the largest of which, in the lower left, is a neural-style learning network composed of 6 neurons, each with its own noise amplifier, and 15 bidirectional synapses which potentially allow the network to be fully connected. In order to study these components separately, there is a also a noise amplifier in the upper left corner of the chip, a neuron in the upper right, and 2 synapses in the lower right.

* Permanent address: University of California, Berkeley; EE Dep't, Cory Hall; Berkeley, CA 94720

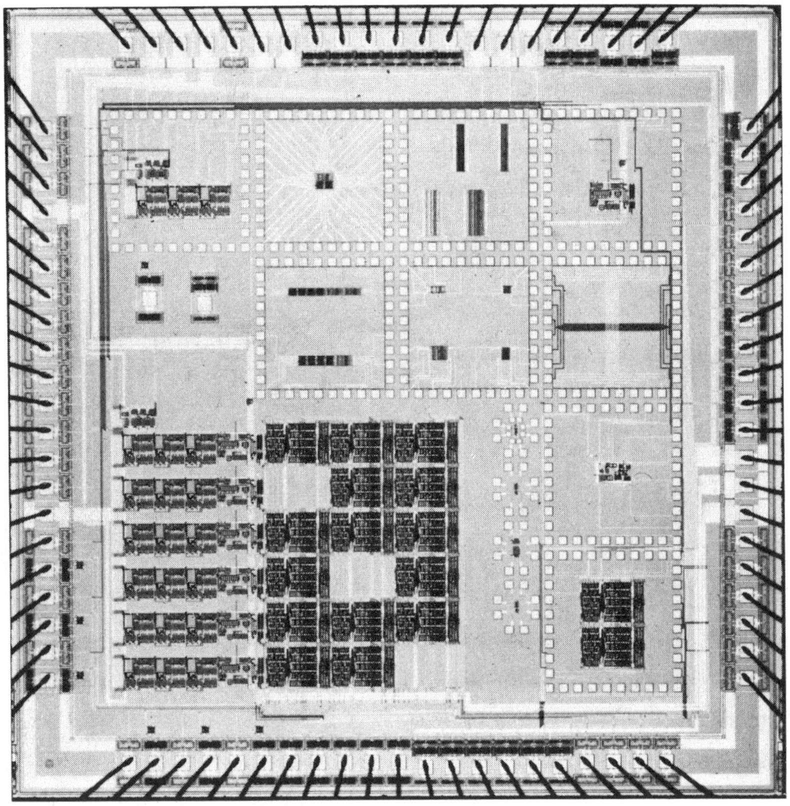

Figure 1. Photograph of Test Chip Containing a Learning Network in Lower Left.

2.1 Neuron

The electronic neuron performs the physical computation:

$$activation = f\,(\Sigma w_{ij}\, s_j + noise) = f\,(gain * net_i)$$

where f is a monotonic non-linear function such as *tanh*. In some of our computer simulations this is a step function corresponding to a high value of *gain*. The signal from other neurons to neuron i is the sum of neural states s_i giving input weighted by the connection strengths w_{ij}, while the *noise* simulates a temperature in a physical thermodynamic system. Their sum is the effective net input net_i.

The model neuron is a double differential amplifier as shown in Fig. 2. Noise and signal have separate differential inputs and are summed at low gain. The differential outputs of this summing stage are converted to a single output by a high gain stage before being fed into a switching arrangement. This selects either the net input or an external clamping signal which forces the neuron into a desired state. The output of the switch is then

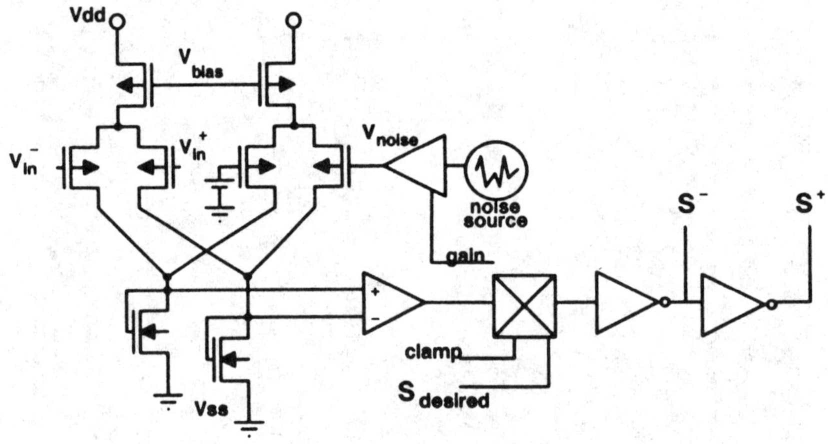

Figure 2. Circuitry of Electronic Analog Neuron.

further amplified before driving the network. The final output approximates a two-state binary neuron.

2.2 Noise amplifier

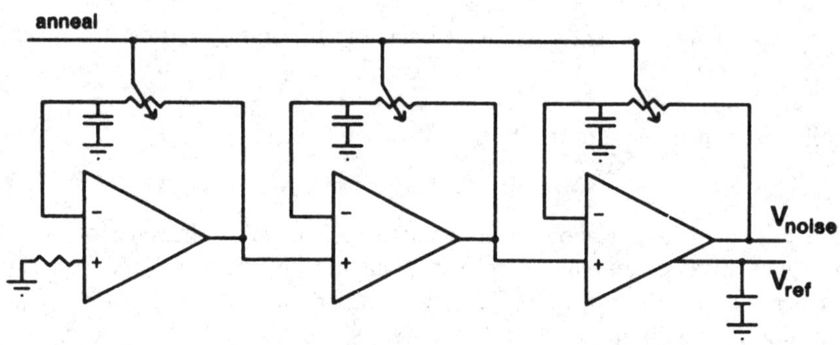

Figure 3. Block Diagram of Noise Amplifier.

Fig. 3 is a block diagram of the noise amplifier. The original idea was to amplify the thermal noise in the channel of a transistor with a gain of nearly a million but to stabilize the dc output using low pass negative feedback in 3 stages. By controlling the feedback, one could control both the bandpass of the noise signal as well as the gain to provide for annealing the temperature (amount of noise) as required by the Boltzmann machine algorithm.[3] Unfortunately this amplifier proved unstable at high gain values leading to oscillations of a few MHz which were highly correlated among all the hoise amplifiers in the network. In spite of this undesirable correlation in the noise signals, the network was still able to learn (see section 3). Rather than a slow "annealing", we used a rapid "heating" and "flash freezing" of the network to randomize it. This was done by momentarily opening a "noise on" switch during the time allotted for annealing. Learning was also demonstrated by clamping the free running neurons momentarily to a pseudo-random state and then releasing them to allow the network to settle.

2.3 Synapse

Fig. 4 is a block diagram of the digitally controlled electronic synapse. The weights are stored as a sign and four bits of magnitude in five flip-flops arranged as an up-down counter. The correlation logic tests whether the two neurons that the synapse connects have the same binary state (correlated) or not at the end of the anneal cycle. If the neurons are correlated in the "teacher" phase (when the teacher is clamping the output neurons in the correct state) and not in the "student" phase (when the output neurons are running free), then a signal to the counter increments the weight by one. If the reverse is true, the counter is decremented. If the "teacher" and "student" phase have the same correlation, no change is made.

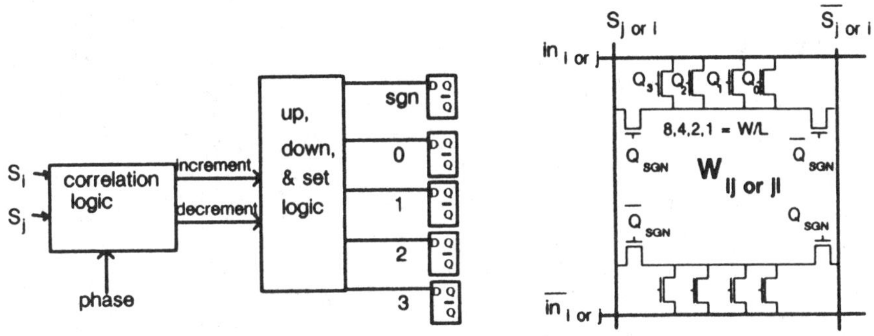

Figure 4. Block Diagram of Synapse.

The digital weight is converted to an analog conductance by a set of pass transistors with graduated binary conductance ratios. Measurements confirmed that the synapse conductance increased monotonically from a value of -15 though +15 as the counter was incremented. The -0 value, when loaded into the synapse, disconnected that link. We usually initialized all the weights to +0 before learning.

3. PERFORMANCE EVALUATION OF NETWORK

3.1 XOR tests

The most difficult test for our 6 neuron network was to have it learn the exclusive-OR function. The network was arranged with 2 input neurons, 2 hidden neurons, and 1 output neuron as shown in Fig. 5. There is also a so-called 'true' neuron which is always clamped on. The negative of the weights from that neuron provide the threshold for the other neurons. The exclusive-OR function is of historical interest because the neural models of the 1960's could not learn it.[4] [5] This is because those learning algorithms did not work when there was a layer of hidden neurons. Networks with only a single layer of modifiable weights could learn the logical OR function but not the exclusive-OR (XOR). The truth table in Fig. 5 shows that the XOR is 1 (on or true) when either one of the two inputs is 1, but not when both are 1. However, recent algorithms such as the Boltzmann machine are able to learn with a hidden layer and hence can solve the XOR.

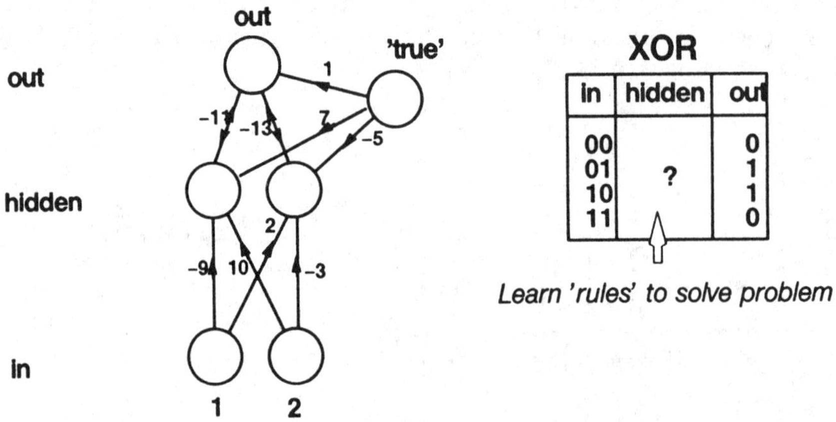

Figure 5. 2-2-1 Network to Learn XOR.

To teach a network to be an XOR, we start with a blank slate where all the weights are zero and then present the patterns of 1's and 0's in the figure with the teacher alternately clamping the output to the correct state and letting it run free. On each presentation, the network is jittered by noise and correlations are counted by each synapse. At the end of each teacher-student cycle, weights are adjusted.

Tests of the chip were conducted using an HP 8180A data generator to present digital patterns to the chip, an HP 8182 data analyzer to capture the chip's digital outputs, and an HP 54112A digitizing oscilloscope to capture waveforms. Analog waveforms were generated using an HP 8770A arbitrary waveform synthesizer feeding a Comlinear E201I amplifier. These instruments were controlled by an HP 9836 computer running UNIX with test programs written in C.

A pattern presentation phase consisted of five subphases and hence five clock cycles of the data generator. The input and/or output pattern to be presented to the clamped neurons is present during all five cycles. The first cycle presents noise or an annealing waveform to the network. The second cycle sends a signal to each synapse to count correlations. The fourth cycle can be used to send a signal to each synapse to adjust weights. This is usually done only after two 5 cycle phases, one for the "teacher" phase and one for the "student" phase. Thus, during learning, ten digital words were used in the data generator for each pattern presentation.

In addition to presenting patterns, digital weights can also be read into the chip with a similar 5 cycle phase. This uses the flip-flop storage arranged as a shift register for weight storage and readout. Because the memory of the data generator was only 1024 bits deep, we would present only 66 patterns (660 words) each time the data generator was loaded by the control computer. The remaining memory was used to initialize the network to its previous value after the destructive readout of weights. In this way, performance of the network was monitored after sets of 66 pseudo-randomly selected patterns. 100 test patterns could also be presented, without learning, to see what performance the network achieved at that point.

For the XOR, we organized the connectivity as in Fig. 5. For example, the connections between input and output neurons were fixed at zero. In order to test the settling of the network, we loaded a set of synapse weights that were learned in one of the computer simulations. We then checked the settling times of the network for various transitions of input states. These varied from 130 to 1700 nanoseconds, with most transitions in the 250 to 600 nanosecond range. The shortest time is a simple settling of the neuron amplifier while the longest time represents several loops of settling of the network before a stable state is found.

For the learning trials, we initialized all weights to zero. Fig. 6 shows three learning curves for a 2-2-1 XOR network (Fig. 5). At first the network performs at chance but it soon learns all the patterns. The values of the weights (which have an accuracy of 4 bits plus a sign) after learning are also shown for one of the trials.

The chip had an easier time learning the XOR function in a network with only one hidden unit provided there were also direct connections from input to output as shown in the inset of Fig. 7. This also demonstrates the flexibility of the connectivity on the chip which would not be possible if we organized it as a strictly layered network. The figure shows the learning curves at various speeds of pattern presentation from 500 to 256,000 patterns per second. The clock rate of the data generator at the highest speed was 2.56 MHz so that the time during which noise was applied was only 400 nanoseconds. The noise amplifier often did not produce an excursion of neural states at these frequencies

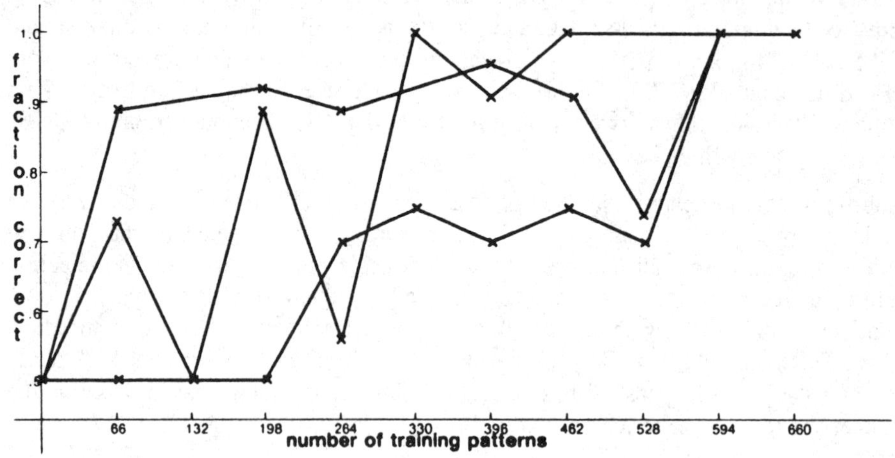

Figure 6. Proportion Correct for On-chip Learning vs. Patterns Presented.

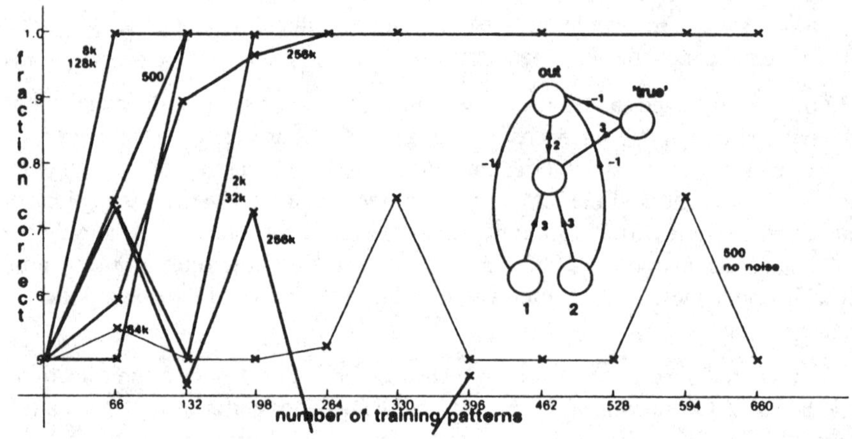

Figure 7. Learning Curves for 2-1-1 XOR at Various Speeds.

effectively limiting learning above this rate. We could have increased the rate by compressing the five cycle phase to three or by random clamping of free running neurons, but probably not by an order of magnitude. Note that noise is necessary for learning by this system as shown by the curve at 500 Hz without noise.

Fig. 8 is an oscilloscope trace of the 4 neural states as a function of time during the pattern presentations.

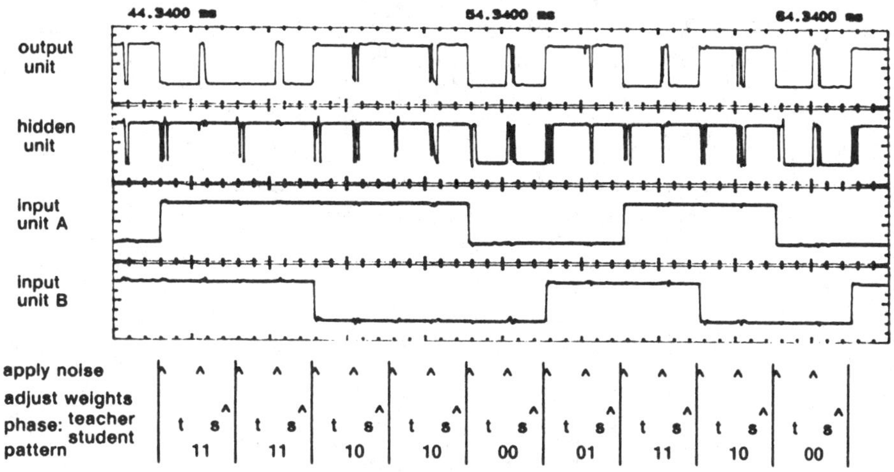

Figure 8. Neural States during Learning.

The time during which noise is applied is apparent from the rapid changes of state in the hidden neuron and also in the output neuron when it is not clamped. Since each pattern presentation can take as little as 5 microseconds, the XOR function can be learned in a few milliseconds. A pattern presentation on a 1 MIP serial computer such as a VAX 11/780 takes about 0.5 seconds with our simulation software.

3.2 Unsupervised Learning

So far, we have described only supervised learning procedures, but the chip can also do unsupervised learning which has no teacher. Nevertheless, the network can learn to classify input patterns according to their similarity to one another. We set the chip connectivity as in Fig. 9 with 4 input neurons and 2 output neurons arranged so that they strongly inhibit each other to form a 'competitive' layer. With noise, this output layer performs a 'winner-take-all' function in that the output neuron which has the strongest net input is on and the other is off. This is because they inhibit each other strongly (are connected to each other with a large negative weight) so that only one can be on. The usual supervised learning rule was effectively simplified by removing the teacher requirement so that correlations always increment weights. Specifically, we stored a comparison pattern in the student phase which consisted of the 'on' state for the two competitive neurons and 'off' for all the input neurons. We then presented patterns to the chip with the "teacher" phase signal on. This has the effect of always decrementing the competitive connections which therefore remain at the lower limit of -15 since it is not possible to have more correlations than the stored "student" phase correlation. On the other hand, the stored "student" phase correlation for the weights leading from the input

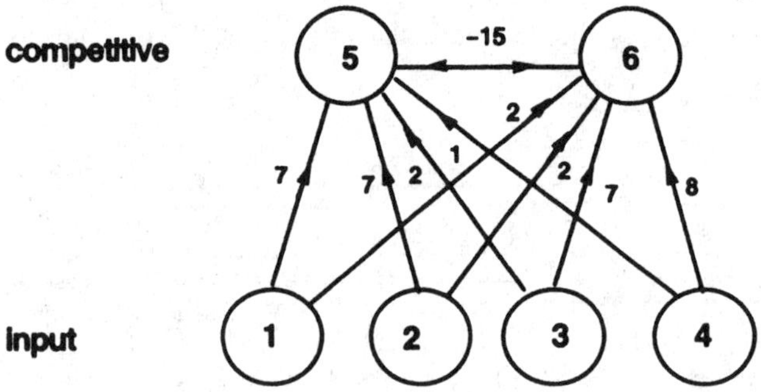

Figure 9. A Competitive Learning Network.

to the competitive layer is zero. Then, the winning output neuron will always be correlated with those input neurons which are 'on' and hence these weights will be incremented. A decay signal decremented weights occasionally to keep them from growing too large. The net effect of such a procedure is for the output neurons to classify the input space among themselves, such that each responds to a particular neighborhood of similar patterns.[2]

To demonstrate competitive learning, an input set was prepared such that the four input bits were not quite random. We picked two input neurons to represent 'left' and the other two to represent 'right'. Patterns were never used with an equal number of left and right neurons on. Eventually one of the two output neurons responded to left weighted patterns and the other to right weighted patterns. Fig. 9 shows one set of weights which were obtained. Therefore the chip learned left from right although nothing in its wiring predisposed it in any way.

3.3 Computer Simulations of Chip Test Conditions

Computer tests were conducted which simulated limitations of the operating chip such as correlated noise. Table 1 presents summaries of 10 replications of 2000 pattern presentations across 5 testing conditions. The Table reports the mean percent correct on the last 100 patterns and, in parentheses, the number of networks which reached 100% performance during at least one block of 100 pattern presentations. The first line of the table shows the performance of the network with no noise. In the next four lines, two parameters of the noise were varied yielding 4 conditions. Specifically, noise was either correlated or uncorrelated across neurons and it was either presented as a single pulse in a "flash freeze" schedule or following a broad annealing schedule.

The 2-1-1 XOR, in which the inputs are directly connected to the outputs, demonstrated very good performance across conditions. Indeed, additional tests of the 2-1-1 in the no-noise condition showed that within 10k patterns all networks reached 100%. This suggests there are deterministic solutions for the 2-1-1.

TABLE 1. Results of Computer Simulations.

noise	schedule	2-1-1 XOR	2-2-1 XOR	4-4-1 parity
no noise	-	92(9)	67(0)	72(0)
correlated	flash freeze	95(9)	83(5)	71(0)
correlated	anneal temperature	99(10)	78(2)	74(0)
uncorrelated	flash freeze	99(10)	84(4)	67(0)
uncorrelated	anneal temperature	99(10)	85(5)	79(0)
no noise	anneal gain	99(9)	81(4)	85(2)

The 2-2-1 networks learned to only 67% correct without noise. Learning with correlated noise degraded performance compared to learning with uncorrelated noise. While the chip contained only 6 neurons it was of interest to consider how limitations such as those studied here might affect solutions to larger problems. Thus, the solution to parity problems were considered and are included in the table.

It is worth noting that the full complexity of the chip's settling and noise distribution is not captured in the discrete time simulations on the computer. The fact that we do not use a circuit simulation may account for some of the differences between the simulations and chip performance. It is interesting to note that learning by the chip was generally faster than learning by the simulation program and that the chip seemed to require noise for learning more than the simulator.

We also considered a system without random noise in which we annealed the inverse gain of the neurons like a temperature through a broad annealing schedule covering the values previously examined[2]. As shown in the last line of the Table this performed comparably to temperature annealing reported above. 10 runs of a 2-2-1 XOR gave a mean performance of 81% with 4 networks reaching 100%. On the 4-4-1 parity problem the mean performance was better than the results of annealing temperature. The mean performance was 85% and 2 networks reached 100%. For still larger problems, such as 6-8-1 parity, performance was comparable to annealing with noise.

4. FUTURE DIRECTIONS

4.1 Applications of Learning Systems

Learning systems give us a way to encode knowledge as a set of training examples rather than as a set of rules. Learned behavior emerges from the training set in ways that depend on the input representation, the network architecture, and the learning procedure. This technique is suitable for problem domains where there are too many rules or where the rules are not known. Two general categories of problems suitable for learning systems are pattern recognition and some types of expert systems.

Pattern recognition of something like an oak leaf is difficult because of the many variations a rule-based system would have to consider even when variations of scale, rotation, and translation are accounted for. Yet, it is quite easy to give a learning system many training examples of oak leaves. Scale, rotation, and translation invariance can be built into the network structure. Similarly, recognition of speech sounds is difficult, but many training examples exist. Here also, pre-processing of the auditory data is important to obtain a useful representation. Another pattern learning task useful in telecommunications is learning the codebook for vector quantization in a real-time visual data compression system.[6]

Expert knowledge is often easier to encode by training examples as well. Experts often do not know the rules they use to troubleshoot equipment or give advice. Again, it is quite easy, by taking a history of such advice, to build a large database of training examples. As knowledge changes, training is a more graceful way of updating a knowledge base than changing the rules. In telephone networks, fault handling or traffic routing are examples of problems for which training is a suitable way of encoding knowledge.

4.2 Future Large-Scale Learning Systems

Because training takes too much computer time in a simulation, physical implementations of learning systems such as ours are necessary for speed. It takes several hours to train a network to recognize a few milliseconds of speech.[7] If we could expand our system to the thousand-neuron level, it would be possible to learn simple speech recognition in real time.

Because the chip uses Ohm's law to multiply, charge conservation to add, device physics to create a threshold step, and a physical noise mechanism for random number generation, we can present training patterns to this chip about 100,000 times faster than the computer simulator. This factor, mostly due to the physical analog computation at this small network size, will increase with the size of the system due to its inherently parallel nature. It would also be possible to build fast special-purpose digital hardware to perform the multiply-accumulate calculations and do fast compares in parallel. Such hardware would take up considerably more silicon area but may be a good way to integrate neural network calculations into existing computer systems. If we could build a large VLSI learning system of, say, 10,000 neurons and 1,000,000 synapses, it would be about a billion times faster than a simulator on a 1 MIP machine. Presumably, such a system will be able to learn things beyond the capability of simulations even if they are run on supercomputers. However, there are several challenges to building these systems.

An algorithmic problem divorced from implementation is the effect of scaling to large size in highly connected networks. The learning time of such a system scales exponentially with the size of the problem.[8] The traditional way of handling complexity in large problems is to break them into smaller subpieces. An effective algorithm is yet to be discovered for doing learning in the modular, hierarchical networks which would be required to handle large problems.

Even from a technological viewpoint, modularity is necessary to manage the connectivity in a typical multiple chip system. A highly connected system, even if it could be built, would take too long to settle even considering the technology and parallel speedups available. Constraints such as power dissipation, capacitive loading across chips, and interchip communication are difficult to solve. If we succeed in these challenges, we will have the problem of presenting data to the system at extremely high rates amounting to several thousand (or more) bits every few microseconds. Biology solves these problems in the visual system, for example, by highly parallel communication via the optic nerve. It is unlikely that we will be able to use a million bit wide bus in our electronic system, however.

Can one take the weights learned by a learning system and simply load them onto a much simpler system with *programmable* rather than *adaptive* synapses? This is perhaps possible for smaller systems where analog inaccuracies and defects can be controlled. Modular networks provide a way of handling inaccuracies. However, for large analog systems, adaptation mechanisms are needed to maintain accuracy. Even if the accuracy were a few percent, a system of only a hundred neurons would be inaccurate across chips. In biological systems, if one were to place the connection strengths found in brain A onto the structures of brain B, the result would be chaos rather than a brain transplant. The robustness of neural systems depends on having the neurons and synapses adapt to the particular environment they find themselves in. Nevertheless, some amount of hard-wiring is probably possible in modular systems if it is modifiable by a trainable portion of the network. A speech recognition system may, for example, adapt in real time to the accents and timbre of a particular speaker. It is also likely that the system would require at least partial training beforehand for robustness.

We plan to design a larger version of our test chip containing both neurons and synapses which can form part of a still larger multiple chip network with the addition of chips containing only synapses. This next chip will have self-powered synapses so that each neuron need only signal its state rather than drive an unknown number of neurons from other chips. In addition, the noise generator will be improved so that true annealing is possible. We may also go further toward a fully analog chip[2] by having a variable gain neuron. Analog charge domain storage of weights and transport of states would further reduce the silicon area necessary but the technology required is not standard.

There are many challenges in scaling learning networks up to the 10^4 neuron and 10^6 synapse range although these large electronic learning networks will have on the order of a billionfold speed advantage over simulations based on serial computers. Thus they may be able to address many longstanding problems in artificial intelligence which have resisted attack by more conventional methods.

References

1. J. Alspector & R.B. Allen, "A neuromorphic VLSI learning system", in *Advanced Research in VLSI: Proceedings of the 1987 Stanford Conference.* edited by P. Losleben (MIT Press, Cambridge, MA, 1987) pp. 313-349.

2. J. Alspector, R.B. Allen, V. Hu, & S. Satyanarayana, "Stochastic learning networks and their electronic implementation", *Neural Information Processing Systems* (Denver, Nov. 1987) pp. 9-21.

3. D.H. Ackley, G.E. Hinton, & T.J. Sejnowski, "A learning algorithm for Boltzmann machines", *Cognitive Science* **9** (1985) pp. 147-169.

4. B. Widrow & M.E. Hoff, "Adaptive switching circuits", *IRE WESCON Convention Record* Part 4, (1960) pp. 96-104.

5. F. Rosenblatt, *Principles of neurodynamics: Perceptrons and the theory of brain mechanisms.* Spartan Books, Washington, D.C. (1961).

6. J. Alspector, "A VLSI approach to neural-style information processing", in *VLSI Signal Processing III.* edited by R.W. Brodersen and H.S. Moscovitz (IEEE Press, New York, 1988) pp. 232-243.

7. T.K. Landauer, C. Kamm, & S. Singhal, "Teaching a minimally structured back-propagation network to recognize speech sounds", *Proceedings of the Cognitive Science Society* (Seattle, Aug. 1987) pp. 531-536.

8. G. Tesauro & B. Janssens, "Scaling relationships in back-propagation learning", *Complex Systems* **2** (1988) pp. 39-44.

Reprinted from *Transactions on Acoustics, Speech, and Signal Processing*, Vol. 36, No. 7, July 1988, pages 1119-1134.

An Analog Electronic Cochlea

RICHARD F. LYON, MEMBER, IEEE, AND CARVER MEAD

Abstract—**An engineered system that hears, such as a speech recognizer, can be designed by modeling the cochlea, or inner ear, and higher levels of the auditory nervous system. To be useful in such a system, a model of the cochlea should incorporate a variety of known effects, such as an asymmetric low-pass/bandpass response at each output channel, a short ringing time, and active adaptation to a wide range of input signal levels. An analog electronic cochlea has been built in CMOS VLSI technology using micropower techniques to achieve this goal of usefulness via realism. The key point of the model and circuit is that a cascade of simple, nearly linear, second-order filter stages with controllable *Q* parameters suffices to capture the physics of the fluid-dynamic traveling-wave system in the cochlea, including the effects of adaptation and active gain involving the outer hair cells. Measurements on the test chip suggest that the circuit matches both the theory and observations from real cochleas.**

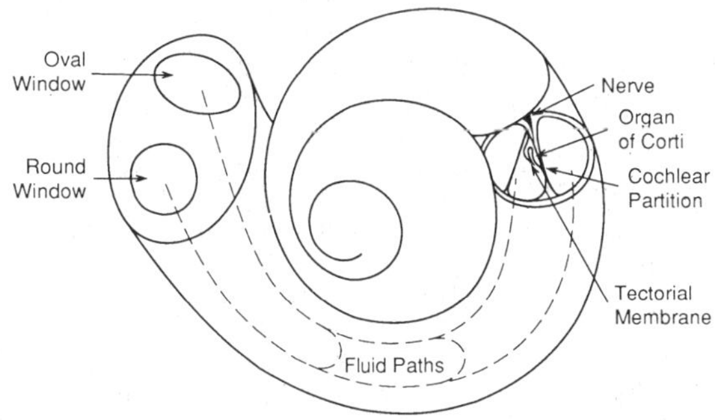

Fig. 1. Artist's conception of the cochlea, with cutaway showing a cross section of a cochlear duct. The bending of the cochlear partition causes a shearing between it and the tectorial membrane, which can be both sensed and amplified by hair cells in the organ of Corti. The dashed lines indicate fluid paths from the input at the oval window and back to the round window for pressure relief.

I. Introduction

WHEN we understand how hearing works, we will be able to build amazing machines with brain-like abilities to interpret the world through sounds (i.e., to *hear*). As part of our endeavor to decipher the auditory nervous system, we can use models that incorporate current ideas of how that system works to engineer simple systems that hear in simple ways. The relative success of these systems then helps us to evaluate our knowledge about hearing, and helps to motivate further research.

As a first step in building machines that hear, we have implemented an analog electronic cochlea that incorporates much of the current state of knowledge about cochlear structure and function. The biological cochlea is a complex three-dimensional fluid-dynamic system, illustrated schematically in Fig. 1. In the process of designing, building, and testing the electronic cochlea, we have had to put together a coherent view of the function of the biological cochlea from the diverse ideas in the literature. This view and the resulting design are the subject of this paper.

The approach used to model the nonuniform fluid-dynamic wave medium of the cochlea as a cascade of filters is based on the observation that the properties of the medium change only slowly and that wave energy is therefore not reflected to any significant degree [1]. The effect of active outer hair cells is included as a variable negative damping term; the variable damping mechanism is shown to be effective as a wide-range automatic gain control (AGC) associated with a moderate change in sharpness of tuning with signal level. The cascade structure enforces unidirectionality, so a coarse discretization in space does not introduce reflections that could otherwise cause instability in an active model. The system is not highly tuned, but rather achieves a high-gain *pseudoresonance* by combining the modest gains of many stages; nevertheless, sharp iso-output tuning curves result from the interaction of the adaptive gains and the filters, as has been observed experimentally in both neural frequency threshold curves and basilar membrane iso-velocity curves.

The cascade filter model is implemented using continuous-time analog CMOS (complementary metal-oxide-semiconductor) VLSI (very large scale integrated) circuits. The building block of the filters is a transconductance amplifier operated in a subthreshold micropower regime, in which the long time constants needed for audio processing can be controlled easily without the use of clock signals. Variable-*Q* second-order filter stages in cascade are adequate to capture most of the important qualitative effects of real cochleas.

Manuscript received February 22, 1988. This work was supported by the System Development Foundation and by Schlumberger Palo Alto Research.
R. F. Lyon is with Apple Computer Inc., Cupertino, CA 95014, and the Department of Computer Science, California Institute of Technology, Pasadena, CA 91125.
C. Mead is with the Department of Computer Science, California Institute of Technology, Pasadena, CA 91125.
IEEE Log Number 8821363.

II. Waves and the Inner Ear

The inner ear, or cochlea, is the interface between sound waves and neural signals. In this section we review several points of view on the purpose, structure, function, and modeling of this complex organ.

A. Background on Hearing

We hear through the sound analyzing action of the cochlea (inner ear) and the auditory centers of the brain.

As with vision, hearing provides a representation of events and objects in the world that are relevant to survival. Just as the natural environment of light rays is cluttered, so is that of sound waves. Hearing systems therefore have evolved to exploit many cues to separate out complex sounds. The same systems that have evolved to help cats catch mice and to warn rabbits of wolves also serve to let human speak with human. Except for the highest level of the brain (the auditory cortex), the hearing systems of these animals are essentially identical.

The mechanical–neural transducer of the hearing system is the hair cell, which evolved from the flow-sensing lateral line organ of fishes and also is used in the inertial equilibrium system of the inner ear. This cell detects the bending motion of its hairs (actually *cilia*) and responds by a change in internal voltage and a release of neurotransmitter. The function of the cochlea is to house these transducers and to perform a first level of separation, so that each transducer processes a differently filtered version of the sound entering the ear. The outer and middle ears gather sound energy and couple it efficiently into the cochlea.

A less obvious but equally important function of the outer, middle, and inner ears is to adapt to a wide range of sound intensities by suppressing loud sounds and by amplifying soft ones. The outer ears are involved by conscious pointing. The middle ear is involved through a protective reflex that contracts the stapedius muscle (and, in some species, the tensor tympani muscle) to reduce the transfer efficiency after detecting a loud sound. The inner ear's involvement is most amazing; it uses hair cells to couple energy back into the acoustic system to amplify weak sounds. Adaptation to signal level continues to be important through higher levels of the nervous system.

Setting aside neural processing for now, let us consider the sound analysis done in the cochlea. Roughly, the cochlea consists of a coiled fluid-filled tube (see Fig. 1) with a stiff *cochlear partition* (the basilar membrane and associated structures) separating the tube lengthwise into two chambers (called ducts or *scalae*). At one end of the tube, called the *basal end*, or simply the *base*, there is a pair of flexible membranes called windows that connect the cochlea acoustically to the middle-ear cavity. A trio of small bones or *middle ear ossicles* couple sound from the eardrum (*tympanic membrane*) into one of the windows, called the *oval window*. When the oval window is pushed in by a sound wave, the fluid in the cochlea moves, the partition between the ducts distorts, and the fluid bulges back out through the *round window* (the elastic round window acts to *complete the circuit*, allowing fluid to move). The hair cells sit along the edge of the partition in a structure known as the *organ of Corti*, and are arranged to couple with the partition motion and the fluid flow that goes with it.

The distortion of the cochlear partition by sounds takes the form of a traveling wave, starting at the base and propagating toward the far end of the cochlear ducts, known as the *apical end*, or *apex*. As the wave propagates, a filtering action occurs in which high frequencies are strongly attenuated; the cutoff frequency gradually lowers with distance from base to apex. The *inner hair cells*, of which there are several thousand, detect the fluid velocity of the wave as it passes. At low sound levels, some frequencies are amplified as they propagate, due to the energy added by the *outer hair cells*, of which there are about three times as many as inner hair cells. As the sound level changes, the effective gain provided by the outer hair cells is adjusted to keep the mechanical response within a more limited range of amplitude.

The propagation of sound energy as hydrodynamic waves in the fluid and partition system is essentially a distributed low-pass filter. The membrane velocity detected at each hair cell is essentially a bandpass-filtered version of the original sound. Analyzing and modeling the function of these low-pass and bandpass mechanisms is the key to understanding the first level of hearing.

A classical view of hearing, known as the *place theory*, is that the cochlea is a spectrum analyzer, and that its output level as a function of *place* (location in the cochlea measured along the dimension from base to apex) is a good characterization of a sound. This view leads to several ways of characterizing the cochlea, such as plots of best frequency versus place, neural firing rate versus place for complex tones, or threshold versus frequency for a given place, that tend to obscure the fact that the cochlea is really a time-domain analyzer. Even the analysis used in this paper, in terms of sinusoidal waves of various frequencies, might give the impression that the cochlea analyzes sounds based on their "frequencies." In fact, the reason sinusoids are used is simply that they are the eigenfunctions of continuous-time linear systems, so the ugly-looking partial-differential-equation formulations of such systems reduce to algebraic equations involving the parameters of the sinusoids.

The mathematical fact that arbitrary finite-energy signals can be represented as infinite sums or integrals of sinusoids should not be construed, as it was by Ohm and Helmholtz [2], to mean that the ear analyzes sounds into sums of sinusoids. The great hearing researcher Georg von Békésy is said to have remarked, "Dehydrated cats and the application of Fourier analysis to hearing problems become more and more a handicap for research in hearing." Animal preparations have improved greatly since then, but there are still too many hearing researchers stuck on the Fourier frequency domain view. The main symptom of this fixation is the widespread interpretation of sharp iso-output tuning curves as implying sharp tuning in the sense of highly resonant or highly frequency-selective filters. Our adaptive nonlinear system view provides a much simpler and more consistent interpretation in terms of unsharp tuning in combination with an AGC.

B. Cochlear Model Background

The cochlea has been modeled by many researchers, from a wide variety of viewpoints. For our purposes, a good model is one that can take real sound as input, in real time, and product output that resembles the signals on the cochlear nerve. The circuit models discussed in this paper are inherently real time, and share important concepts of structure and function with a previous generation of computational models [3], [4].

The two most important concepts kept from the computational models are that the filtering is structured as a cascade of low-order filter stages, and that adaptation is accomplished by some form of *coupled* AGC that is able to change the gains to different output taps separately, but not independently.

Three significant differences between the older computational models and our current circuit models are: first, that pseudoresonance concepts from two-dimensional (2-D) and three-dimensional (3-D) models replace the older resonant-membrane one-dimensional (1-D or *long-wave*) model; second, that adaptive active outer hair cells replace hypothetical mechanisms of gain control; and third, that the implementation is continuous-time analog rather than discrete-time digital.

A cascade of filters is a direct way to model wave propagation in a distributed nonuniform medium. It results in overall transfer functions with sharp (high-order) cutoff using low-order stages. The filter stages can be designed directly from the dispersion relation that characterizes the wave medium. In the previous computational models, the dispersion relations used were based on the long-wave approximation and analysis of Zweig [5] and other researchers, which included an unrealistically large basilar membrane mass in order to achieve a sharp resonant response. For the circuit models, we have used a more accurate hydrodynamic analysis to derive a pseudoresonant response without requiring membrane mass.

A coupled AGC is a functional requirement of a hearing system that must cope with a wide range of loudness and spectral tilt. In the computational models, the AGC was implemented in several layers, following a time-invariant linear filtering layer. In the circuit models, the filtering layer is allowed to be slowly time varying; large gain changes are realized by small changes in the cascaded filter stages. This time-varying nearly linear system approach is in agreement with recent measurements of cochlear mechanics by Robles and his associates [6].

The implementation difference is not entirely an independent issue. Because analog filters cannot easily be made to be precise, they must be made self-adjusting; if the circuits must adjust for their own long-term offsets and drifts, they might as well also adjust to the signal. This seems to be a pervasive principle in perception systems, which are built from sensitive but imprecise components. *Lateral inhibition* is one term often applied to physiological systems that self-adjust, much as our circuit model does [7].

C. Traveling Waves and Sinewave Response

As sounds push on the oval window, a pressure wave starts to move along the scala tympani. The fluid is incompressible and the bone around the cochlea is incompressible, so as the pressure wave mores, it displaces the basilar membrane. When the eardrum is tapped, the middle-ear ossicles will tap on the oval window, and a pressure pulse will travel down the length of the cochlea. In propagating, the pressure pulse deforms the basilar membrane upward; if we could watch, we would see a little bump traveling along the basilar membrane. There is a well-defined velocity at which a signal will travel on such a structure, depending on the physical parameters.

If the basilar membrane is thick and stiff, the wave will travel very fast along the cochlea; if it is thin and flexible, the wave will travel very slowly. The changing properties of the basilar membrane control the velocity of propagation of a wave. Hearing starts by spreading out the sound along a continuous traveling wave structure. The velocity of propagation is a nearly exponential function of the distance along the membrane. The signal starts near the oval window with very *high* velocity of propagation, because the basilar membrane is very thick and stiff at the basal end. As the signal travels toward the apical end, away from the oval window, the basilar membrane becomes thinner and more flexible, so the velocity of propagation *decreases*—it changes by a factor of about 100 along the length of the cochlea.

When the sound is a sine wave of a given frequency, it vibrates the basilar membrane sinusoidally. The wave travels very fast at the basal end, so it has a long wavelength. A constant energy per unit time is being put in, but, as the wave slows down and the wavelength gets shorter, the energy per unit length builds up, so the basilar membrane gets more and more stretched by the wave. For any given frequency, there is a region beyond which the wave can no longer propagate efficiently. The energy is dissipated in the membrane and its associated detection machinery. Past this region, the wave amplitude decreases very rapidly.

Fig. 2 is an artist's conception of what the membrane deflection might look like for a given sine wave. There is a maximum point very near the cutoff point. Fig. 2 depicts only a small section of the basilar membrane. The propagation velocity changes by only about 5 : 1 over the length shown.

D. Neural Machinery

The auditory nerve signal comes out of the machinery, called the organ of Corti, built on the top of the basilar membrane. A protrusion called the *tectorial membrane* is located just above the basilar membrane. We can think about the tectorial membrane's relation to the organ of Corti this way: as the pressure wave travels along the cochlea, it bends the basilar membrane up and down. When the basilar membrane is pushed up, the tectorial membrane moves to the right relative to the basilar mem-

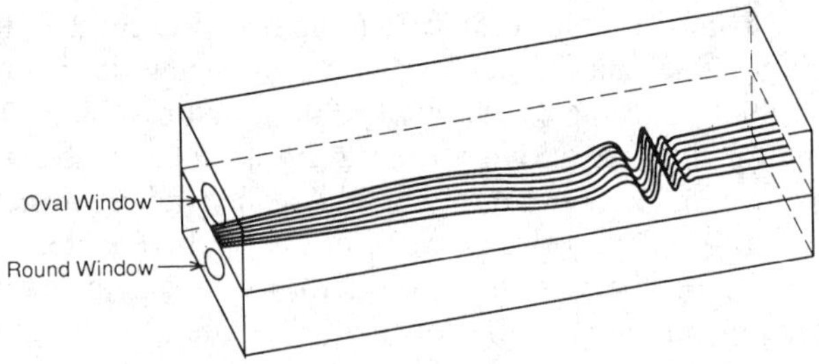

Fig. 2. A sinusoidal traveling wave on the basilar membrane, in a simplified rectangular box model. The basilar membrane (the flexible part of the cochlear partition between the bony shelves) starts out stiff and narrow at the base and becomes more compliant and wider toward the apex. Thus, a wave's propagation velocity and wavelength decrease—the wavenumber, or spatial frequency, increases—as the wave travels from base to apex.

brane. This linkage arrangement is a way of converting up-and-down motion on the basilar membrane to shearing motion between it and the tectorial membrane.

Mounted on the top of the basilar membrane (within the organ of Corti) is a row of inner hair cells. The single row of 3500 (in humans) inner hair cells that runs along the length of the membrane is the primary source of the nerve pulses that travel to the cochlear nucleus and on up into the brain. All the auditory information is carried by about 28 000 (in humans) nerve fibers that originate at the inner hair cells and extend into the brain. Everything heard is dependent on that set of hair cells and nerve cells. Fine hairs, called *stereocilia*, protrude from the end of the inner hair cells; they detect the shearing motion of the membranes and act as the *transducers* that convert deflection to an ion current.

There also are three rows of outer hair cells. These cells do not send information about the sound to the brain. Instead, they function as part of an active amplifier and AGC. Three times as much machinery is dedicated to gain control as to sensing the signal.

On the scale of a hair cell's stereocilia—a small fraction of a micron—the viscosity of the fluid is high. The fluid travels back and forth because of the shearing action between the top of the basilar membrane and the bottom of the tectorial membrane. The fans of cilia sticking out of the hair cells have enough resistance to the motion of the fluid that they bend. When the cilia are bent one way, the hair cells stimulate the primary auditory neurons to fire. When the cilia are bent the other way, no pulses are generated. When the cilia are bent to some position at which the neurons fire, and then are left undisturbed awhile, the neurons stop firing. From then on, bending them in the preferred direction away from that new position causes firings. So the inner hair cells act as auto-zeroing half-wave rectifiers for the velocity of the motion of the fluid. For that reason, all reasonable hearing models assume that the output is a half-wave-rectified version of any signal traveling down the basilar membrane.

Based on the threshold of hearing and linear extrapolations from observations on loud signals, researchers once estimated that a displacement of the cilia by less than one-thousandth of an angstrom (10^{-3} Å or 10^{-13} m) would be enough to give a reasonable probability of evoking a nerve pulse. The actual motion sensed is probably on the order of 1 Å of basilar-membrane displacement or hair-cell bending, which is achieved by active mechanical amplification of sounds near the threshold of hearing.

E. Outer Hair Cells

The large structure of the organ of Corti on top of the membrane absorbs energy from the traveling wave. In the absence of intervention from the outer hair cells, the membrane response is reasonably damped. The membrane itself is not a highly resonant structure—the ear was designed to hear transients.

What then is the purpose of the outer hair cells? There are only a few slow nerve fibers coming back into the auditory nerve from the outer hair cells. On the other hand, there are a large number of fibers coming *down* from higher places in the brain into the cochlea, and they synapse onto these outer hair cells. The outer hair cells are *not* used primarily as receptors—they are used as *muscles*. If they are not inhibited by the efferent (*from* the brain) fibers, they provide *positive* feedback into the membrane. If they are bent, they push even harder in the same direction. They can put enough energy back into the basilar membrane that it will actually oscillate under some conditions; the resulting ringing in the ears is called tinnitus.

Tinnitus is not caused by an out-of-control sensory neuron as one might suppose. It is a *physical oscillation* in the cochlea that is driven by the outer hair cells. The cells pump energy back into the oscillations of the basilar membrane, and they can pump enough energy to make the traveling-wave structure unstable, so it creates an oscillatory wave that propagates back out through the eardrum into the air. In 1981, Zurek and Clark [8] reported spontaneous acoustic emission from a chinchilla that made such a squeal that it could be heard from several meters away by a human's unaided ear. An excellent and insightful overview of the role of outer hair cells for active gain control in the auditory system is given by Kim. In a classic monument of understatement, he comments on the chinchilla results, "It is highly implausible that such an intense and sustained acoustic signal could emanate from a passive mechanical system" [9, p. 251].

So, the outer hair cells are used as muscles and their function is to reduce the damping of the basilar membrane when the sound input would be otherwise too weak to hear.

F. Gain Control

The function of the outer-hair-cell arrangement is to provide not just gain, but control of the gain, which it

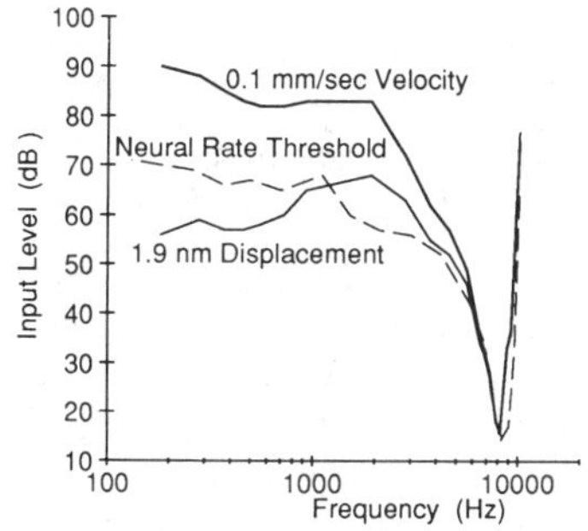

Fig. 3. Mechanical and neural iso-output tuning curves, based on data from Robles and his associates [6]. The mechanical measurements (amount of input needed to get 1 mm/s basilar membrane displacement velocity or 19 Å basilar membrane displacement amplitude) were made by measuring Doppler-shifted gamma rays (Mössbauer effect) from a small radioactive source mounted on the cochlear partition. The neural tuning curve was measured by looking for a specified increase in firing rate of a single fiber in the cochlear nerve.

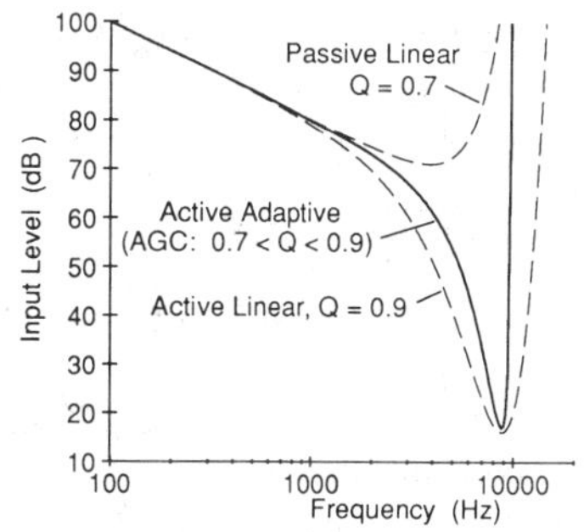

Fig. 4. Model iso-output tuning curves for linear models (dashed curves) and for a particular nonlinear AGC scheme (solid curve) that varies the model gain by varying the Q of the cascaded filter stages. The similarity in the response area shape and width between the active adaptive model and the biological system (Fig. 3) is striking. For this simulation, all filter stage Q values are equal, and are computed from a feedback gain α that is a maximum value minus a constant times the total output of 100 channels. The relation of Q values to overall gains and overall transfer functions is discussed in the text.

does by a factor of about 100 in amplitude (10 000 in energy).

When the signal is small, the outer hair cells are not inhibited and they feed back energy. They reduce the damping until the signal reaching the higher brain centers is large enough. The AGC system works for sound power levels within a few decades of the bottom end of our hearing range by making the structure slightly more resonant and thereby much higher gain—by reducing the damping until it is negative in some regions.

Fig. 3 shows the sound pressure level required to produce a fixed membrane displacement amplitude or velocity, compared to the level required to produce a certain increase in the rate of firing of a single auditory nerve fiber. The data were obtained by Robles and his associates [6], using the Mössbauer effect in chinchilla cochlea. Curves such as these are termed *iso-output* curves, because the input level is adjusted to produce the same output level at each frequency; the region above an iso-output curve is known as the *response area*. The curves show reasonable agreement between neural and mechanical data, implying that the response area is already determined at the mechanical level. Without the outer hair cells, the sensitivity is at least 30 dB less, and the curve tips are much broader [9]. The sharpness of such tuning curves (i.e., response area widths of only about one-fourth to one-tenth of the center frequency) often misleads model developers into thinking that the system is narrowly tuned, when in fact the curves are quite different from transfer functions. As frequency changes, the input level and AGC gains change enormously, in opposite directions, to keep the output at a constant level. The filter-gain shapes are difficult to infer from this kind of measurement, but they must be broader than are the iso-output tuning-curve shapes.

Fig. 4 shows iso-output curves for a cochlear model as described in this paper, under two linear conditions (a passive low-gain condition, as in a cochlea with dead or damaged outer hair cells, and an active high-gain condition, as in a hypothetical cochlea with active outer hairs of constant gain and unlimited energy), and under the condition of an AGC that acts to adapt the gain between the two linear conditions in response to the average output level. The curves show that a simple gain-control loop can cause a broadly tuned filter to appear to have a much narrower response when observed with an iso-output criterion; further examples of this effect have been shown by Lyon and Dyer [10].

This neural/mechanical AGC is an intelligently designed gain-control system. It takes effect before the signal is translated into nerve pulses, just as does the visual gain-control system in the retina [11]. Nerve pulses are by their very nature a horrible medium into which to translate sound. They are noisy and erratic, and can work over only a limited dynamic range of firing rates. It makes sense to have a first level of AGC *before* the signal is turned into nerve pulses, because this approach reduces the noise associated with the quantization of the signal.

III. Mathematical Approach

As we have discussed above, sounds entering the cochlea initiate traveling waves of fluid pressure and cochlear partition motion that propagate from the base toward the apex. The fluid-mechanical system of ducts separated by a flexible partition is like a waveguide, in which wavelength and propagation velocity depend on the frequency of a wave and on the physical properties of the waveguide. In the cochlea, the physical properties of the partition are not constant with distance, but instead change radically from base to apex. The changing parameters lead to the desirable behavior of sorting out sounds by their frequencies or time scales; unfortunately, the parameter variability makes the wave analysis a bit more complex. This section discusses the mathematics of waves in such varying media.

A. Mathematical Waves

The instantaneous value W of the pressure or displacement of a wave propagating in a one-dimensional medium often is described in terms of single frequencies as the real part of a complex exponential, to simplify the analysis of the wave equations. For our current purposes, the real-valued formulation is adequate:

$$W(x, t) = A(x) \cos (kx - \omega t). \quad (1)$$

If frequency ω and wavenumber k (spatial frequency) are positive and real and A is constant, W is a wave propagating to the right (toward $+x$) at a phase velocity $c = \omega / k$ with no change in amplitude.

Differential equations involving W generally are derived from the physics of the system (or from an approximation, such as a 2-D cochlear model). We can then convert the differential equations to algebraic equations involving ω, k, and parameters of the system by noting that W can be factored out of its derivatives when $A(x)$ is constant (or if A is assumed constant when it is nearly so). These algebraic equations are referred to as *eikonal equations* or *dispersion relations*. Pairs of ω and k that satisfy the dispersion relations represent waves compatible with the physical system.

From the dispersion relations, we can calculate the velocity of the wave. If c is independent of ω, all frequencies travel at the same speed and the medium is said to be *nondispersive*. Real media tend to be lossy and dispersive; in the cochlea, higher frequencies are known to propagate more slowly than lower frequencies. In dispersive media, the group velocity U, or the speed at which wave envelopes and energy propagate, is the derivative $d\omega / dk$, which differs from the phase velocity ω / k.

Dispersion relations generally have symmetric solutions, such that any wave traveling in one direction has a corresponding solution of the same frequency, traveling with the same speed in the opposite direction. If, for a given real value of ω, the solution for k is complex, then the equations imply a wave amplitude that is growing or diminishing exponentially with distance x. If the imaginary part k_i of $k = k_r + jk_i$ is positive (depending on the complex exponential wave conventions adopted), the wave diminishes toward the right ($+x$); in a dissipative system, a wave diminishes in the direction that it travels. The wave may be written as the damped sinusoid.

$$W(x, t) = A \cos (k_r x - \omega t) e^{-k_i x}. \quad (2)$$

In the cochlea, working out the relations between ω and k is more complex than in a one-dimensional wave system, such as a vibrating string. The fluid-flow problem must be worked out first in two or three dimensions, but ultimately it is possible to represent displacement, velocity, and pressure waves on the cochlear partition in one dimension as k varies with ω and x.

B. Nonuniform Media and Filter Cascades

As we will see, the dispersion relations that must be satisfied by values of ω and k involve the physical parameters of the cochlear partition and cochlear ducts, which are changing with the x dimension (conventionally referred to as the cochlear *place* dimension, or simply place). The differential equations that describe the nonuniform physical system are not solvable except under specific restrictions of form. Nevertheless, excellent approximate solutions for wave propagation in such nonuniform media are well known, and correspond to a wave propagating locally according to local wavenumber solutions. Any small section of the medium of length Δx over which the properties do not change much behaves just as would a small section in a uniform medium. It contributes a phase shift $k_r \Delta x$ and a log gain $-k_i \Delta x$. The amplitude $A(x)$ also may need to be adjusted to conserve energy as energy-storage parameters such as spring constants (membrane stiffness) change, even in a lossless medium (these observations are equivalent to the *WKB approximation* often invoked to solve cochlear model differential equations).

The wave amplitudes $A(x)$ for pressure or velocity potential in a passive lossless cochlea are roughly constant (in the case of a 2-D short-wave approximation, their amplitudes are exactly constant as the wavenumber k increases). Conversion to basilar-membrane displacement or velocity involves a spatial differentiation, so amplitudes will increase proportional to k as the waves travel. Loss terms tend to be high order (i.e., roughly proportional to a high power of frequency), so losses reduce the wave energy quickly near cutoff, more than cancelling the slowly increasing $A(x)$. The resulting rise and fall has been termed a *pseudoresonance* [12]; it does not involve a resonance between membrane mass and stiffness, as some models do, and it is not sharply tuned. Low-order passive-loss or active-gain terms mainly affect the height of the pseudoresonance, and have relatively less effect on its peak position and cutoff sharpness.

A wave-propagation medium can be approximated (for waves traveling in one direction) by a cascade of filters (single-input, single-output, linear, continuous-time, or discrete-time systems). A filter is typically characterized by its transfer function $H(\omega)$, sometimes expressed as $H(s)$ or $H(Z)$, with $s = j\omega$ for continuous-time systems or $Z = e^{j\omega\Delta t}$ for discrete-time systems. A nonuniform wave medium such as the cochlea can be spatially discretized by looking at the outputs of N short sections of length Δx; the section outputs, or *taps*, can be indexed by n, an integer place designator that corresponds to the x location $n\Delta x$. A cascade of filters $H_1, H_2, \cdots, H_n, \cdots, H_N$ can be designed to approximate the response of the wave medium at the output taps. In passing from tap $n - 1$ to tap n, a propagating (complex) wave will be modified by a factor of $H_n(\omega)$, which should match the effect of the wave medium.

The equivalent transfer function $H_n(\omega)$, a function of place (tap number n) and frequency, is thus directly related to the complex wavenumber $k(\omega, x)$, a function of place and frequency. The relation between the filter cascade and the wave medium is

$$H_n(\omega) = e^{jk\Delta x} \quad \text{with } k \text{ evaluated at } x = n\Delta x. \quad (3)$$

Because H and k can both be complex, we can separate

the phase and loss terms using $\log H = \log |H| + j \arg H$:

$$\log H = jk\Delta x = jk_r\Delta x - k_i\Delta x. \quad (4)$$

Therefore, if we want to model the action of the cochlea by a cascade of simple filters, each filter should be designed to have a phase shift or delay that matches k_r and a gain or loss that matches k_i, all as a function of frequency

$$\text{gain} = e^{-k_i \Delta x} \quad (5)$$

$$\text{group delay} = \frac{d\text{ phase}}{d\omega} = \frac{dk_r}{d\omega}\Delta x = \frac{\Delta x}{U} \quad (6)$$

(where U is the group velocity; the equation implies that the previous definition of group velocity, $d\omega/dk$, is correctly generalized to $d\omega/dk_r$). The overall transfer function of the cascade of filters, from input to tap m, which we call $\boldsymbol{H}^m$, is

$$\boldsymbol{H}^m(\omega) = \prod_{n=0}^{m} H_n(\omega)$$

$$= \exp j \sum_{n=0}^{m} k(\omega, n\Delta x)\Delta x. \quad (7)$$

The integral form of the sum in the last line in (7) is the form usually used as the WKB approximation: $\int k\, dx$. This formulation implies that we could be more exact by using k values averaged over sections of x, rather than values at selected points.

In the cochlea, k is nearly real for frequencies significantly below cutoff; that is, the filters are simply lossless delay stages at low frequencies. The gains may be slightly greater than unity at middle frequencies, when the input signal is small and the cochlea is actively undamped; at high frequencies, however, the gains always approach zero. Near cutoff, a small change in the value of k_i corresponds to a small change in the gain of a section and a potentially large change in the overall gain of the cascade.

These formulas provide a way to translate between a distributed-parameter wave view and a lumped-parameter filter view of the cochlea. The filter-cascade model can be implemented easily, with either analog or digital circuits, and will be realistic to the extent that waves do not reflect back toward the base and that the sections are small enough that the value of k does not change much within a section. In our experimental circuits, k may change appreciably between the rather widely spaced output taps, so several filter stages are used per tap.

C. Scaling

A filter cascade or wave medium is said to *scale* (or be *scale-invariant*) if the response properties at any point are just like those at any other point with a change in time scale. It is particularly easy to build filter cascades that scale, because each stage is identical except that time constants change by a constant ratio from one stage to the next. In general, all numeric characteristics such as cutoff frequencies and component values in such a system will be geometric (exponential) functions of x, the place dimension, or of n, the stage index.

In a system that scales, the response for all places can be specified as a single transfer function $H(f)$, where f is a nondimensional normalized frequency

$$f = \omega/\omega_N \quad (8)$$

where ω_N is any conveniently defined natural frequency that depends on the place (e.g., we choose $\omega_N = 1/\tau$ to characterize filters made with time constants of τ). Because of the assumed geometric variation of parameters, we can write ω_N as

$$\omega_N = \omega_0 e^{-x/d_\omega} \quad (9)$$

where ω_0 is the natural frequency at $x = 0$ (at the base) and d_ω is the characteristic distance in which ω_N decreases by a factor of e.

Changing to a log-frequency scale in terms of $l_f = \log f$, we define the function $G(l_f) = H(f)$, which may be written as

$$G(l_f) = G\left(\log \frac{\omega}{\omega_N}\right) = G\left(\log \frac{\omega}{\omega_0} + \frac{x}{d_\omega}\right). \quad (10)$$

This equation shows that the transfer function G expressed as a function of log frequency l_f is identical to the transfer function for a particular frequency ω expressed as a function of place x, for an appropriate offset and place scaling. Thus, we can label the independent axes of transfer function plots interchangeably in either place or log frequency units, for a particular frequency or place respectively.

In the cochlea, the function G will be low-pass. Above a certain cutoff frequency, depending on the place, the magnitude of the response will quickly approach zero; equivalently, beyond a certain place, depending on frequency, the response will quickly approach zero.

The stiffness is the most important parameter of the cochlear partition that changes from base to apex, and has the effect of changing the characteristic frequency scale with place (ω_N varies as the square root of stiffness if other parameters, such as duct size, are constant). Over much of the x dimension of real cochleas, the stiffness varies approximately geometrically [13].

In the real cochlea, responses scale only for frequencies above about 1 kHz. The scaling assumption simply allows us the convenience of summarizing the response of the entire system by a single function G, and does not prevent us from adopting more realistic parameter variations later. The scaling property also simplifies the design of analog CMOS circuits.

IV. Active Fluid Mechanics of the Cochlea

The lowest-order loss mechanism in the cochlea probably is a viscous drag of fluid moving in a boundary layer near the basilar membrane and through the small spaces of the organ of Corti. The sensitive cilia of the inner hair cells that detect motion are moved by viscous drag. The outer hair cells also interact with the fluid and membranes in the organ of Corti, and are known to be a source of energy, rather than a sink. Apparently, at low sound levels, the outer hair cells can supply more than enough energy to make up for the energy lost to viscous drag. In this section we discuss such active fluid mechanical effects.

A. Active and Adaptation Undamping

Looking at the effect of the outer hair cells as negative resistances (being added to the positive resistances of viscous loss), we find that the low-order viscous loss term becomes a low-order gain term; that is, the wavenumber has a negative imaginary part until, at high enough frequency, a higher-order loss mechanism dominates.

A system with active gain can be modeled easily as a time-invariant linear system; it will have the same gain no matter how loud the sound input is. The live cochlea, however, is known to be highly adaptive and compressive, such that the mechanical gain is must less for loud inputs than for soft inputs. This nonlinear (but short-term nearly linear) behavior makes sense for several reasons: first, the mechanism that adds energy must of necessity be energy-supply limited; and second, even at relatively low levels, the variation of the gain can be useful in compressing inputs into a usable dynamic range, without causing excessive distortion.

In the analog circuit model we shall describe below, the gain of a filter at middle frequencies is controlled by the filter's Q value. For Q less than 0.707, the gain of a two-pole filter stage will be less than unity at all frequencies; for slightly higher Q values, the filter stage is a simple but reasonable model of an actively undamped section of the cochlear transmission line, with gain exceeding unity over a limited bandwidth. By varying the filter's Q value adaptively in response to sound, the filter can model a range of positive and negative damping, and can thereby cause large overall gain changes.

Researchers who attempted previously to model active wave amplification in the cochlea often met with difficulties, especially when the place dimension was discretized for numerical solution. It has been shown recently that slight irregularities in the cochlea can reflect enough energy to make the system break into unstable oscillations (as in tinnitus) [14]; models that use discrete sections and allow waves to propagate in both directions sometimes suffer from the same problem. By taking advantage of the known normal mode of cochlea operation by propagating signals in only one direction, our circuit model avoids the stability problem as long as each section is independently stable.

B. Fluid Mechanical Results

The analysis of the hydrodynamic system of the cochlea yields a relation among frequency, place, and complex wavenumber. The analyses we used are based on three good approximations normally employed to make the hydrodynamics problem relatively simple. First, we assume that the cochlear fluids have essentially zero viscosity, so the sound energy is not dissipated in the bulk of the fluid, but rather is transferred into motion of the organ of Corti. Second, we assume that the fluid is incompressible or, equivalently, that the velocity of sound in the fluid is large compared to the velocities of the waves on the cochlear partition (see [15] for more on the two wave speeds). Third, we assume fluid motions to be small, so we can neglect second-order motion terms; for sound levels within the normal range of hearing this is a good approximation.

The 3-D hydrodynamics problem has been considered from several points of view, including a 2-D analysis (assuming that fluid velocities do not vary across the width of the membrane, but do vary within the depth of the ducts), a 2-D analysis corrected for the difference between the membrane width and the duct width in the region of long wavelengths, and a full 3-D fluid-motion analysis. By comparing these models and results, we observe that the extra *width* of the ducts relative to the membrane has the approximate physical effect of extending the short-wave behavior further into the region that would be considered long-wave if the membrane covered the full width of the duct. Because of this, the 2-D shortwave model matches the 3-D results quite well (better than the full 2-D model does), except in the extreme long-wave region (i.e., it overestimates wavelengths and velocities in the base region for low frequencies). The beauty of the 2-D shortwave analysis is that both the physical model and the dispersion relations derived from it are greatly simplified relative to the other models (hyperbolic and trigonometric functions are entirely avoided) [16].

The details of the hydrodynamic analysis and reasoning about physical approximations are too lengthy to include in this paper, but we can summarize the results by the short-wave dispersion relation (with complex k), which is

$$\omega^2 \rho = \pm k[S - j\omega(\beta + k^2\gamma)] \tag{11}$$

where β is a low-order (viscous) loss coefficient (which may be negative in the actively undamped case), γ is a high-order (bending) loss coefficient, S is the membrane stiffness, and ρ is the mass density of the fluid. Parameters S, β, and γ change with place, but only β is considered to change with time as the system adapts.

C. Approximate Wavenumber Behavior

It is instructive here to look at approximations that make clear the dependence of the wavenumber on the parameters, since it is this dependence that relates the circuit model to the fluid dynamics. In practice, more exact solutions for k may be achieved by Newton's method, starting from simple approximations such as those we discuss here.

Starting with real k, an approximate dispersion relation is

$$k_r \approx \frac{\omega^2 \rho}{S}. \tag{12}$$

This equation implies zero group delay (infinite group velocity) at dc ($\omega = 0$), which is not quite right. We can find the correct limit for low frequencies from the long-wave approximation, which gives a velocity of $\sqrt{hS/\rho}$, where h is the effective duct height (duct cross-section area divided by membrane width, to be consistent with our interpretation of stiffness S).

Given an approximate solution for k_r, we can obtain a first approximation for the imaginary part k_i by solving the imaginary part of the dispersion relation, assuming $k_i << k_r$ and ignoring terms with k_i^2 and k_i^3.

$$\begin{aligned} k_i &\approx \frac{k_r \beta \omega}{S} + \frac{k_r^3 \gamma \omega}{S} \\ &\approx \frac{\beta \omega^3 \rho}{S^2} + \frac{\gamma \omega^7 \rho^3}{S^4}. \end{aligned} \tag{13}$$

Using $f = \omega/\omega_N$, the two k_i terms are proportional to βf^3 and γf^7. In the long-wave region, the k_i terms are proportional to βf^2 and γf^4. Filter transfer functions and wavenumbers are symmetric about 0 frequency; the apparent antisymmetry in the odd-order terms of the short-wave approximation is due to dropping the sign change from (11) (which came from a tanh kh term saturated at ± 1).

We can interpret these complex wavenumber approximations either as *frequency-dependent* at a constant place (constant S, β, and γ), or as *place-dependent* at a constant frequency (constant ω). Thus, a wave of frequency ω will propagate until the damping gets large; the loss per distance, k_i, grows ultimately as ω^7 or e^{7x/d_ω} (assuming the geometric dependence of S discussed earlier, and with geometric γ proportional to ω_N or e^{-x/d_ω}). Therefore, the damping is near zero for low x and then becomes dominant very quickly at a *cutoff place* x_C. Similarly, at a given place, low frequencies are propagated with little loss; as ω grows, however, the loss quickly kills waves above a *cutoff frequency* ω_C.

The *best* frequency, or frequency of highest wave amplitude, will be somewhat less than the cutoff frequency, for any place. The best frequency ought to be calculated on the wave of displacement or velocity (or acceleration) of the cochlear partition, however, not on the pressure wave or the velocity-potential wave. Conversion from pressure to acceleration or from velocity potential to velocity involves a spatial differentiation, contributing another factor of k, or a tilt of about 12 dB per octave ($k \propto \omega^2$) below the best frequency (or 6 dB per octave at very low frequencies, according to the long-wave analysis). When there is no negative damping, the pressure-wave peak amplitude will be at dc (or at the base), but the displacement wave will peak within about an octave of cutoff.

The effect of the variable damping on the cutoff points is not included in our approximation, due to the assumption that the higher-order loss mechanism mainly determines the sharp cutoff. The best frequency shifts by nearly an octave (depending on parameters) as the damping changes in response to changing signal levels, whereas the cutoff point measured as the point of a particular high rolloff slope changes relatively little. Correspondingly, the observed shift in CF (neural best frequency) from healthy to traumatized cochleas has been observed to be up to 0.75 octave [17], whereas the steep high side of the response is unchanged. Also in agreement with physiological observations, higher signal levels cause an increase in effective bandwidth and a reduction in phase shift or delay near the best frequency (but a slightly increased phase lag below best frequency) [18], [19].

V. Silicon Cochlea

All auditory processing starts with a cochlea. Silicon auditory processing must start with a *silicon cochlea*. The fundamental structure in a cochlea is the basilar membrane. The silicon basilar membrane is a transmission line with a velocity of propagation that can be tuned electrically. Signal output taps are located at intervals along the line. We can think about the taps as crude inner hair cells. Unfortunately, we cannot build a system with as many taps as living systems have hair cells. Human ears have about 3500; we will be lucky to have 1000. On the other hand, we can make many delay line elements; the delay element we use in this delay line is the second-order section, which we expect to be good enough to duplicate approximately the dynamics of the second-order system of fluid mass and membrane stiffness.

A. CMOS Circuit Building Blocks

The most useful fundamental building blocks used in all our analog integrated circuit work are transconductance amplifiers and capacitors, both of which are made up of p-type and n-type MOS transistors.

The MOS transistor is used in strong inversion (above threshold) as a capacitor, and in weak inversion (subthreshold) as an active device. In the subthreshold region, the transistor's drain current is exponential in the gate–source voltage. The relative advantages of operating transconductance amplifiers in this low-current exponential region are discussed by Vittoz [20].

We can think of the transconductance amplifier as an operational amplifier with well-controlled limitations; in particular, although we can think of open-loop voltage gain as being very high (greater than 1000), the gain from voltage difference input to current output (i.e., the transconductance) is limited and well controlled. A single bias-control voltage input on the transconductance amplifier sets the current through a differential-amplifier stage, thereby setting both the transconductance and the saturated output current.

The ideal transfer characteristic of the transconductance amplifier, for MOS transistors in the subthreshold region, is

$$I_{\text{out}} = I_B \tanh \frac{V_+ - V_-}{V_T} \tag{14}$$

where I_B is the amplifier's bias current and V_T is a characteristic voltage near 40 mV equal to $\mathrm{k}T/q\kappa$, in which k is Boltzmann's constant, T is absolute temperature, q is the charge of an electron, and κ is a capacitive divider ratio, typically around 0.6, that characterizes how much of the potential change on the gate of a transistor causes a change in surface potential in the channel region of the transistor.

For input voltage differences $V_+ - V_-$ less than about 40 mV, we can approximate the tanh function as an identity, so that the amplifier is roughly linear with a transconductance of I_B/V_T. For large input differences, the output current saturates smoothly at $\pm I_B$.

Fig. 5 shows two transconductance amplifier circuits. The basic transconductance amplifier circuit uses only five transistors, but has a limited voltage gain and a limited range of output voltages over which it operates correctly. For the cochlea chip, we use the wide-range transconductance amplifier circuit, which uses nine transistors; the final output transistors are made extra long to maximize output impedance and hence voltage gain.

The next-level building block used in many analog systems is a first-order low-pass filter, shown in Fig. 6, which we refer to as a follower-integrator [21]. For low frequencies, it acts as a unity-gain follower; for high frequencies, it acts as an integrator. The follower-integrator is implemented in CMOS VLSI technology using a single transconductance amplifier and a single fixed capacitor. The bias control terminal, often refered to as the "τ knob," sets the transconductance G, and hence the time constant $\tau = C/G$ in the first-order transfer function

$$\frac{V_2}{V_1} = \frac{1}{\tau s + 1}. \tag{15}$$

The pole (root of the denominator) at $s = -1/\tau$ determines the natural frequency $\omega_N = 1/\tau$ beyond which the filter response declines at about 6 dB per octave.

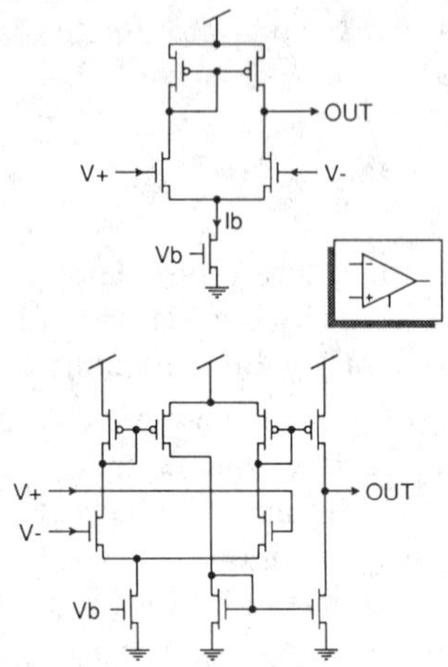

Fig. 5. Basic and wide-range CMOS transconductance amplifier circuits. The wide-range transconductance amplifier was chosen for the CMOS cochlea test chips, due its higher dc gain and wider range of output voltages.

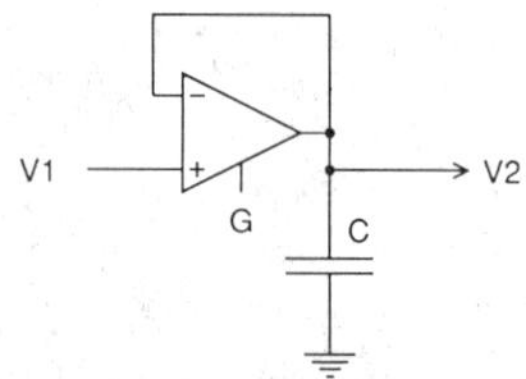

Fig. 6. Follower-integrator circuit, or first-order low-pass filter. The output follows slowly varying inputs with unity gain, but acts more like an integrator for rapidly varying inputs. The control terminal sets the amplifier bias current to control the transconductance G and the time constant $\tau = C/G$.

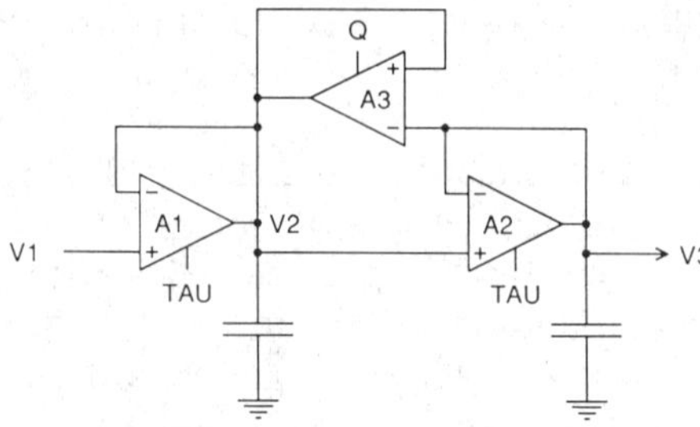

Fig. 7. Second-order filter section circuit. The TAU (τ) and Q control inputs set amplifier bias currents to control both the characteristic frequency and the peak height of the low-pass filter response.

B. Second-Order Section Circuit

The second-order circuit is shown in Fig. 7; it contains two cascaded follower-integrators and an extra amplifier. The capacitance C is the same for both stages ($C_1 = C_2 = C$), and the transconductances of the two feed-forward amplifiers, $A1$ and $A2$, are the same: $G_1 = G_2 = G$ (approximately—if G is defined as the average of G_1 and G_2, small differences will have no first-order effect on the parameters of the response). An underdamped response is obtained by adding the *feedback amplifier* $A3$, with transconductance G_3; its output current is proportional to the difference between V_2 and V_3, but the sign of the feedback is *positive*. For small signals, $I_3 = G_3(V_2 - V_3)$.

If we reduce the feedback to zero by shutting off the bias current in $A3$, each follower-integrator will have the transfer function given in (15). Two follower-integrators in cascade give an overall transfer function that is the product of the individual transfer functions, so the transfer function has two poles at $s = -1/\tau$

$$\frac{V_3}{V_1} = \left(\frac{1}{\tau s + 1}\right)^2 = \frac{1}{\tau^2 s^2 + 2\tau s + 1}. \tag{16}$$

We can understand the contribution of $A3$ to the response by following through the dynamics of the system when a perturbation is applied to the input. Suppose we begin with the input biased to some quiescent voltage level. In the steady state, all three voltages will settle down, and $V_1 = V_2 = V_3$. If we apply to V_1 a small step function on top of this dc level, V_2 starts increasing, because we are charging up the first capacitor $C1$. Eventually, V_2 gets a little ahead of V_3, and then amplifier $A3$ makes V_2 increase even faster. Once V_2 is increasing, the action of $A3$ is to keep it increasing; the feedback around the loop is positive. If we set the transconductance G_3 of amplifier $A3$ high enough, V_2 will increase too fast, and the circuit will become unstable.

The transfer function of the circuit is

$$H(s) = \frac{V_3}{V_1} = \frac{1}{\tau^2 s^2 + 2\tau s(1 - \alpha) + 1} \qquad (17)$$

where $\tau = C/G$ and $\alpha = G_3/(G_1 + G_2)$.

The roots are located on a circle of radius $1/\tau$; they move to the right from the negative real axis as we increase the transconductance of the feedback amplifier. The angle of the roots is determined by the ratio of feedback transconductance to forward transconductance, and is independent of the absolute value of τ. When $\alpha = 1$, the real part is 0, and we are left with a pair of roots on the $\pm j\omega$ axis. When $\alpha = 0$, the root pair is at the point $-1/\tau$ on the negative real axis; the distance between that point and the real part of the roots for general α is just α/τ.

The second-order transfer function can be expressed in terms of the Q parameter that describes the degree of resonance (or *quality*) of a second-order system:

$$H(s) = \frac{1}{\tau^2 s^2 + \frac{1}{Q}\tau s + 1}. \qquad (18)$$

By comparison to (17), we find that

$$Q = \frac{1}{2(1 - \alpha)}.$$

Note that Q starts from 0.5 with no feedback ($\alpha = 0$), and grows without bound as the feedback gain approaches the total forward gain ($\alpha = 1$, or $G_3 = G_1 + G_2$); beyond this point, small signals grow exponentially and large-signal nonlinearities dominate the circuit behavior

Examination of this well-known transfer function reveals that the gain is always less than unity whenever Q is less than 0.707. We will use this region in modeling the cochlea without active gain. When active gain is included, a gain slightly greater than unity is needed at middle frequencies, and this can be achieved by using Q values up to about 1.0. At low frequencies ($\omega/\omega_N = f \ll 1$), the response of a stage initially grows quadratically as f is increased, provided $Q^2 > 1/2$ or $Q > 0.707$. The response will reach a maximum at a frequency given by

$$f_{\max}^2 = 1 - \frac{1}{2Q^2} \qquad (19)$$

at which point the peak gain is

$$|H|_{\max} = \left|\frac{V_3}{V_1}\right|_{\max} = \frac{Q}{\sqrt{1 - \frac{1}{4Q^2}}}. \qquad (20)$$

When $Q^2 = 0.5$, the peak gain is 1.0 at zero frequency and the response is maximally flat (that is, the lowest-order frequency dependence is f^4). When the Q value is high, the peak gain is just above Q, and the peak frequency is just below $f = 1$. For $Q = 1$, the peak gain is about 1.16 at $f = 0.707$.

We have not yet defined damping quantitatively. In second-order systems, damping often is defined as $\xi = 1/2Q$, which goes to 0 as Q goes to infinity, and becomes negative for poles in the right half of the s plane. Second-order systems with any amount of negative damping are unstable—any small disturbance will grow exponentially, at a controlled rate but without bound. We have used damping differently, as applied to wave propagation. When wave damping is negative, a disturbance will grow exponentially in space, but the growth will be limited due to the limited range of places for which the damping remains negative. Therefore, in second-order stages cascaded to model wave propagation, negative damping corresponds to a stage gain greater than unity, or $Q^2 > 0.5$.

C. Basilar Membrane Delay Line

Our fabricated basilar membrane model has 480 stages in a boustrophedonic arrangement, as shown in a 100-stage version in Fig. 8. The only reason for using this serpentine structure instead of a straight line is that there are many stages, each of which is longer than it is high. The chip has a reasonable aspect ratio with this floorplan. Circuit yields are good enough that we regularly are able to propagate a signal through the entire 480-stage delay line on chips from several fabrication runs. A photomicrograph of one of the test chips in shown in Fig. 9.

The τ and Q bias inputs on the second-order sections are connected to polysilicon lines that run along one edge of the stages. We connect both ends of each of these resistive polysilicon lines to pads so that we can set the voltages from off chip. Due to the subthreshold characteristics of the bias transistors in the amplifiers, the time constants of the stages are exponentially related to the voltages on the τ control line. If we put a different voltage on the two ends of the τ line, we get a gradient in voltage along the length of the polysilicon line. A linear gradient in voltage will turn into an exponential gradient in the delay per stage. We can thereby easily make a transmission line with exponentially varying propagation velocity and cutoff frequency. Adjusting all the stages to have the same Q value then simply requires putting a similar gradiant on the Q control line, with a voltage offset that determines the ratio of feedback gain to forward gain in each stage.

For a cochlea operating in the range of human hearing, time constants of about 10^{-5} to 10^{-2} s are needed. A convenient capacitor size is about 1 pf (10^{-12} f), so the range of transconductance values needed is about 10^{-7} to 10^{-10} Ω^{-1}. If V_T is 40 mV, the range of bias currents will be 4×10^{-9} to 4×10^{-12} A. This range leaves several orders of magnitude of leeway from room-temperature thermal leakage currents at the low end, and from space-charge limited behavior (strong-inversion effects) at the high end,

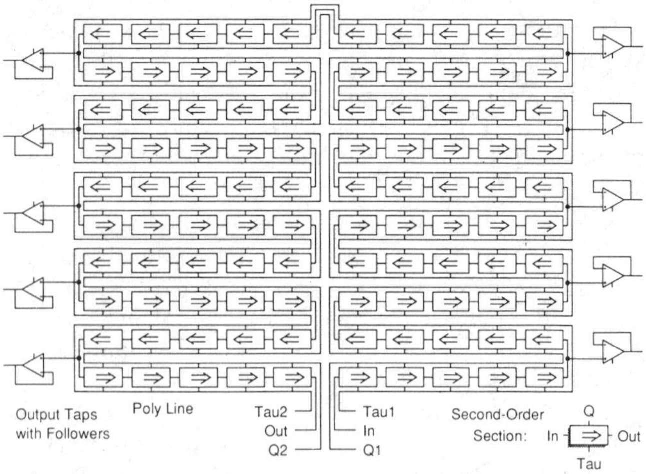

Fig. 8. Floorplan of 100-stage cochlea chip, in serpentine arrangement. The wires that are shown connecting the TAU and Q control terminals of the filter stages are built using a resistive polysilicon line, to act as a voltage divider that adjusts the bias currents in the cascade as an exponential function of distance from the input.

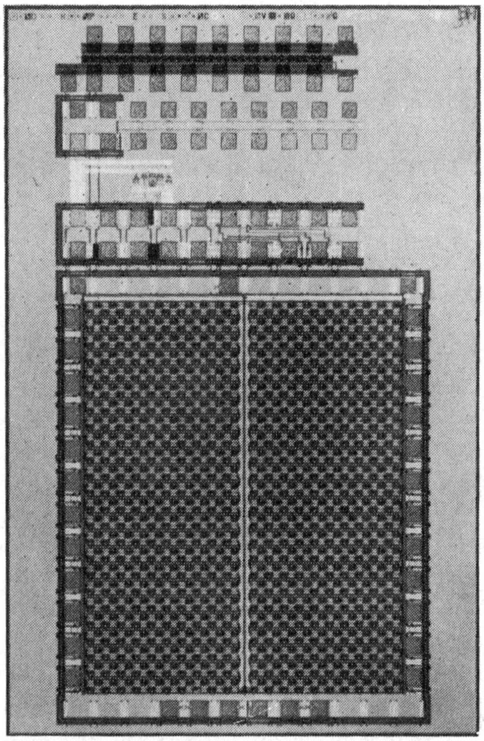

Fig. 9. Photomicrograph of 480-stage cochlea test chip. The large project in the bottom two-thirds of this MOSIS die is the cochlea. The pads visible on the left and right edges are for output taps, and on the bottom edge are for the other signals shown in Fig. 8.

so the circuits are in many ways ideal. The total current supplied to a cascade of 480 stages is only about a microampere.

D. Second-Order Sections in Cascade

Fig. 10(a) shows the response of a single second-order section from the transmission lines, for Q values 0.7, 0.8, and 0.9; scaled versions of the $Q = 0.9$ transfer function, from earlier stages in a cascade, also are shown. For this application, we use Q values of less than 1.0, which means that the peak of the single-stage response is very broad and has a maximum value just slightly greater than unity (for $Q > 0.707$).

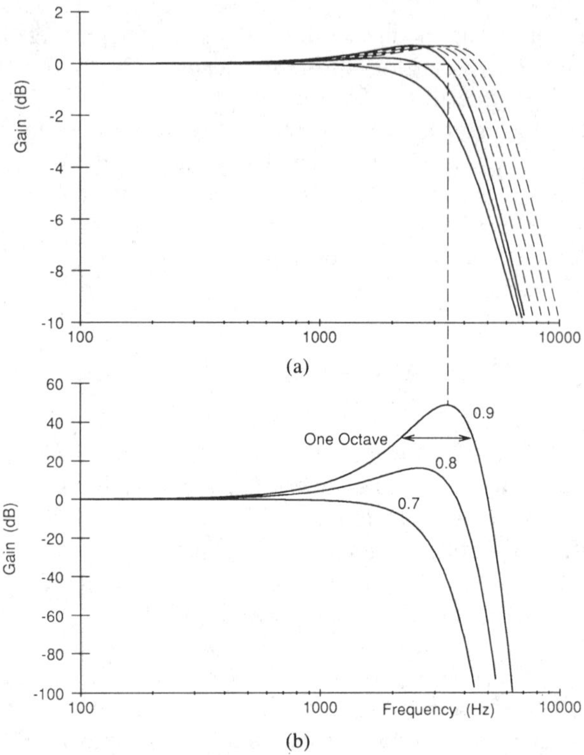

Fig. 10. (a) Log-log frequency response of a single second-order filter section, for Q values 0.7, 0.8, and 0.9, including scaled copies of the $Q = 0.9$ response to represent earlier sections in a cascade. (b) Corresponding overall response of a cascade of 120 stages with a factor 1.0139 scaling between adjacent stages. The dashed line between part (a) and part (b) indicates that the overall response peak occurs at the frequency for which the final section gain crosses unity. Note the different dB scale factors on the ordinates.

Because the system scales, each second-order section should have a similar response curve. The time constant of each stage is larger than that of its predecessor by a constant factor $e^{\Delta x/d_\omega}$, so each curve will be shifted along the log-frequency scale by a constant amount $\Delta x/d_\omega$. The overall response is the product of all the individual gains; the log response is the sum of all of the logs. In terms of the normalized log-log response G, the overall response is simply

$$\log H^m(\omega) = \sum_{n=0}^{m} \log G\left(\log \frac{\omega}{\omega_0} + \frac{n\Delta x}{d_\omega}\right). \quad (21)$$

Taking the stage illustrated in Fig. 10(a) as the last stage before the output tap and working backward to stages of shorter time constants, we obtain the overall log response in Fig. 10(b). There are many stages, and each one is shifted over from the other by an amount that is small compared to the width of the peak (in this case, 120 stages differing by a factor of 1.0139, to match the experimental conditions we shall describe). Although there is not much gain in each section, the cumulative gain causes a large peak in the response. This overall gain peak is termed a pseudoresonance, and is much broader (less sharply tuned) than is a single resonance of the same gain.

Fig. 11 shows the s-plane plot of the poles of an exponentially scaling cascade of second-order sections. For clarity, only six stages per octave (factor of 1.122) covering only three octaves are used for this illustration, although the 480-stage line would be tuned for about 48 stages per octave (factor of 1.014) to cover the 10 octaves from 20 Hz to 20 kHz.

Because each stage of the delay line has nearly unity gain at dc, we interpret the propagating signal as a pressure wave in the cochlea, which should propagate with a nearly constant amplitude in the passive case with zero damping. In the active case, a significant gain (e.g., 10–100) can be achieved, measured in terms of the pressure wave.

We can design output tap circuits to convert the pressure wave into a signal analogous to a membrane deflection-velocity wave. Ideally, this would be done by a spatial differentiation to convert to acceleration, followed by a time integration to convert to velocity. The combination would be exactly equivalent to a single time-domain filter, which can be approximated in the short-wave region by the approximate differentiator $\tau s/(\tau s + 1)$, with τ adjusted to correspond roughly to the τ of each stage; this filter tilts the low side of the response to 6 dB per octave, without much effect on the shape or sharp cutoff of the pseudoresonance. We have built and tested several such circuits, as well as more complex hair-cell circuits, but the results reported in this paper are based on the filter cascade alone (except that in the numerical calculation of Fig. 4, an ideal differentiator was included to model the low-frequency tail more reasonably).

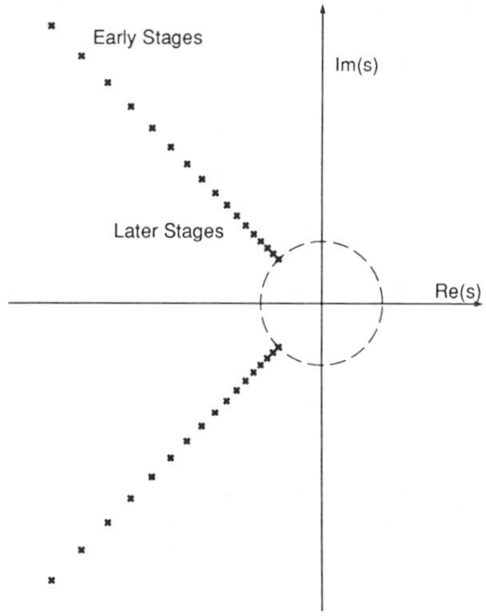

Fig. 11. Plot in the s-plane of the poles of an exponentially scaling cascade of second-order sections with $Q = 0.707$. The time constant τ of the final stage of the cascade determines the smallest ω_N, indicated by the circle. Six stages per octave (factor of 1.122 scaling between stages) are used for this illustration, covering three octaves.

E. Effect of MOS Transistor Variation

It would be ideal if Fig. 10 showed the real picture. MOS transistors, however, are not inherently well matched. For a given gate voltage, the current (in the subthreshold region where our circuits operate) can vary randomly over a range of a factor of about 2 (depending on how well controlled the fabrication process is—the relevant variation is conventionally called a threshold variation, although that is not a useful view when operating in the subthreshold or weak-inversion region). In the real curves, there is a dispersion in the center frequencies of the stages because of this random variation in currents. That would not be too great a problem, but the Q values also vary, because the threshold of the Q control transistor varies randomly and is not correlated with the τ adjustment on the same stage.

If the responses of too many stages fall off without peaking, then the collective response will get depressed at high frequencies and we will not be able to maintain a good bandwidth and gain in the transmission line. If we try to increase the value of Q too much, however, to make up for the depressed response, some of the stages may start to oscillate. Thus, there is a range of variations beyond which this scheme will not work. Fortunately, ordinary CMOS processes are capable of producing currents that are sufficiently well controlled to obtain cochlear behavior with no oscillation.

Fig. 12 illustrates a possible random distribution of pole positions, based on a uniform distribution of threshold voltage offsets that would cause currents and transconductances to vary over a factor of two range. The nominal Q and the τ scaling factor are as in the experimental conditions discussed below. The bounded distributions allow us to compute that α will change by a factor of two above and below nominal. Measured distributions of threshold offsets are sometimes a little worse than these, since the CMOS processes we have used are optimized for digital circuits with little attention to analog details.

F. Frequency Response

The most straightforward behavior of the silicon cochlea that can be compared to theory is the magnitude of the frequency response. The circuit was set up with a gradient in the τ such that each stage was slower than its predecessor by a factor of 1.0139. With this value, the auditory range was covered in the 480 stages. The Q-control voltage was set so that the peak response was about 5 times the dc response, as seen at several different output taps. Experimental data were taken with a sine wave of 14 mV peak-to-peak amplitude applied to the input. Results for two taps 120 stages apart are shown in Fig. 13. The solid points are measured values, and the smooth curves are theoretical predictions. Each curve is constructed as a product of individual stage response curves as given by (17). The value of the dc gain of the amplifiers was determined from the ratio of the response peaks. The value of Q used in the theory was adjusted until the predicted peak heights agreed with the observed ones. The resulting Q value was 0.79. The lower frequency peak corresponds to a tap further from the input by 120 stages than the

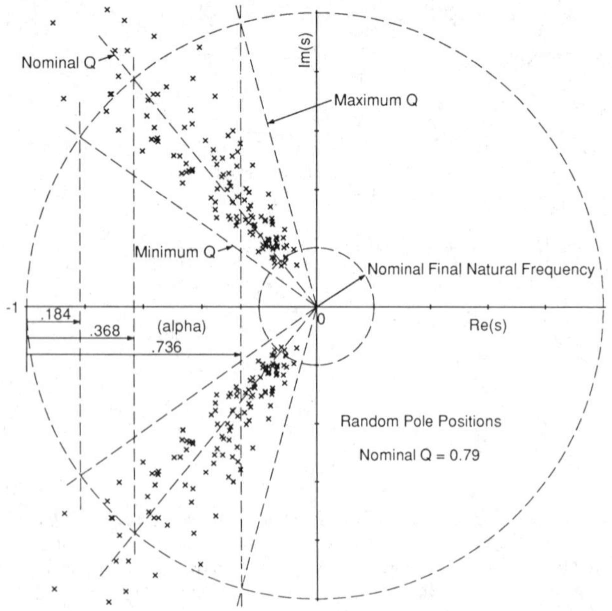

Fig. 12. Plot in the s-plane of the poles of an exponential cascade of second-order filter sections with random threshold offsets ($Q = 0.79$ nominal, stage ratio = 1.0139, 120 stages covering about a factor of five in frequency). Threshold offset was modeled as a uniform distribution of bias current over a factor of two range, resulting in α parameter variation of up to a factor of two above and below nominal (factor of four range).

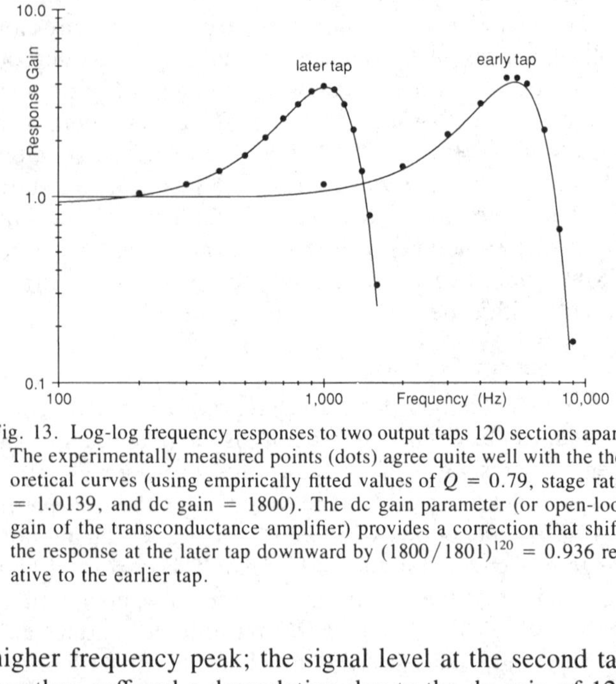

Fig. 13. Log-log frequency responses to two output taps 120 sections apart. The experimentally measured points (dots) agree quite well with the theoretical curves (using empirically fitted values of $Q = 0.79$, stage ratio = 1.0139, and dc gain = 1800). The dc gain parameter (or open-loop gain of the transconductance amplifier) provides a correction that shifts the response at the later tap downward by $(1800/1801)^{120} = 0.936$ relative to the earlier tap.

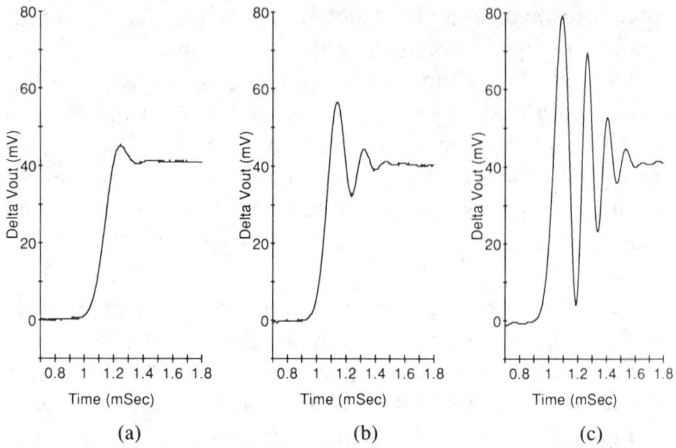

Fig. 14. Step response at one tap of the cochlea. In (a), the Q of the delay line has been adjusted to be just less than maximally flat (about 0.69); the trace shows only a slight overshoot. In (b), the Q has been increased to about 0.74, and more overshoot is evident. In (c), the Q is still higher (about 0.79), and delay line "rings" for several cycles.

higher frequency peak; the signal level at the second tap has thus suffered a degradation due to the dc gain of 120 followers in cascade. The open-circuit amplifier gain inferred from this observation is 1800, in good agreement with measurements on other amplifiers of similar design.

The remarkable agreement between theory and experiment is surprising in view of random variations in transistor input offset voltages (thresholds). We would expect a variation in Q and τ values for each stage that is much larger than the systematic progression between adjacent amplifiers. This variation need not, however, have a drastic effect on the result. The total response is the product of the responses of a large number of amplifiers. The product is an associative operation—it does not depend on the order of the terms. The fact that amplifiers in a particular physical location do not have precisely the τ value that we desire does not matter. Some amplifier somewhere will have the τ value, and it will make its contribution as required. It is more surprising that the random variation of the value of Q does not affect the result in a more violent way. As of now, we do not have a satisfactory explanation for the composite response curve as a result of many curves of different individual Q values.

G. *Transient Response*

The response at one tap of the cochlea to a step input is shown in Fig. 14. In (a), the Q of the delay line has been adjusted to be just slightly less than critically damped; the trace shows only a slight resonant overshoot. In (b), the Q has been increased, and more overshoot is evident. In (c), the Q is considerably higher, and the delay line "rings" for several cycles. If the Q were automatically adjusted, as it is in living systems, (a) would correspond to the response at high background sound levels, and (c) would correspond to a very quiet environment. With the Q adjustment corresponding to (c), we can observe the response at the two taps along the delay line where the frequency response of Fig. 13 was measured. The result is shown in Fig. 15. Note that the large delays are a natural result of using simple minimum-phase filters to model wave propagation; it is not necessary to design filters and then add extra delay as some modelers do.

These results illustrate the scale invariance property that is so unique and valuable about this structure: when we adjust the time scale on the oscilloscope to correspond to the τ of the particular section being observed, we obtain a similar output waveform at every tap. Living systems use this principle so the detection machinery does not depend on the position along the basilar membrane. We will use it for the same purpose.

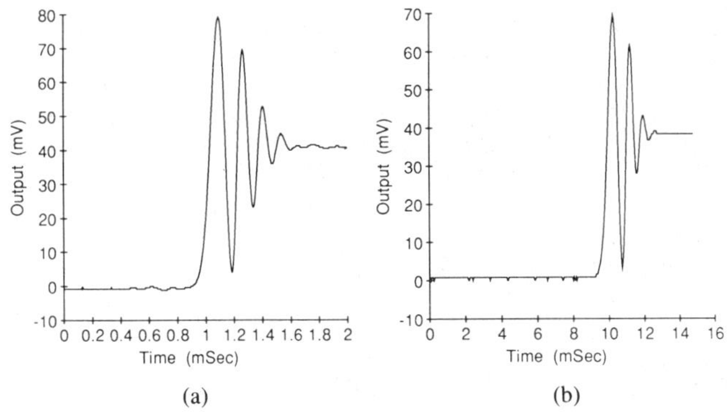

Fig. 15. Step responses at two taps separated by 120 delay stages. Note that the second response has about ten times as much delay as the first, and a slightly faster rise time relative to the delay. The Q is adjusted as in Fig. 14(c).

VI. Application of Cochlear Output Information

Applying the output of our cochlear model circuits will require several more levels of modeling. First, we need good hair cell model circuits and neuron model circuits to obtain outputs that are truly representative of the signal on the cochlear nerve. Second, we need to implement the sensory feedback loop that controls the gains of the cochlea stages; so far, we have made such adjustments manually, from off chip. Ultimately, we need to understand and model the processing done by the rest of the auditory nervous system.

Several steps toward modeling the auditory nervous system for binaural localization, for monaural sound characterization, and for sound separation combining these cues have been reported by Lyon and Weintraub [22]–[24]. These are examples of correlation-based neural-processing stages, which are natural to model in terms of analog circuits. Further stages of processing, for example, for speech recognition, are easy to conceive, but will take time to develop into a useful state.

VII. Summary and Conclusions

The problems we must solve to build perception machines are mostly similar to those that nature had to solve biologically in the evolution of intelligent animal behavior. The key problems in sound perception are to cope with a very wide dynamic range of loudness and to separate sounds on the basis of their properties, such as frequency content and time structure. We believe that, by developing circuits that solve the same problems using imprecise analog components, we will increase our understanding of how animals hear.

We believe that to make further progress in hearing research it is important for researchers to adopt a coherent set of working hypotheses, such as those presented by Kim [9], that emphasize the nonlinear, active, and adaptive aspects of hearing. The circuit model presented in this paper incorporates some of Kim's ideas as well as other observations on hearing and on circuits, as follows.

- Outer hair cells provide active and adaptive undamping to boost weak sounds and attenuate loud ones, thereby providing the gain-control element of an AGC loop.
- The AGC action of the cochlea is effectively coupled, in that a large detected signal at one place can reduce the overall gain to other places.
- Hydrodynamic analysis and recent experimental data imply a low-mass cochlear partition and an unsharp pseudoresonant response.
- Iso-output curves, whether measured neurally, mechanically, or theoretically, are sharpened by the coupled AGC action.
- Variable-Q second-order filter sections in cascade can implement delay, a high-gain pseudoresonance, sharp rolloff, and wide-range coupled gain control.
- CMOS subthreshold transconductance amplifiers are appropriate circuit building blocks for analog hearing models.
- Exponential variation of time constants is easy to achieve using a linear voltage gradient on transistor gates, yielding a log frequency scale.
- VLSI technology limitations such as threshold variation present an important challenge in designing systems with appropriate collective behavior.
- Test circuits of 480 filter stages work with reasonable yield in a 3-μ generic CMOS logic process.

Acknowledgment

The assistance of DARPA's MOSIS chip fabrication service was vital to this research and is greatly appreciated.

References

[1] E. de Boer and R. MacKay, "Reflections on reflections," *J. Acoust. Soc. Amer.*, vol. 67, pp. 882–890, 1980.
[2] H. Helmholtz [A. J. Ellis (Transl.)], *On the Sensations of Tone*. New York: Dover (reprint of 1885 English transl. of 1877 fourth German ed.), 1954.
[3] R. F. Lyon, "A computational model of filtering, detection, and compression in the cochlea," in *Proc. IEEE Int. Conf. Acoust., Speech, Signal Processing*, Paris, France, May 1982.
[4] R. F. Lyon and N. Lauritzen, "Processing speech with the multi-serial signal processor," in *Proc. IEEE Int. Conf. Acoust., Speech, Signal Processing*, Tampa, FL, Mar. 1985.
[5] G. Zweig, R. Lipes, and J. R. Pierce, "The cochlear compromise," *J. Acoust. Soc. Amer.*, vol. 59, pp. 975–982, 1976.
[6] L. Robles, M. A. Ruggero, and N. C. Rich, "Mössbauer measurements of the mechanical response to single-tone and two-tone stimuli at the base of the chinchilla cochlea," in *Peripheral Auditory Mechanisms*, J. B. Allen *et al.*, Eds. New York: Springer-Verlag, 1985.
[7] G. von Békésy, *Sensory Inhibition*. Princeton, NJ: Princeton University Press, 1967.
[8] P. M. Zurek and W. W. Clark, "Narrow-band acoustic signals emitted by chinchilla ears after noise exposure," *J. Acoust. Soc. Amer.*, vol. 70, pp. 446–450, 1981.
[9] D. O. Kim, "Functional roles of the inner- and outer-hair-cell subsystems in the cochlea and brainstem," in *Hearing Science*, C. Berlin, Ed. San Diego, CA: College-Hill, 1984.
[10] R. F. Lyon and L. Dyer, "Experiments with a computational model of the cochlea," in *Proc. IEEE Int. Conf. Acoust., Speech, Signal Processing*, Tokyo, Japan, Apr. 1986.
[11] F. S. Werblin, "The control of sensitivity in the retina," *Sci. Amer.*, Jan. 1973.
[12] M. Holmes and J. D. Cole, "Pseudo-resonance in the cochlea," in *Mechanics of Hearing*, E. de Boer and M. A. Viergever, Eds. The Hague, The Netherlands: Martinus Nijhoff, 1983.
[13] P. Dallos, "Biophysics of the cochlea," in *Handbook of Perception*,

vol. IV, E. C. Carterette and M. P. Friedman, Eds. New York: Academic, 1978, ch. 4.
[14] E. de Boer, "Wave reflection in passive and active cochlea models," in *Mechanics of Hearing*, E. de Boer and M. A. Viergever, Eds. The Hague, The Netherlands: Martinus Nijhoff, 1983.
[15] J. Lighthill, "Energy flow in the cochlea," *J. Fluid Mech.*, vol. 106, pp. 149–213, 1981.
[16] R. F. Lyon and C. A. Mead, "Cochlear hydrodynamics demystified," Caltech Comput. Sci. Tech. Rep. Caltech-CS-TR-884, Pasadena, CA, Feb. 1988.
[17] A. R. Cody and B. M. Johnstone, "Single auditory neuron response during acute acoustic trauma," *Hearing Res.*, vol. 3, pp. 3–16, 1980.
[18] J. O. Pickles, "Recent advances in cochlear physiology," *Prog. Neurobiol.*, vol. 24, pp. 1–42, 1985.
[19] P. M. Sellick, R. Patuzzi, and B. M. Johnstone, "Measurement of basilar membrane motion in the guinea pig using the Mössbauer technique," *J. Acoust. Soc. Amer.*, vol. 72, pp. 131–141, 1982.
[20] E. A. Vittoz, "Micropower techniques," in *Design of MOS VLSI Circuits for Telecommunications*, Y. Tsividis and P. Antognetti, Eds. Englewood Cliffs, NJ: Prentice-Hall, 1985, ch. 4.
[21] C. A. Mead, *Analog VLSI and Neural Systems*. Reading, MA: Addison-Wesley (in press).
[22] R. F. Lyon, "A computational model of binaural localization and separation," in *Proc. IEEE Int. Conf. Acoust., Speech, Signal Processing*, Boston, MA, Apr. 1983.
[23] —, "Computational models of neural auditory processing," in *Proc. IEEE Int. Conf. Acoust., Speech, Signal Processing*, San Diego, CA, Mar. 1984.
[24] M. Weintraub, "The GRASP sound separation system," in *Proc. IEEE Int. Conf. Acoust., Speech, Signal Processing*, San Diego, CA, Mar. 1984.

Richard F. Lyon (M'78) received the B.S. degree in engineering and applied science from California Institute of Technology, Pasadena, in 1974, and the M.S. degree in electrical engineering from Stanford University, Stanford, CA, in 1975.

He has worked on a variety of projects involving communication and information theory, digital system design, analog and digital signal processing, VLSI design and methodologies, and sensory perception at Caltech, Bell Labs, Jet Propulsion Laboratory, Stanford Telecommunications Inc., Xerox PARC, and Schlumberger Palo Alto Research. In his current position at Apple Computer, he is involved in research in speech recognition using models of hearing. He is also currently on the Computer Science Faculty at Caltech, where he works on sensory modeling research and analog VLSI techniques for signal processing.

Carver Mead is the Gordon and Betty Moore Professor of Computer Science, and has taught at the California Institute of Technology, Pasadena, for over 20 years. He worked in the fields of solid-state electronics and the management of complexity in the design of very large scale integrated circuits, and has been a leading force in the development of a design methodology for VLSI. He has written, with L. Conway, the standard text for VLSI design, *Introduction to VLSI Systems*. His recent work is concerned with modeling neuronal structures, such as the retina or the cochlea, using analog VLSI systems. His new book on this topic, *Analog VLSI and Neural Systems*, is to appear in 1988.

Prof. Mead is a Fellow of the American Physical Society, a member of the National Academy of Engineering, foreign member of the Royal Swedish Academy of Engineering Science, and has been elected to Life Membership in the Franklin Institute.

A DIGITAL IMPLEMENTATION OF A BEST MATCH CLASSIFIER

Stuart Mackie and John S. Denker

AT&T Bell Labs,
Holmdel,
NJ 07733, U.S.A

Abstract

In this paper we discuss why special purpose chips are needed for useful implementations of algorithms in such applications as pattern recognition and classification. We describe one design in particular, the key feature of which is simple arithmetic processors distributed amongst data storage to minimize data movement.

Introduction

It is clear that conventional electronic computers lag far behind organic computers when it comes to dealing with very large data rates in problems such as computer vision and speech recognition. Why is this? One reason is that the brain performs a huge number of operations in parallel, in contrast to a conventional computer where there is a very fast processor that can perform a variety of instructions very quickly, but operates on only two pieces of data at a time. The rest of the many megabytes of RAM is idle during any instruction cycle. The duty cycle of the processor is close to 100%, but that of the stored data is very close to zero. If we wish to make better use of the data, we have to distribute processing power amongst the stored data. Figure 1 illustrates where distributed computation chips lie in comparison to conventional computer chips as regard number and complexity of nodes per chip.

In order for a distributed strategy to work effectively, each processing element must be small in order to accommodate many on a chip, and communication must be local and hard-wired. Whereas the processing element in a conventional computer may be able to execute many hundred different operations, in our scheme the processor is able to perform just one and obviously must be tailored to some particular application. In neural network and pattern recognition algorithms, the dot products of an input vector with a series of stored vectors is often required. The general calculation is:

$$\text{Sum of Products} \qquad V \cdot F(i) = \sum_j v_j f_{ij}$$

where **V** is the input vector and **F(i)** is one of the stored vectors. Two variations of this are of particular interest. In feature detection, we wish to find all the stored vectors for which the dot product with the input vector is greater than some threshold **T**, and say that such vectors (referred to as features) are *present* in the input vector.

$$\text{Feature Detecion} \qquad V \cdot F(i) = \sum_j v_j f_{ij} > T$$

In pattern classification we wish to find the single stored vector that has the largest dot product with the input vector, and we say that the input is a *member of the class* represented by that vector, or simply that that stored vector is *closest* to the input vector.

$$\text{Classification} \qquad \max(V \cdot F(i)) = \max\left(\sum_j v_j f_{ij}\right)$$

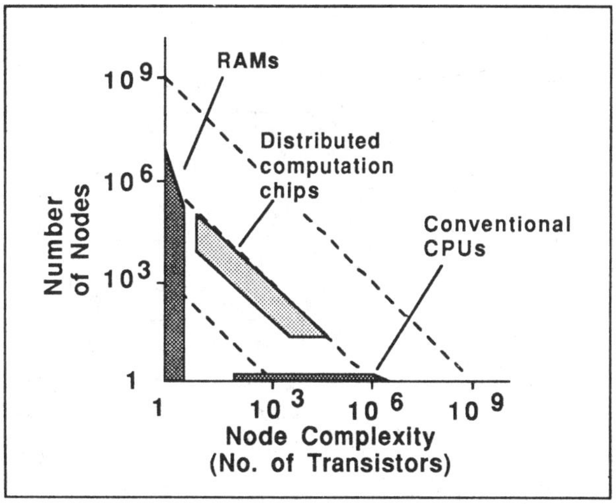

Fig.1 A schematic graph of addressable node complexity and size for conventional computer chips. Memories can contain millions of very simple nodes each with a very few transistors but with no processing power. CPU chips are essentially one very complex node. Neural network chips are in the distributed computation region where chips contain many simple fixed instruction processors local to data storage. (After Reece and Treleaven[5])

Reprinted from *IEEE 1988 Custom Integrated Circuits Conference*, pages 10.4.1-10.4.4.

The design strategy may be summed up as follows: we recognize that in typical pattern recognition applications, the feature vectors need to be changed infrequently compared to the input vectors, and the calculation that is performed is fixed and low-precision. We therefore distribute simple fixed-instruction processors throughout the data storage area, thus minimizing the data movement and optimizing the use of silicon. Our ideal would be to have every transistor on the chip doing something useful during every instruction cycle. Such a specialized chip would be used as a coprocessor in a larger system.

The design described below is primarily for classification, but could also be used for feature extraction in some cases.

Digital Classifier Chip

This chip was designed as part of a project to compare analog and digital implementations of neural network algorithms. The design is an implementation of a classifier whose architecture is a pipeline of digital processors, rather than a hybrid digital/analog interconnection matrix as described elsewhere. It is nearing completion of the design stage, and will be fabricated using 0.9µm CMOS. It calculates the largest five $V \cdot F(i)$ using an all-digital pipeline of identical processors, each attached to one stored word. Each processor is also internally pipelined to the extent that no stage contains more than two gate delays. This is important, since the throughput of the processor is limited by the speed of the slowest stage. In this first version of the design, the elements of the input and stored vectors are binary valued. The dot-product operator is switchable between AND an NXOR, corresponding to finding the number of common 1's and the number of bits the same, respectively. Each processor calculates the dot product of an input word and its stored word, and then compares value obtained with each of the largest 5 values previously found for that input word. An updated list of 5 best matches is then passed to the next processor in the pipeline. At the end of the pipeline the best 5 matches overall are output.

The data paths on chip are one bit wide and all calculations are bit-serial. This means that the processing elements and the data paths are compact and maximizes the number of stored words per chip. The layout of a single processor is shown in Fig. 2 and a schematic of operation is shown in Fig. 3. The features are stored as 128-bit words (in 8 16-bit ring shift registers) and associated with each feature is a 14-bit tag or name string that is stored in a static register. The input vector passes through the processor and is

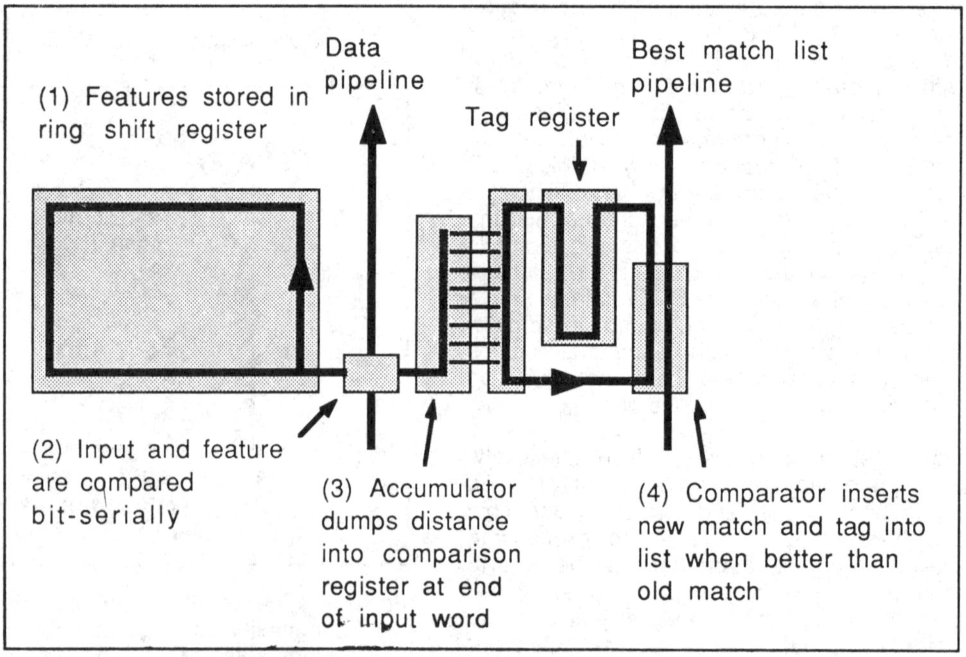

Fig. 2 Schematic of one of the 50 processors in the digital classifier chip. The Hamming distance of the input vector to the feature vector is calculated, and if better than one of the five best matches found so far, is inserted into the match list together with the tag and passed onto the next processor. At the end of the pipeline the best five matches overall are output.

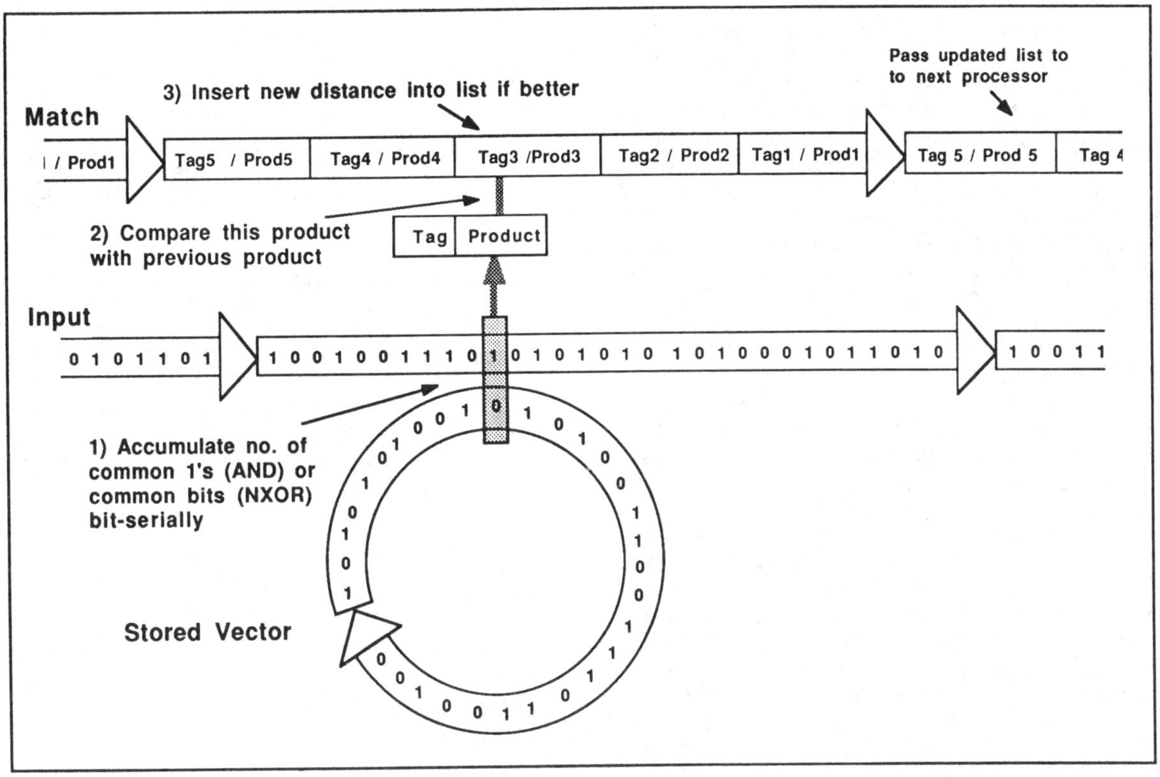

Fig. 3 Schematic of operation of a processor.

operated on bit-by-bit with the stored vector, whose shift registers are cycled in turn. The outcomes of each bit-wise operation (AND or NXOR) are summed in an accumulator. After a vector has passed through a processor, the total dot product is loaded into the comparison register together with the tag. At this time, the match list for the input vector arrives at the comparator. It is an ordered list of the 5 largest products found in the pipeline so far, together with associated tag strings. The product just calculated is compared bit-serially with each of the values in the list in turn. If the current product is larger than one of the ones in the list, the output streams of the comparator are switched, having the effect of inserting the current product and tag into the list and deleting the previous fifth best product. After the last processor in the pipeline, the list stream contains the best five products overall, together with the tags of the stored vectors that generated them. The data stream and the list stream are loaded into 16-bit wide registers ready for output. The design enables chips to be connected together to extend the pipeline if more than 50 stored vectors are required. The throughput is constant, irrespective of the number of chips connected together; only the latency increases as the number of chips increases.

The chip has been designed to operate with an on-chip clock frequency of at least 100MHz. This high speed is possible because stage sizes are very small and data paths have been kept short. Although bit-serial, the overall throughput is high because of the high clock speed. Assuming a clock frequency of 100MHz, the chip will produce a list of 5 best distances with tag strings every 1.3µs, with a latency of about 2.5µs. Even if a thousand chips containing 50,000 stored vectors were pipelined together, the latency would be only 2.5ms, low enough for most real time applications. The chip is expected to perform 5 billion bit operation/sec. A single chip will calculate at a rate in excess of 1000 times faster than a conventional computer.

While it is important to have high clock frequencies on the chip, it is also important to have them much lower off the chip, since frequencies above 50MHz are hard to deal on circuit boards. The 16-bit wide communication paths onto and off the chip ensure that this is not a problem here.

Conclusion

The approach to classification discussed here, in some sense represents an opposite computational approach to interconnection matrices[1,2,3]. In one, many local calculations are done, in the other, a single global computation is performed for each match. Both the approaches have their advantages and it remains to be seen which type of circuit will be more efficient in applications, and how closely an electronic implementation of a neural network should resemble the highly interconnected nature of a biological network.

This design represents one of the first distributed computation chips for pattern recognition. These are characterized by having simple processors distributed amongst data storage. (See Ref. 4 for a pipelined bit-serial multiplier that does not, however, have any on-chip memory). The algorithm performed by the chip is mapped exactly into the silicon and is tailored to the application in a trade-off of flexibility for speed. The mapping of the algorithm is such that there are never bus conflicts or memory sharing; this allows every computing element to operate at maximum efficiency. It is interesting to note some of the reasons why these designs can now be made: minimum linewidths on circuits are now small enough that enough processors can be put on one chip to make these designs of a useful size, sophisticated design tools are now available that enable a single person to design and simulate a complete circuit in a matter of months, and fabrication costs are low enough that highly speculative circuits can be made without requiring future volume production to offset prototype costs.

We expect a flurry of similar designs in the coming years, with circuits becoming more and more optimized for particular applications. However, it should be noted that the impressive speed gain achieved by putting an algorithm into custom silicon can only be done once. Further gains in speed will be closely tied to mainstream technological advances in such areas as transistor size reduction and wafer-scale integration. It remains to be seen what influence these kinds of custom circuits will have in useful technology since at present their functions cannot even be simulated in reasonable time. What can be achieved with these circuits is very limited when compared with a three dimensional, highly complex biological system, but is a vast improvement over conventional computer architectures.

The authors gratefully acknowledge the contributions made by L.D. Jackel and R.E. Howard for advice and support, by Bob Clark and the MULGA team for the design tools, and by N.F. Foster of AT&T Bell Labs in Allentown for fabrication.

References

[1] H.P. Graf, L.D. Jackel, R.E. Howard, B. Straughn, J.s. Denker, W. Hubbard, D.M. Tennant, and D.B. Schwartz, "VLSI Implementation of a Neural Network Memory with Several Hundreds of Neuron", Neural Networks for Computing, J.S. Denker (Ed.), AIP Press (1986)

[2] H.P. Graf and P. deVegvar, "A CMOS Implementation of a Neural Network Model", in "Advanced Research in VLSI", Proceedings of the 1987 Stanford Conference, P. Losleben (ed.), MIT Press 1987.

[3] H.P. Graf and P. deVegvar, "A CMOS Associative Memory Chip Based on Neural Networks", Tech. Digest, 1987 IEEE International Solid-State Circuits Conference.

[4] M. Hatamian and G. Cash, "A 70-MHz 8-bit × 8-bit Parallel Pipelined Multiplier in 2.5µm CMOS", IEEE J. Sol. St. Circ. **SC-21** 505 (1986).

[5] M. Reece and P.C. Treleaven, "Parallel Architectures for Neural Computers", Neural Computers, R. Eckmiller and C. v.d. Malsburg, (Eds.) Springer-Verlag, Heidelberg, (1988)

A Generic Architecture for Wafer-Scale Neuromorphic Systems*

Jack Raffel, James Mann, Robert Berger, Antonio Soares, and Sheldon Gilbert
M.I.T. Lincoln Laboratory
244 Wood Street, Lexington, MA 02173-0073

Introduction

Wafer-scale integration is ideally matched to the extraordinary interconnect requirements of neuromorphic systems. The very high fanout associated with connectionist architectures results in designs which will ultimately be constrained by the pinout limitations of conventional packages. The Restructurable VLSI approach to wafer-scale integration[1] uses a laser to both form and remove connections between conductors on a silicon wafer after fabrication and test. This technique accomplishes two important objectives: the incorporation of redundancy in order to circumvent defects and provide acceptable yields in very large monolithic systems, and the flexible configuration of interconnect between modular cells in order to program the functionality of the wafer-scale device for rapid turnaround customization. Whole wafer systems developed previously at Lincoln Laboratory using this technology include a 16-point-FFT[2], a Hough Transform Processor, and a system for implementing the Dynamic Time Warping[3] algorithm for a speech recognizer.

A generic wafer-scale architecture is being developed which should be capable of implementing a wide variety of different network types. For example, it should be possible to build Hopfield, Grossberg, multilevel perceptron[5] and other net types or combinations thereof, from a common set of prefabricated wafer resources. The network architecture for a particular application would then be hard-wired after fabrication by laser programming.

Restructurable VLSI

The critical technological advance which underlies the RVLSI approach to building wafer-scale circuits is the development of a very high yield laser-linking technique which enables both additive and deletive modification of interconnect wiring after fabrication and test. This approach allows the incorporation of operable, redundant devices and the removal of defective ones without the need for time-consuming and defect-prone custom

*This work was sponsored by the Department of the Air Force, and the Defense Advanced Research Projects Agency. The views expressed are those of the author and do not reflect the official policy or position of the U.S. Government.

"A Generic Architecture for Wafer-Scale Neuromorphic Systems" by J. Raffel, J. Mann, R. Berger, A. Soares, and S. Gilbert from *The Proceedings of the IEEE 1st Annual International Conference on Neural Networks*, 1988, Vol. II, pages 173-180.

masks and extra fabrication steps. The laser restructuring facility is shown in Figure 1. The beam from an argon cw laser, running at power levels of about 2 watts, is focused on a silicon substrate through a rotating shutter which produces pulses of 1 msec duration. A number of link structures have been developed, but two have been demonstrated in working whole-wafer systems. The first, a vertical device, shown in Figure 2, comprises two levels of metal separated by a dielectric sandwich of amorphous silicon with thin oxide barriers on both sides to prevent interdiffusion of metal and silicon during high temperature anneals. This device provides resistances of under one ohm with extremely high yields over a wide range of laser power. Its main drawback is that it requires unconventional link dielectric processing steps which are not easily transferred to a standard industrial process line. In order to expedite the transfer of the RVLSI technology, a new link was developed which requires no additional processing steps and can be fabricated using any conventional CMOS process sequence. This lateral device, shown in Figure 3, is formed by two substrate diodes separated by a gap of approximately the size of the laser beam, (typically 2 to 4 microns). Exposure at power levels and pulse widths comparable to those used for the vertical link causes the silicon in the gap to melt and the dopant to diffuse across the gap resulting in connections in the 100 ohm range. Recently, this link was demonstrated in building a wafer-scale system which was fabricated entirely in the MOSIS foundry, thus dramatically demonstrating the transferability of this technology. The same laser system can be used to segment wires on both first and second level metal.

Depending on the circuit details of the approach to neural net implementation, it is likely that either of these devices could be used to build a wafer-scale system. Since it is probable that such systems will operate at very high impedance levels and low currents, the higher resistance of the lateral links should not be a significant factor. In addition to the laser linking technology, it has been necessary to develop a set of special-purpose CAD tools to automate the linking procedure for routing tested resources to implement a particular system function. Figure 1 shows a block schematic of the procedures and equipment necessary to restructure a wafer. It is likely that these tools can be utilized to implement the wafer-scale neural net architecture described in this paper with a minimum of additional software.

Wafer-scale Design

The wafer design begins with the definition of a basic building block and its placement in a matrix of conductors and programmable links. Such a block is shown schematically in Figure 4, where m inputs enter the block horizontally, are connected through multiplying digital to analog converters (MDACs) to n outputs and then exit vertically. These MDACs correspond to the weighted connections present in virtually all neural net models. Their output current is the product of the input voltage and the conductances of the transistors which are controlled by the associated storage bits which correspond to the digital value of the connection weight.[4] The circles at the intersections of the vertical and horizontal

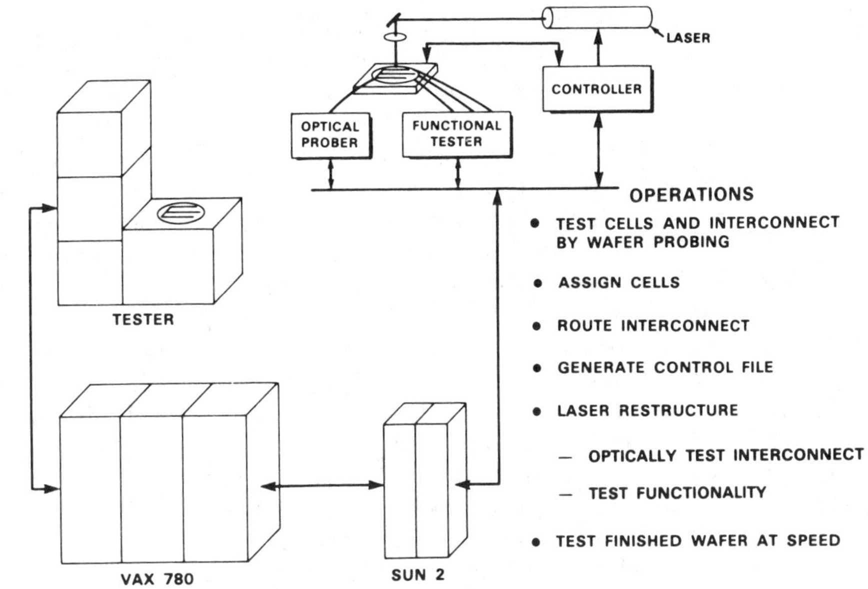

Figure 1. CAD & Test of RVLSI Wafers.

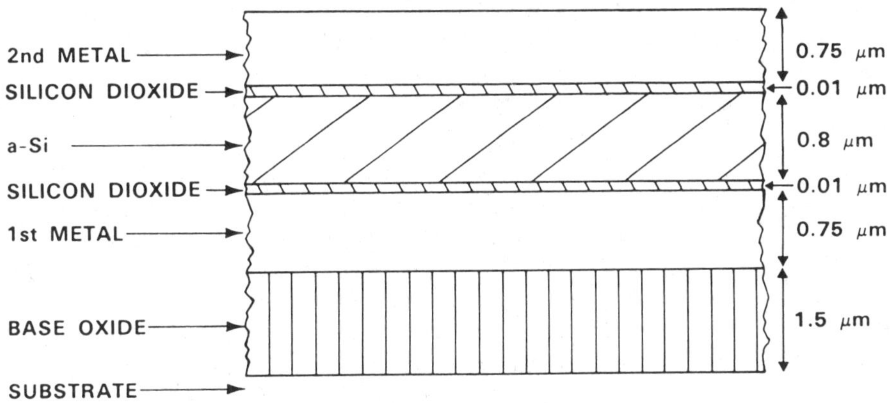

Figure 2. Vertical Laser Link.

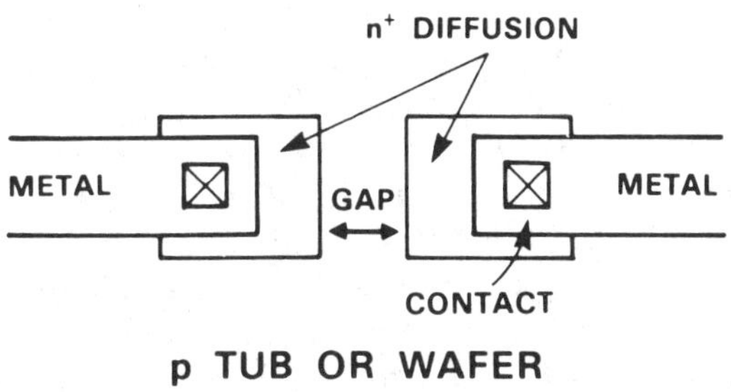

Figure 3. Laser-Diffused Link.

wires represent locations at which it is possible to form a connection using the laser linking technique. It is assumed that cutting of conductors can take place at any point along either first or second level metal.

The values of m and n for wafer-scale implementation would be selected on the basis of an estimate of the average expected neuron fan-in and fan-out respectively rather than the package limitations characteristic of discrete systems. In order to allow complete flexibility in connecting the outputs of any block to the inputs of any other block with a low probability of interference, a matrix of links and conductors of size i x m is located to the left of each block and a matrix of size j x n is located below each block as shown in Figure 4. While connectionist architectures are usually characterized as being highly redundant and therefore robust with regard to individual component failures, the systems which are likely to be built in the near future will fall far short of their neurological counterparts in redundancy and therefore will benefit from the complete testability of both interconnect and active devices. Therefore, the matrix layout is arranged so that each MDAC is accessible from the wafer periphery for testing. A second feature is that blocks are extendible in size so that fan-in and fan-out can be increased in increments of the block width and length. Both horizontal input lines and vertical output lines are made continuous across block boundaries, extending the full length of the wafer to its periphery, thereby providing such access as well as allowing complete testing of the interconnect itself. Above each j x n link matrix are located a row of amplifiers whose outputs are all connected to a common horizontal line labelled "amplifier test out" and each of whose inputs is connected to a vertical line, labelled "amplifier test in", which is shared by all other amplifiers in the same column. Not shown on this diagram are the power lines which must also be brought out on separate column conductors in order to allow selective accessability to amplifier terminals for complete testing of these components. After testing, amplifiers are separated by segmenting the "amplifier test out" line with the laser. To further enhance the flexibility of the design, a small number of summing nodes with relatively few (1 to 4) inputs could be distributed strategically around the wafer for those special cases in which it would be particularly wasteful of mdacs to use an amplifier with full fan-in capability.

Chip-Level Design

As a first step in exploring a potential wafer-scale design, a chip was designed and fabricated in the MOSIS foundry. The chip uses external connectivity because its purpose was the evaluation of the active circuits, (MDACs and their storage bits), not the already well characterized laser links. This chip comprises a matrix of interconnect lines including 32 analog inputs, each of which is connected through 4-bit MDACs to 16 pairs of output lines. In series with the weight transistors are switch transistors. An extra bit associated with each MDAC pair controls these switches and thereby determines whether the excitation or the inhibition MDAC contributes current to its associated output line. Figure 5 shows the circuit diagram for an MDAC pair with polarity control. Figure 6 shows the plot of output current vs. input voltage for a single MDAC as the storage bits are incremented from 0 to 15. It is estimated from measurements on working MDACs that current increments are uniform to within about 5%. Note that it is possible to increase the weight precision beyond four bits by connecting two input lines in parallel for five bits, or four input lines for six bits, etc. It is also possible to provide for threshold offset control by using one of the analog inputs connected to a fixed voltage as a programmable bias control. Figure 7 shows a photograph of the chip. It is packaged in an 84-pin package using 64 pins (32 plus 2 x 16) for analog inputs and outputs, 5 pins for digital data in, and 10 bits for MDAC address. The active area occupies 28 mm^2 using 3-micron design rules, and the present circuit uses 28,500 transistors to implement 1024 4-bit MDACs. It is estimated that this area could be shrunk by almost an order of magnitude using 2-micron design rules and circuit simplifications. The decision was made to avoid on-chip amplifiers in this first experimental design in order to allow flexibility for building small systems in which there is complete control over amplifier gain, saturation characteristics and output drive capability, as well as the ability to experiment with various means for performing the subtraction necessary for combining the exciting and inhibiting outputs. The off-chip amplifiers for this preliminary system are provided by a pair of operational amplifiers run in the transimpedance mode, one each attached to the exciting and inhibiting lines. The outputs of the two amplifiers are then fed into a differential amplifier which provides the output drive to other analog inputs.

Experimental Results

Two MDAC chips have been installed in a printed circuit board which provides the summing amplifiers and a flexible wiring arrangement which allows modification of input/output connections with jumpers as shown in Figure 8. The board is operated by a Tektronix S3260 tester which can input analog voltages and measure analog outputs on up to 64 pins, under control of a stored program. The first experiment performed was the implementation of a Hamming net which is an optimum classifier for binary patterns corrupted by noise.[6] This was aimed at characterizing the summing and amplification circuits, measuring the uniformity of the weights and verifying the operation of a winner-take-all or max-picker circuit, which served as the second stage of the network and will be described later in this paper. The first stage utilized the linear region of the neuron response to implement a linear correlator between a series of 16-bit binary input vectors and 6 pre-selected 16-bit "stored" vectors. These vectors were stored in the sense that the network weights from the 16 input neurons to 6 output neurons were chosen, by an algorithm described below, so that

$$\text{nth output} = k\ (16 - \text{Hamming distance to nth stored vector})$$

By breaking the circuit into two separate stages it was possible to examine the behavior of each separately, although these two were later combined and found to operate with equivalent behavior. Because negative

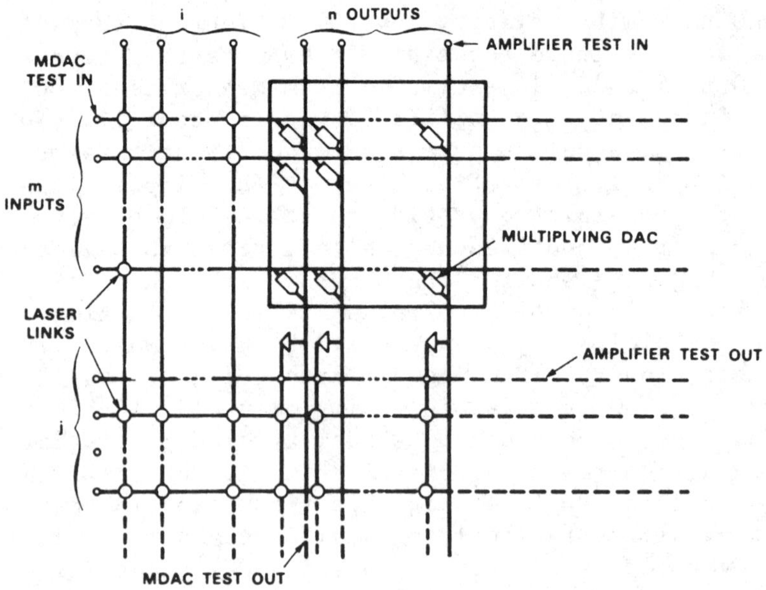

Figure 4. Wafer-Scale Neural Net Architecture.

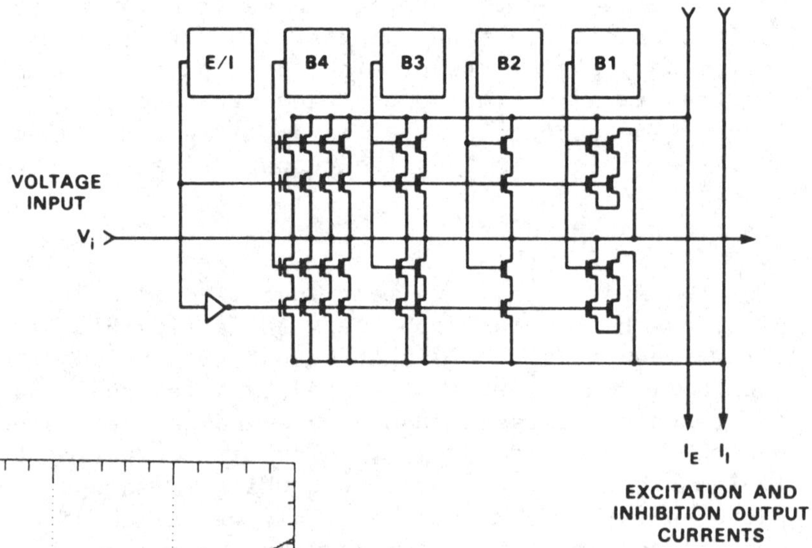

Figure 5. 4 Bit MDAC with Polarity Control.

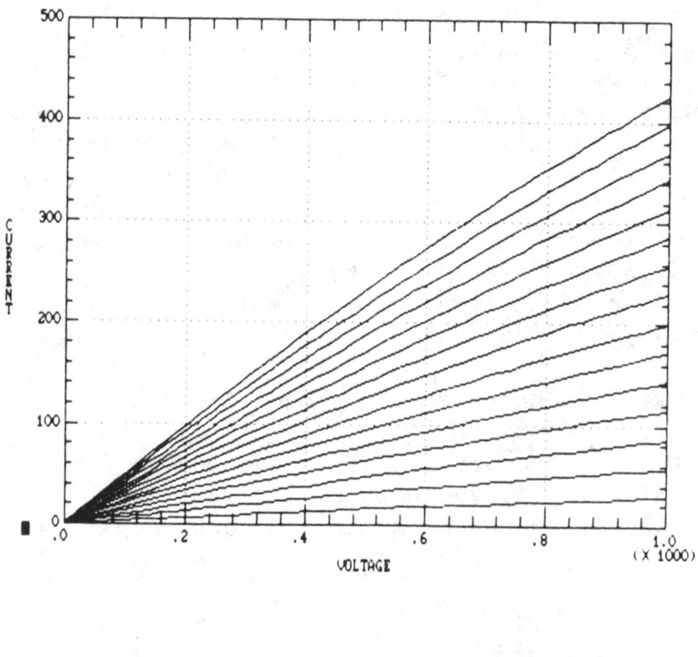

Figure 6. Current (microamps) vs. Voltage (millivolts) for one MDAC.

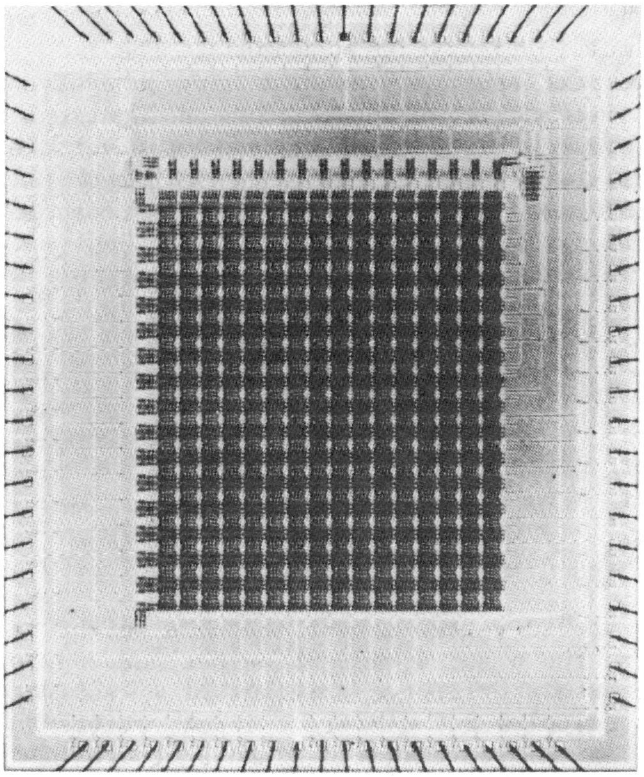

Figure 7. The MDAC Test Chip.

Figure 8.
The Network Board for MDAC Chips.

input voltages were never used and the weight representations for ONES and ZEROS were realized as algebraic multiplicative connections to the excitatory and inhibitory lines respectively, it was necessary to apply biases to each output neuron so as to realize the exclusive-or function required for computing Hamming distance. Table 1 shows the input voltages, weight combinations and the necessary biases to achieve the required output. Weights to inhibitory lines are indicated by negative entries in the table.

V_{in} x	W_i +	B =	I_{out}
1	+1		+1
0	+1		0
1	-1	+1	0
0	-1	+1	+1

Table 1

In other words a ZERO in bit j of stored vector n contributed a weight of -1 from input neuron j to output neuron n and a bias at output neuron n of +1. A ONE in bit j of stored vector n contributed a weight of +1 and no bias. Table 2 shows the results of applying 9 different input vectors to the first stage of the network, 6 of the stored vectors and 3 others.

Applied Vector	Nearest Stored Vector	Outputs in Millivolts A	B	C	D	E	F
1	A	(1130)	695	[556]	[556]	775	300
2	B	710	(1125)	[554]	700	636	559
3	C	[556]	[560]	(1125)	[555]	637	[560]
4	D	[556]	695	[558]	(1125)	493	845
5	E	780	631	629	485	(1130)	353
6	F	303	[556]	[557]	840	358	(1130)
7	A	1065	628	480	627	705	352
8	C	428	[556]	705	[557]	640	[560]
9	A&B	705	695	[557]	415	493	300

Table 2
Final Results from Hamming Net Experiment

The resulting outputs follow the equation above with a k of about 70 millivolts, with a variation of less than 5%. The circled numbers along the diagonal starting at the upper left hand corner correspond to a full match in all 16 bits. The variation in this maximum output is approximately 5 parts in 1100 or less than 0.5%. The boxed numbers correspond to a distance of eight. Ideally they should all be the same; experimentally they vary by less than 2%. When this experiment was originally performed differences between nominally equivalent outputs showed much larger column-to-column variation than within a single column which is serviced by a single set of amplifiers. This was found to be largely due to offset variation between amplifiers. The effect was minimized by using low-offset amplifiers and raising the input voltage operating range so as to increase the signal-to-offset voltage ratio.

The Hamming net used single bit weights. In order to demonstrate the 4-bit weight capability, a system was configured to serve as a Gaussian classifier for the first 7 monosyllabic spoken digits. This network implements in hardware the simulations described in detail elsewhere in these proceedings.[6] An input vector consisting of 22 continuous analog variables was fed through programmed weights into each of 7 summing nodes as shown in Figure 9. These inputs represent 11 cepstral components derived from two 10 msec frames of speech samples comprising the 7 digits. Reference 6 describes how the first stage, acting as a biased linear correlator, can effectively calculate the square of the Euclidean distance between the applied vector and each of the 7 stored vectors.

The outputs from this first level were then each fed into one of 7 nodes which were configured to perform the winner-take-all function. All 7 outputs were fed to a single summing node whose output was fed back to the inhibitory inputs of all 7 nodes. The negative excursions of the 7 outputs were clamped nearly to ground by diodes. This clamping, along with the high gain used in the 7 output neurons, resulted in the feedback voltage tracking the largest output. The inputs of all the other neurons saw a net inhibiting voltage which caused their output nodes to be clamped to ground. The net result was a circuit in which the winner of the seven output nodes reproduced its positive input value and all other nodes produced very small voltages. In order to present a graphic demonstration of net operation the clamp diodes on the winner-take-all or max-picker circuit were replaced with LEDs which, while performing the clamping function, also light up on all losing nodes and remain unlit on the single winning node. This can be observed in the photograph of Figure 8, where six out of the seven LEDs are shown in the ON condition.

The results of this experiment are shown in Table 3. Here 182 vectors were applied to the circuit and the outputs compared with the results of a computer simulation to determine discrepancies between the hardware implementation and the idealized simulation. Simulated and experimental winners are tabulated for each of the seven output nodes.

The numbers along the diagonals indicate the number of matches between the two categories. Off-diagonal components indicate misclassifications, of which there were 7 out of the 182 trials. Five of these resulted from misidentifying type 1 vectors as belonging to type 5. This confusion is not too surprising, because vectors 1 and 5 are far closer than any other pair, although not so close that they should not be distinguishable by the circuit. These errors are presently under investigation.

Winners by Network

Winners by Simulation		0	1	2	3	4	5	6
	0	19						
	1		19				5	1
	2			24				
	3				28			
	4	1				30		
	5						29	
	6							26

Table 3
Histogram of Results with Guassian Classifier Net

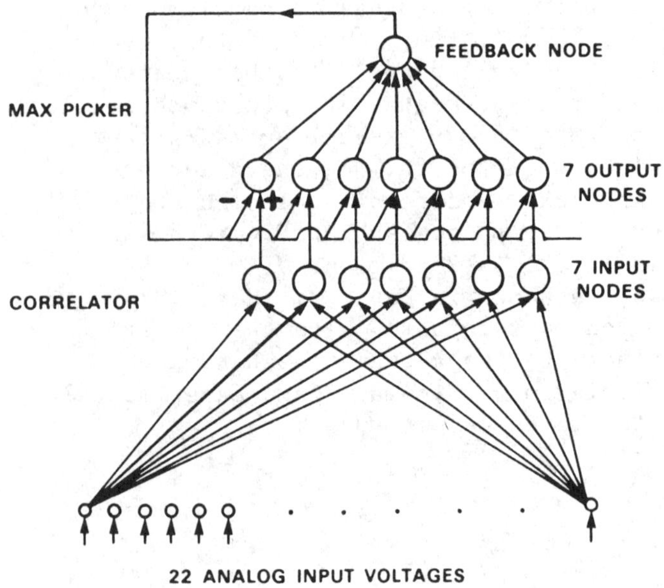

Figure 9. Neural Net Using MDAC Chip.

Alternative Circuit Realization

The MDAC circuit fabricated and used to implement the networks described above operates in the linear region of the conductance curve for the transistor up to a range of Vds = 1 volt where the percentage deviation from linearity varies directly with signal voltage in this range. It is possible instead to operate transistors in saturation performing the multiplication operation by driving the gate instead of the drain. A second version of the MDAC chip has been designed and is in fabrication using this approach. Here the subtraction of inhibiting current from exciting current is performed using current mirrors. The MDAC, shown at the top of figure 10, uses a one's complement representation to realize the weight strength and the polarity of connection. As in the previous design, the storage bits B0 through B3 turn on transistors corresponding to the desired weight. For negative weights, B4 gates on the lower row of transistors as well, forming the one's complement by exciting both inbitory and excitatory lines. The analog input Vin is applied to the second and third rows of transistors and is used to generate a current in each "on" transistor path which is proportional to the output generated at some other neural node. One of the principal motivations for using current mirrors is to allow the direct connection of neuron outputs to inputs. Also the high impedance input is desirable for distributing signals in a wafer-scale environment in which interconnect impedances are not negligible.

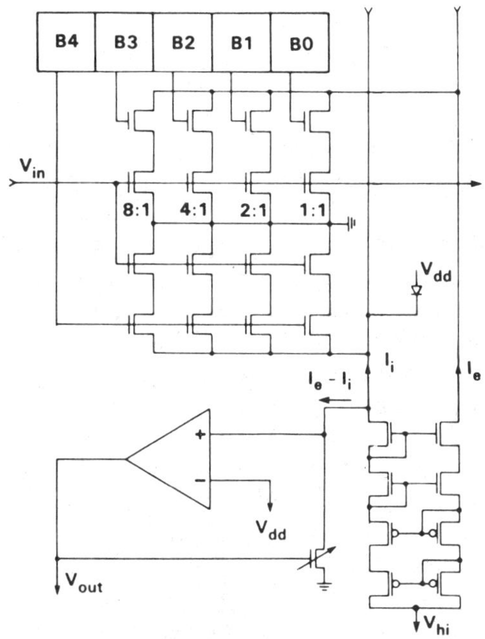

Figure 10. Current-Mirror MDAC.

The cascode mirror circuit shown at the bottom right subtracts the inhibition current from the excitation current. The current set up in the excitation branch is reflected in the other leg of the mirror. Any current in excess of the inhibition current is passed to ground through the lower transistor whose conductance corresponds to the maximum MDAC weight. (The arrow indicates that this transistor can be varied in conductance by programming a storage register controlling a bank of variable width transistors). The gate of this transistor is maintained at the voltage necessary to cause this transistor to sink the required signal current, Ie - Ii through the action of the difference amplifier whose output, Vout, is the neural node output voltage. If inhibition exceeds excitation, the diode connected to the inhibition leg prevents the internal node (I_i) from being pulled to ground.

This cascode mirror arrangement was selected for its insensitivity to voltage variations at the input and for its ability to hold the input ports at the same potential. The latter property guarantees that all of the MDACs are operating at the same Vds, eliminating any effects due to "Early" voltage. Because of its high impedance however, the transistor sizes necessary to handle any appreciable currents prohibit both a homogeneous distribution of the mirrors throughout the connection matrix or the ability to accommodate the entire operating range of MDAC currents. A single mirror at the output of each neuron was used in this implementation. The mirror was designed to operate linearly over the range 0-2 mA which is nearly the output range of a single MDAC (whose range is constrained by process geometry). Operation of the MDACs over a reduced range is accomplished by scaling the input/output mirrors which set up the gate voltages distributed across the chip. The conductances are variable with respect to the full conductance of an MDAC in ratios from 1:1 to 15:1 through a 4 bit coefficient stored in RAM.

Conclusions

Encouraging experimental results have been obtained for small networks built from integrated arrays of multiplying analog-to-digital converters controlled by writeable storage registers to implement the programmable weights common to virtually all neuromorphic systems. Design techniques used previously to build wafer-scale signal processing systems based on a laser-linking technology can be applied to the design of very large monolithic neural networks. It is estimated that a four-inch wafer, employing 2 micron design rules, will allow a network size of about 10,000 summing nodes with an average fan-in of 16. This will provide the capability for implementing in hardware networks comparable to the largest which have been simulated on general purpose computers. This will improve computation rates by many orders of magnitude, corresponding to operation in microseconds rather than seconds to minutes. An area which has clearly not been addressed by this work is that of on-wafer circuitry for adaptive weight modification or learning. This is a major objective of future design efforts but has been temporarily deferred in the interest of proceeding with the first wafer-scale implementation.

Acknowledgements: The authors which to express their appreciation to Professors H.S. Lee and John Wyatt of MIT for helpful discussions and to the MOSIS foundry for chip fabrication.

References

1. J. I. Raffel, et al, A Wafer-Scale Digital Integrator Using Restructurable VLSI, IEEE Journal of Solid-State Circuits, Vol. SC-20, No. 1, Feb 1985.

2. S. L. Garverick, E.A. Pierce, A Single Wafer 16-Point 16 MHZ FFT Processor, IEEE Proceedings of the Custom Integrated Circuits Conference May, 1983.

3. J. R. Mann, F. M. Rhodes, A Wafer-Scale DTW Multiprocessor, Presented at ICASSP'86, Tokyo, Japan, April 8-11, 1986.

4. J. Alspector and Allen, R.B., A Neuromorphic VLSI Learning System, Advanced Research in VLSI, Proceedings of the 1987 Stanford Conference.

5. R. Lippman, Computing with Neural Nets, IEEE ASSP Magazine, volume 4, number 2, April 1987.

6. R. Lippman, B. Gold, Neural Net Classifiers Useful for Speech Recognition, IEEE First International Conference on Neural Networks, San Diego, California, 1987.

Why VLSI Implementations of Associative VLCNs Require Connection Multiplexing†

Jim Bailey and Dan Hammerstrom

Dept. of Computer Science / Engineering
Oregon Graduate Center
Beaverton, Oregon

1. Abstract

This paper discusses some of the implementation constraints imposed upon VLSI architectures for emulations of Very Large Connectionist/Neural Networks (VLCNs). Specifically it shows that multiplexing interconnections is necessary for networks exhibiting poor locality.

2. Introduction

In recent years there has been a great deal of interest in Connectionist/Neural Networks (CNNs). These are networks of simple processors, where the network state is represented by the outputs of the processors and the strengths of the connections between them. They are characterized by asynchrony, a high degree of connectivity, and good fault tolerance. CNNs are seen as providing solutions to problems that are difficult or impossible to solve with the traditional approach of symbolic processing on von Neumann computers. Pattern recognition, constraint satisfaction, and data completion are some examples of these types of problems.

Many demonstrations have shown the feasibility of CNNs. Unfortunately, research efforts have been limited by time and memory requirements of simulating CNNs on general purpose computers. For example, NETtalk, a system that learned to generate speech from text [16], required more than twelve hours of VAX-780 time for the necessary learning trials. Network sizes have been restricted to a few hundreds nodes for all but the largest simulations. In addition to limiting problem size, the lack of appropriate tools has kept researchers from empirically investigating the effects of scaling on network algorithms.

A variety of computational solutions have been proposed. They include the use of supercomputers, networks of simple microprocessors, vector co-processor boards, and specialized systems based on fast numeric processors. While all help alleviate the problem, increasing network sizes will require even larger and faster VLCN emulators. In addition, the development of applications requires the availability of inexpensive emulation systems. It is impractical to use a hundred thousand dollar system on someone's desk for speech recognition.

We feel the most promising arena of research for inexpensive, but powerful, emulation engines is VLSI CMOS. Microprocessor and memory competition has pushed the development of faster and denser CMOS processes and has provided a well understood, powerful, yet relatively inexpensive and easy to use medium. Many exotic technologies are being investigated in various research labs, but they are not expected to contribute practical, mass manufacturable solutions for years [8]. Included in this category are optical networks that have wonderful theoretical properties, but are too expensive and installation critical to be presently feasible for consumer products.

In designing custom VLSI circuits for VLCNs, a range of possible implementations are available. Very fast, dedicated processors tuned for the required computations can be used alone or in small groups to process an entire network. This, the network processor

†This work was supported in part by the Semiconductor Research Corporation contract no. 86-10-097, and jointly by the Office of Naval Research and Air Force Office of Scientific Research, ONR contract no. N00014 87 K 0259.

Reprinted from *IEEE 2nd Annual International Conference on Neural Networks*, 1988, pages II-173--II-180.

EH2029-3/90/0000/0112$01.00 © 1988 IEEE

model, is the approach used by SAIC, TI, HNC, and TRW in their *neurocomputer* products. The other end of the spectrum is systems directly implementing CNNs in silicon with a processor, usually analog, for each *neuron*. This is the approach used by researchers at Bell Labs, Synaptics, Lincoln Labs, JPL, and Cal Tech.

This paper looks at CNN connectivity requirements and proposes a solution for *general purpose associative* VLCNs that lies toward, but not at, the direct end of this spectrum. We feel that, while direct implementation matches the connectivity requirements of highly localized primary sensory processing as exemplified by the visual processing chips of Carver Mead and his associates [13], it does not scale well for the greater degree of interconnect required by associative networks. Our approach differs from direct by multiplexing connections. Also, we provide the potential sharing of a physical processor by a small number of CNN nodes. Not only does our alternative scale better, it also delivers better cost/performance. The comparative cost is determined by the silicon area required, since manufacturing costs are directly correlated with increasing chip module size. Comparative performance is determined by system speed.

3. Terms and Definitions

The communication requirements of a CNN model can be expressed as a directed graph where the vertices are the connection nodes (CNs), or neurons, and the edges are the computational dependencies between them. That is, if there exists an edge (p,q) in a CNN, then the output of CN p is an input to CN q. Such a graph will be called a *c-graph* (connection graph) in the remainder of this paper.

Similarly the physical system used to emulate the CNN has communication capabilities that can be viewed as a directed graph. Here the vertices are the physical nodes (PNs), or computational processors, and the edges represent communication paths between them. Physical system communication graphs will be referred to as *p-graphs*.

Before an emulation of a CNN by a physical system can be done, there must be a partitioning of the set of CNs into small subsets, where the computation for each subset is performed by a single PN. Each such partitioning requires the establishment of communication channels so each PN can receive the necessary update information, or inputs, for its set of CNs. A partitioning can be viewed as a mapping M of c-graph c to p-graph p. M assigns each vertex in c to a single, not necessarily unique, vertex in p. Each edge in c is mapped to a path in p such that if (a,b) is an edge in c, $M(a) = r$, $M(b) = s$, then $M(a,b)$ is a path from r to s in p.

Note that the above definitions are not concerned with either the computational function required in the c-graph nodes or the capabilities of the PNs. This model is strictly one of communication dependencies and capabilities. Specifically, it is possible to use either analog or digital communications without restricting the form of computation. For example, our research is investigating hybrid digital communication and analog computation [11].

The final concepts to define are distance and locality. *P-graph distance* is the length of a minimal path between the two points of interest. *C-graph distance* is the p-graph distance under some mapping. Thus, the distance between two CNs is a function of the c-graph structure and the quality of the mapping involved. It is only defined in the context of a particular mapping.

The *locality* of a CN is a function of both the number and length of its connections. Intuitively, a CN with few connections exhibits better locality than one with many. Similarly, having long distance connections implies poorer locality than short distance ones. The locality of a c-graph, or subsection of a c-graph, is the average of the localities of the nodes within it.

Only the spatial, or static, aspect of locality is considered in this paper. Temporal, or dynamic, locality refers to the firing pattern in time of the CNs. A more formal, in depth, treatment of both types of locality can be found in [2].

Locality not only depends on the quality of the mapping, it is also affected by the availability of connections within the p-graph. CNNs with good locality scale better than those with poor locality. Network locality depends on network function. General associative processing appears to be less localized than sensory data processing. One possible source of solutions for locality related problems is biological systems. They appear to display locality, even in association cortex [10]. Due to physical connectivity limitations, as network locality decreases, the c-graph to p-graph mapping (for planar silicon implemented p-graphs) becomes increasingly inefficient.

4. Interconnection Possibilities

There are currently two widely differing interconnect models for VLSI implementations. The first uses short length internode connections, i.e. each node communicates only with nodes within a small physical radius. This is the model used by Carver Mead *et alia* in building the "silicon retina" chip [13]. The other model is more general and provides for all possible connections. This second approach is being used by Jackel, Graf, *et alia* in their associative network chips [6, 9], and by Alspector and Allen in their Boltzman Machine chip [1].

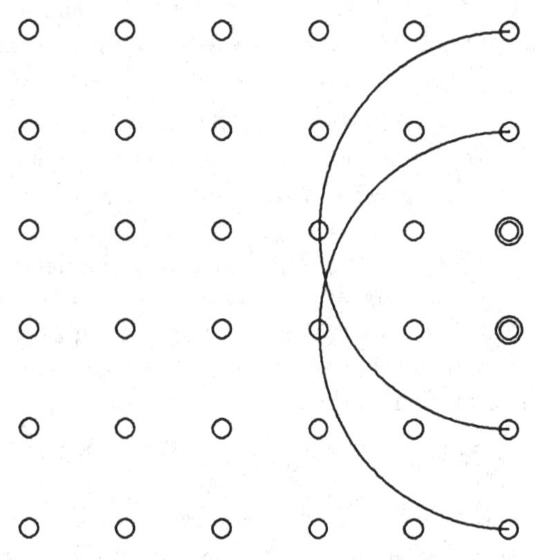

Figure 1 Limited connection radius graph

It is obvious that both models work for the size networks currently being built - chips either exist or are under development. The question is: "how do they scale for VLCNs?". If each PN is connected only to its nearest neighbors, then the size of the system can be increased indefinitely with no scaling problems. To illustrate this, consider a planar layout of PNs and add new PNs along one edge. New connections are made between the new PNs and the old border PNs, which were not fully connected before. PNs more than the radius of connection from the edge are not impacted, as shown in figure 1, where the two nodes on the right have *interconnection radius* of two and do not reach any PNs in the three left columns.

Unfortunately, the total interconnect model does not scale as well. Figure 2 shows how a Hopfield Network chip may be laid out with an $O(N^2)$ area requirement for N connections. In figure 2, the horizontal lines transmit the new CN output states and the vertical wires sum them. Thus, one vertical line is *shared* among a number of connections. If the computation performed in the CN does not sum all inputs, then this approach is infeasible. Consider a node that computes a function with two or more classes of inputs, it requires a vertical summing wire for each class. When the computational model requires N discrete inputs at the CN, N vertical wires for each CN are needed. Such a model requires $O(N^3)$ area.

No one is seriously proposing global interconnect for VLCNs due to the $O(N^3)$ area requirement. More important for VLCN design is how the area required grows with less than global, but still non-planar, interconnect.

The width of the area needed by the inter-PN connections is the product of the wire pitch, or wire width plus interwire spacing, times the number of wires. Assume a grid of PNs. With no loss of generality choose two that are adjacent and horizontal to each other. Assume a *uniform* distribution of sources and destinations and count the number of wires that cross a vertical *bisector* drawn between them. This sum will be a function of the number of PNs that a

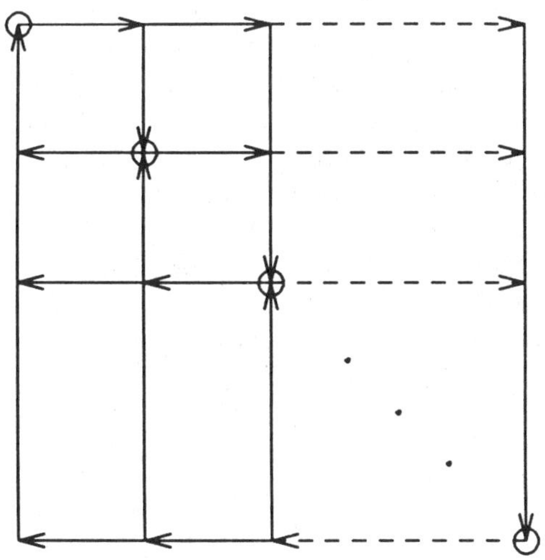

Figure 2 A Possible Hopfield Network Layout

connection can be made to, times the probability that a given connection is long enough to cross the bisector, summed over all nodes on one side, and multiplied by two. A formal restatement is:

$$C = 2\left(\sum_{i=1}^{\infty}\sum_{j=0}^{\infty} f(i+j) + \sum_{i=1}^{\infty}\sum_{j=0}^{\infty}\sum_{k=1}^{\infty} f(i+j+k)\right)$$

This reduces to:

$$C = 2\sum_{i=0}^{\infty} i\,(f(i) + 1/2\,(i+1)f(i+1))$$

Where C is the number of connections and $f(x)$ gives the probability of a connection between two PNs x distance apart. Setting $f(x)$ to allow connections between all nodes within a fixed distance k,

$$f(x) = 1 \quad (for\ x \leq k)$$

$$f(x) = 0 \quad (otherwise)$$

yields

$$C_k = 1/3\,(k^3 + 2k)$$

Since k, or the radius of the circle of connections, is a function of the number of nodes connected to, the area required is $O(n^3)$ where n is the number of connections required. A similar limit is developed differently by Hammerstrom in [7]. CNN models with increased degree of interconnect locality must be found to limit the rapid growth of silicon area as the number of nodes increases.

5. A Layout Example

To see the possible gains in layout density due to multiplexing of interconnect, compare the area and response time of two equivalent systems of 10^6 CNs with 10^3 connections for each, for a total of 10^9 connections or synapses. The first, or *direct*, model has one CN per PN and every c-graph edge explicitly present as a p-graph edge. The second, or *grid*, alternative has 16 CNs per PN and connections are made only to nearest neighbors and messages are relayed to further destinations.

Both models assume that the PNs are laid out in a hexagonal grid. In addition, it is assumed that wire widths and interwire spacing are each 1 μ, three levels of metal are available, and that a memory cell takes 50 μ^2. Also, the processor area required for computation is ignored, since it is a small percentage of the total area and is the same in both models. One bit of state is transmitted between nodes and weights are 4 bits. The specific values of these assumptions are not critical since only a measure of relative performance is intended.

5.1. Direct Implementation

Communication delays in a direct connect system are due to the length of the interconnect lines. Message length is minimal, each node can readily identify the source of a given message for weight assignment and no destination addresses are needed for routing. The delay in transmitting a one bit message is therefore equal to the time it takes for the signal to transit the wire.

Fault tolerance is equivalent to that of the underlying CNN model, the only possible points of failure are the CNs themselves and the connections between them. With the number of CNs in the system, and the ability of the CNN model to change connection weights to adjust for invalid inputs, such a system should be very defect tolerant.

Consider the best case from an implementation viewpoint: a system with every PN connected to the nearest 10^3 PNs. For a hexagonal grid layout of PNs, the radius of a *connection group* is 18 since

$$\sum_{i=0}^{n} 6i \geq 1000$$

has minimal solution $n = 18$.

The total processor area is then $\pi r^2 \times 10^6$, for a processor radius r; the total interconnect area is $2/3 \times l \times 10^9$, where l is the average length of an interprocessor connection; and $l = 1/3 \times (2 \times 18 + 1) \times 2r$, since l is the length of an average connection spanning a circular region of radius 18 PN diameters ($2r$). Solving this set of equations yields $r = 5.2 \times 10^3 \mu$, PN area of $8.6 \times 10^7 \mu^2$ and a total chip area of $8.6 \times 10^{13} \mu^2$ or **86 square meters**. The area required for memory is only 4 *bits per weight* $\times$ 50 μ^2 *per bit* $\times$ 10^3 *weights* $\times$ 10^6 PNs or 2×10^{11} μ^2, showing how the interconnect requirements dwarf the processor requirements.

The worst case delay is over a wire 18 $\times$ $2r$ μ long with a delay of 10^{-2} *nsec per* μ, or 1.9×10^3 *nsec*, and the average delay is 1.3×10^3 *nsec*.

This analysis is limited in accuracy because the CN of origin is assumed to be in the center of the system and there will be some CNs on the periphery, with wider interconnect groups. It is impossible for three metal layers to be routed as closely as the calculations assume or to have this optimal mapping of c-graph to p-graph. Further, a real system would have some number of long, or non-local, connections making the required area even worse. For these reasons, and because of the use of approximate values in all computations, the results are lower bounds of roughly the correct magnitude.

It is clear from this analysis that direct interconnection is not feasible for silicon implementations of large associative networks. We now look at a virtual connection approach.

5.2. Grid

The contrasting model uses multiple CNs per PN and multiplexed interconnect. The analysis of this model is similar to direct. Because of the lack of non-local connections, grid should exhibit minimum interconnect cost and maximum communication delays.

One potential problem with having multiple CNs per PN is the required interprocessor communication bandwidth. Obviously, if there are an infinite number of PNs and they are all connected to each other then the bandwidth is infinite. With an infinite array of PNs, as long as the probability of a connection between any two is a function decreasing with the distance d at least as fast as α^{-d}, for some $\alpha > 1$ (not unreasonable for a model of cortical interconnectivity), then the required bandwidth is finite. The limit is

$$\beta\left(\frac{\alpha^3}{(\alpha-1)^4}+\frac{\alpha^2}{(\alpha-1)^2}+\frac{\alpha}{(\alpha-1)^2}+\frac{\alpha}{3(\alpha-1)^3}\right)$$

where β is the message length. A proof can be found in [2]. Placing the PNs in a hexagonal pattern reduces both the bandwidth required and the diameter of the interconnect region. Each PN both transmits to and receives from its six neighbors. Any messages that need to be routed to a non-adjacent PN are relayed by the intermediate nodes using a routing algorithm based on the destination address of the message.

There are sixteen CNs in a PN. Each CN requires 10^3 weights, 16 local addresses and 984 global addresses, assuming optimal mapping. Using the routing information as the address, a global address requires 19 bits. This is established by each of five intermediate PNs requiring three bits to determine routine direction and the destination PN needing four bits to determine the correct CN. A local address is 4 bits.

The source address in each message is used to determine which weight to apply. There are two sets of addresses required for each CN, one for destinations and one for weight selection. The total memory required is thus $4 \times 10^3 + 2 \times (4 \times 16 + 984 \times 19)$ or 41520 *bits per CN*. This predicts a PN area of $6.6 \times 10^5 \times 50$ μ^2 or 3.3×10^7 μ^2. The complete system would require 2.1×10^{12} μ^2 (2.1 square meters), or one fortieth the area of the direct implementation.

A message sent between two PNs consists of the routing information, which functions as both source and destination address, and one bit of state, for a total of 20 bits. The expected path length can be calculated by solving the equation:

$$\sum_{i=1}^{n} 6i \geq (1000 - 16) \;/\; 16$$

The smallest such integral n is 5, so the maximum number of intervening links expected is 5 and the average is $(2 \times 5 + 1) / 3$ or 3.7, assuming the PNs are uniformly distributed within the area of the circle with radius 5. All connections are to nearest neighbors, so the communication latency is the time required to relay the message through intermediate PNs. Given the above figure for PN area, the diameter is $\sqrt{3.3 \times 10^7}\ \mu$. With a wire transit time of 10^{-2} *nsec per* μ *per bit*, this works out to a minimal relay time of 57 *nsec per node per bit*.

For a rough approximation of the added delay due to contention, assume 10% of the CNs firing at any given time and six wires available in each direction for carrying messages. This yields a contention factor of 525 (984 *messages per CN* $\times$ 16 *CNs per PN* $\times$ 10% *firing rate* $\times$ 62500 *PNs* /(6 *wires per PN* $\times$ 62500 *PNs* / 2)) and a serialization factor of 164 (984 *wires* / *fanout of* 6).

The above contention factor greatly underestimates the delays due to contention since it assumes that the message traffic is uniformly distributed over all wires in the system, both temporally and physically. It ignores the increased contention in the center of the system. The serialization factor could be decreased by the use of more wires between nodes, but at the cost of increased complexity in the routing hardware. For these reasons, these numbers are order of magnitude approximations only.

The average cycle time, or the time for a 20 *bit* message to reach the CN an average distance away and come back, is 3.6×10^8 *nsec* $(2 \times 20 \times 57 \times 3.7 \times 525 \times 164 / 2)$ and the worst case time is 1.0×10^9 *nsec* $(2 \times 20 \times 57 \times 5 \times 525 \times 164)$. This delay is **five to six orders of magnitude slower** than in the direct implementation and two to three orders of magnitude slower than neural systems.

Changing the assumption of 16 CNs per PN impacts the comparison to a limited extent since the area required becomes $5.4 \times 10^{12}\ \mu^2$ and the delay times go to 1.3×10^8 and 2.5×10^8 *nsec*. (These latter numbers are suspect since the degree of contention is greater than allowed for.)

Both examples suffer from requiring optimal mappings of c-graph to p-graph, since otherwise some connections would be to remote PNs, and ignoring edge discontinuities. They are thus for comparative purposes only and not indicative of the actual costs involved other than as order of magnitude approximations.

5.3. The CAP Alternative

While the above arguments show that sharing interconnect is a big win over direct interconnect, both alternatives presented suffer from weaknesses. The Cognitive Architecture Project (CAP) at Oregon Graduate Center has developed an architecture that solves some of these problems. This paper does not have room to present much of our work, but we have designed the ABH (Augmented Broadcast Hierarchy*) architecture, which uses a hierarchy of overlapping broadcast regions to support local communication and a point-to-point communication structure for long distance messages. Area requirements are less than grid due to data sharing and address compression. The performance is significantly better because of the reduction in the number of messages each PN must generate. More information on the architecture and the results of test chips can be found in [2,15].

6. Multiplexing Advantages and Disadvantages

In addition to reducing interconnect area, multiplexing of communication lines provides more flexibility in use. By changing the addresses stored in the PNs, new connections can be made or changed dynamically,

*patent pending

even while the system is running.

While the concept of sharing wires does not force the use of digital communication, analog multiplexing is more difficult and would probably not be used in practice. Digital communication has the added advantages of increased robustness and easier debugging. Also, digital communication does not preclude the use of analog computation.

Multiplexing interconnect is not a panacea, it brings with it a variety of problems that need to be solved before VLCN emulation systems can be built. These problems include decreased fault tolerance, since the loss of a single line or of the multiplexing hardware causes the loss of multiple connections; the need for more complex addressing and routing algorithms; increased power dissipation and heat generation; and increased contention problems with resultant degradation of repeatability of transit delays, which is a problem for algorithms where temporal behavior is critical. This section provides some possible solutions, but detailed answers are beyond the scope of this paper.

Decreased fault tolerance can be solved by using multiple instances of structures that might fail. For example, three communication lines might be used with required agreement among any two. Alternatively there can be a final processing step that removes flawed connections and substitutes working ones [3, 14]. A third possible solution is to use intelligent routing that attempts to send messages around flaws. Unfortunately, all of these approaches increase the amount of area required and the cost of the final product. Research is being done at OGC [12] into characterizing the reliability of multiplexed implementations and the behavior of the resulting CNN models in the face of a variety of flaws. The engineering of better solutions is part of that research.

When considering the effect of fabrication defects, it is important to realize that current defect densities are on the order of fifteen to twenty-five per square inch. This compares to millions of transistors in the same area. Since much of the area of the system consists of memory for storage of weights, addresses, and CN states, the loss of a few bits should be tolerable and will rarely have a major impact. Thus added redundancy may not be needed.

There is no avoiding the need to have routing information and data packets when multiple messages are sent across a single communication link. It is also necessary to decode the arriving packet and determine for which CNs it is intended. Since all messages must include a source address, it is possible to use broadcast communication. This reduces the length of packets and solves some of the congestion problems. More information on this approach can be found in [2, 15]. A factor offsetting the problems of communication complexity is the speed differential between communication and computation. With chips being clocked at twenty megahertz or more, a clock cycle is less than 5×10^{-8} seconds. We believe computational systems will not need to update more than once every 10^{-4} seconds to be fast enough for most applications. The difference, a factor of four orders of magnitude, provides sufficient time to resolve message traffic problems.

Finally, there is the problem of congestion and contention. Research has been proposed into the effects of losing packets of information on network functionality, but nothing has yet been done on this question. Our simulation results [15], together with that of other researchers in the field [4], indicate that delay repeatability and magnitude is critical in CNN models when it becomes large relative to the CN update ratio. Since the communication times are orders of magnitude faster than computation times, reasonable contention should be tolerable. More research on this is in pending work at OGC [2].

7. Conclusions

As the above analyses have shown, it is more feasible to build a VLCN system with sharing or multiplexing of interconnect than to build one with dedicated wires for each connection. This is true unless the network exhibits extreme locality and all CNs are connected to others within some small radius region. Unfortunately, association requires some global connectivity. The advantages of sharing wires agrees with the work of Dally at CalTech where he shows that it is more efficient to use lower dimensional shared interconnect than high dimensional dedicated connections for VLSI designs [5].

The problems associated with multiplexing are solvable and some solutions are provided, although more research is needed. Techniques are available for providing analog computation, even when multiplexing indicates the need for digital communication. Finally, once communication lines are multiplexed, it is possible to provide for further reductions of area by combining several CNs on a single PN.

8. References

[1] Alspector, J. and Allen, R. B., "A Neuromorphic VLSI Learning System," *Advanced Research in VLSI: Proceedings of the 1987 Stanford Conference*, Cambridge, MA, 1987.

[2] Bailey, J., "A VLSI Interconnect Structure for Neural Networks," Ph.D. Dissertation, Oregon Graduate Center. In Preparation..

[3] Cole, B., "Inova Brings Wafer-Scale Integration to Market," *Electronics*, January 8, 1987, pp. 91-95.

[4] Conwell, P. R., *Effects of Connection Delays in Two State Model Neural Circuits*, Proceedings of the ICNN, San Diego, CA, June 1987.

[5] Dally, W. J., "A VLSI Architecture for Concurrent Data Structures," Ph.D. Dissertation, California Institute of Technology, 1986.

[6] Graf, H. P. and Vegvar, P., "FAM 22.1: A CMOS Associative Memory Chip Based on Neural Networks," *IEEE International Solid-State Circuits Conference*, 1987, pp. 304-305,437.

[7] Hammerstrom, D., "A Connectivity Analysis of Recursive, Auto-Associative Connection Networks," Tech. Report CS/E-86-009, Oregon Graduate Center, August 1986.

[8] Hecht-Nielsen, R., "Performance Limits of Optical, Electro-Optical, and Electronic Neurocomputers," *Artificial Neural Networks*, August 1986.

[9] Jackel, L. D., Howard, R. E., Graf, H. P., Straughn, B. and Denker, J. S., "Artificial Neural Networks for Computing," *Journal of Vacuum Science Technology*, , pp. 61-63.

[10] Lynch, G., Granger, R., Larson, J. and Baudry, M., Cortical encoding of memory: Hypotheses derived from analysis and simulation of physiological learning rules in anatomical structures, Unpublished Manuscript, 1987.

[11] Mates, J. and Owens, S., "Microarchitecture Specification for the Analog Processor Node, APN," Tech. Report CS/E-88-014, Oregon Graduate Center , March 1988.

[12] May, N., "Fault Simulation of a Wafer-Scale Integrated Neurocomputer," Tech. Report CS/E-88-020, Oregon Graduate Center , March 1988.

[13] Mead, C. A. and Mahowald, M. A., "A Silicon Model of Early Visual Processing," *Neural Networks*, , pp. 91-97.

[14] Raffell, J., Mann, J., Berger, R., Soares, A. and Gilbert, S., "A Generic Architecture for Wafer-Scale Neuromorphic Systems," *Proceedings of the ICNN*, San Diego, CA, June 1986.

[15] Rudnick, M. and Hammerstrom, D., "Physical Broadcast Structure," Tech. Report CS/E-88-018, Oregon Graduate Center , April 1988.

[16] Sejnowski, T. J. and Rosenberg, C. R., "NETtalk: A Parallel Network that Learns to Read Aloud," JHU/EECS-86/01, The Johns Hopkins University, 1986.

A Unifying Algorithm/Architecture for Artificial Neural Networks*

S. Y. Kung

Princeton University
Deptartment of Electrical Engineering
Princeton, NJ 08540

J. N. Hwang

University of Southern California
Deptartment of Electrical Engineering
Los Angeles, CA 90089

Abstract

This paper proposes a generic iterative model for a wide variety of artificial neural networks (ANNs): single layer feedback networks, multilayer feed-forward networks, hierarchical competitive networks, and hidden Markov models. Unifying mathematical formulations are provided for both the retrieving and learning phases of ANNs. Based on the unifying mathematical formulation, a programmable universal ring systolic array is derived for both phases, which maximizes the strength of VLSI in terms of intensive and pipelined computing and yet circumvents the limitation on communication. Hardware implementation for the processing units based on Cordic techniques is also discussed.

1 A Generic Iterative Model for ANNs

A basic ANN model consists of a large number of *neurons*, linked to each other with *synaptic weights*. Each, say i-th, neural processing unit (PU) has an activation value a_i. This value is propagated through a network of synaptic weight denoted as w_{ij} which dictates the effect the j-th PU has on the i-th PU (see Figure 1(a)).

From algorithmic point of view, the ANN processing can be divided into two phases: *retrieving* and *learning*. Given a fixed configuration of a neural network, the retrieving phase specifies the iterative updating of activation values of each neuron, based on the (nonlinear) *system dynamics*, in response to the stimulus inputs (test patterns). On the other hand, the learning phase specifies the iterative updating of the connection strength of each synaptic weight, based on the adopted *learning rule*, in response to the input training patterns.

Retrieving Phase of the Generic Iterative ANN Model The system dynamics in the retrieving phase of a generic (L-iterations) iterative model for ANNs can be written as:

$$u_i(l+1) = \sum_{j=1}^{N_l} w_{ij}(l+1)a_j(l) + \theta_i(l+1) = \sum_{j=0}^{N_l} w_{ij}(l+1)a_j(l) \quad (1)$$

$$a_i(l+1) = f_i(u_i(l+1), a_i(l)) \quad (2)$$

where $1 \leq i \leq N_{l+1}$ and $0 \leq l \leq L-1$. The initialization activation values $\{a_i(0)\}$ are often regarded as stimulus inputs and the termination activation values $\{a_i(L)\}$ are often regarded as retrieved outputs. This system dynamics result in an L-layer feed-forward neural network with N_l neural units at l-th layer as shown in Figure 1(b).

Each PU, say i-th neuron at $(l+1)$-th iteration, receives the weighted inputs from other PUs at l-th iteration together with the external input $\theta_i(l+1)$ to yield the net input $u_i(l+1)$ according to the *propagation rule* (see Eq. 1). For simplicity, the external inputs $\{\theta_i(l+1)\}$ are often treated as synaptic weights $\{w_{i,0}(l+1)\}$ which have clamped inputs $a_0(l) = 1$. The net input value $u_i(l+1)$, along with its forward propagated activation value (if any) $a_i(l)$, will determine the new activation value $a_i(l+1)$ by the *nonlinear activation* function f_i (see Eq. 2).

Learning Phase of the Generic Iterative ANN Model The weight updating (credit assignment) problem in a multilayer feed-forward network shown in Figure 1(b) is to find a set of synaptic weights (and also external inputs), so that a predefined measure function E can be optimized given a set of P input training patterns. The learning phase usually involves two steps: In the first step, the input training pattern (or patterns) is (are) passing through the iterations of the network, which is the same as in retrieving phase. Based on the resulting information, the weights are updated correspondingly in the second step based on the adopted learning rules. Due to the nature of adaptive training inputs and the high complexity involved in finding a closed form solution, recursive procedures are highly desired. A unifying recursive weight updating formulation (learning rule) for the generic iterative ANN model can be given:

$$w_{ij}^{(m+1)}(l) = \Phi(w_{ij}^{(m)}(l),\ \eta_{ij}(l),\ \frac{\partial E}{\partial w_{ij}^{(m)}(l)}) \quad (3)$$

The new weight value $w_{ij}^{(m+1)}(l)$ at $(m+1)$-th recursion can be determined by the current weight value $w_{ij}^{(m)}(l)$, the updating rate parameter $\eta_{ij}(l)$, and the derivative term $\frac{\partial E}{\partial w_{ij}^{(m)}(l)}$ which represents the derivative of a measure function E with respect to the specific weight $w_{ij}^{(m)}(l)$.

2 Formulations of the Iterative Model

Given a specific formulation of the system dynamics in the retrieving phase (see Eqs. 1 and 2) and a specific formulation of the learning procedure in the learning phase (see Eq. 3) of the generic iterative ANN model, a unique neural network model can be determined.

2.1 Formulations in the Retrieving Phase

Iterations in the Retrieving Phase The iteration indices $\{l\}$ used in the generic iterative ANN model denote either type of the three possible iterations: *time spatial*, and *pattern*. If l represents the time iteration, then the network is a single layer feedback network with each neuron being updated synchronously (in parallel) at each iteration. The resulting time-iterated generic multilayer feed-forward network has equal number of N neuron at each layer, and a homogeneous set of synaptic weights $\{w_{ij}\}$ used for all the layers. If l represents the spatial iteration, then the network is usually heterogeneous in both the number of neurons and the synaptic weights at each layer. It is also possible that each pattern input forms a separate layer.

Nonlinear Activation Functions The nonlinear activation function f_i in Eq. 2 can be a stochastic or a deterministic function (for ease of reading, we will denote the position invariant activation function as f). There are three popular deterministic nonlinear activation functions: thresholding, squashing, and sigmoid. In some applications, winner-take-all type of nonlinear mechanism implemented by lateral inhibitions can be used so that only the neuron receives largest input is activated.

2.2 Formulations in the Learning Phase

Recursions in the Learning Phase The recursion indices $\{m\}$ used in the unifying recursive weight updating formulation denote either type of the two possible recursions: *pattern* and *sweep*. If m denotes the pattern recursion, then the network update the synaptic weights after the presentation of each training pattern. If m denotes the sweep recursion, the network update the synaptic weights after the presentation of all the P training patterns.

* This research was supported in part by the National Science Foundation under Grant ECS-82-13358, and by the Innovative Science and Technology Office of the Strategic Defense Initiative Organization, administered through the Office of Naval Research under Contract No. N00014-85-K-0469 and N00014-85-K-0599.

Reprinted from *The Proceedings of the International Conference on Acoustics, Speech, and Signal Processing*, Vol. 4, 1989, pages 2505-2508.

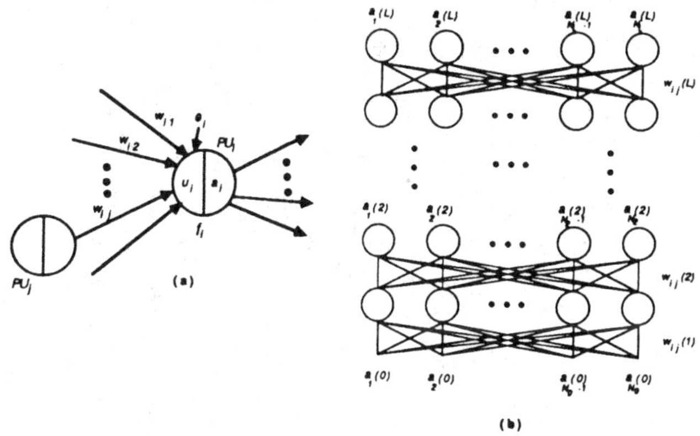

Figure 1: (a) A basic ANN model with two operations: propagation rule, and nonlinear activation. (b) A generic iterative model (L-iterations) for ANNs.

The Measure Functions The measure function E in Eq. 3 is introduced to perform an iterative optimization task. It can be a metric function in a maximization problem, or it can be a cost function in a minimization problem. The measure function can be optimized in a global network basis, or it cab be optimized in a layer-by-layer (or neuron-by-neuron) basis, these result in a local measure function for each layer $\{E(l), \forall l\}$, or for each neuron $\{E_i(l), \forall i, l\}$.

Additive or Multiplicative Formulations The Φ function in Eq. 3 can be in additive formulations or in multiplicative formulations. The additive formulations lead to the gradient descent (ascent) approach:

$$w_{ij}(l) \equiv w_{ij}(l) \pm \eta \frac{\partial E}{\partial w_{ij}(l)} \tag{4}$$

where $\pm$ is determined based on either the maximization or minimization formulation. On the other hand, if $\{w_{ij}(l)\}$ satisfy the following constraints, i.e., $w_{ij}(l) \geq 0$ and $\sum_{i=1}^{N_l} w_{ij}(l) = 1$, then the multiplicative formulation has been proven to lead to an iterative optimization technique [12].

$$w_{ij}(l) \equiv w_{ij}(l) \cdot \eta \frac{\partial E}{\partial w_{ij}(l)} \tag{5}$$

where proper choice of the updating step η is necessary.

Back-Propagated Signals In both of the additive and multiplicative formulations, the chain rule can be used to simplify the computations, i.e., the derivative term can be decomposed into:

$$\frac{\partial E}{\partial w_{ij}(l)} = \frac{\partial E}{\partial a_i(l)} \frac{\partial a_i(l)}{\partial w_{ij}(l)} = \delta_i(l) \frac{\partial a_i(l)}{\partial w_{ij}(l)} \tag{6}$$

where the backward propagated signal $\delta_i(l)$ is defined to be $\frac{\partial E}{\partial a_i(l)}$. The change in $w_{ij}(l)$ will first influence the activation value $a_i(l)$ of the outgoing neuron of this weight, and the change in the activation value will further influence the global E measure function. In some neural network models, due to the difficulty of computing $\delta_i(l)$ quantitatively, approximations are proposed;

$$\frac{\partial E}{\partial w_{ij}(l)} = \frac{\partial E}{\partial a_i(l)} \frac{\partial a_i(l)}{\partial w_{ij}(l)} \approx \frac{\Delta E}{\Delta a_i(l)} \frac{\Delta a_i(l)}{\Delta w_{ij}(l)} \tag{7}$$

For a more precise calculation, the backward propagated signal $\delta_i(l)$ can be recursively calculated based on signal one layer above (where $L-1 \geq l \geq 1$).

$$\begin{aligned} \delta_i(l) &= \frac{\partial E}{\partial a_i(l)} = \sum_{j=1}^{N_{l+1}} \frac{\partial E}{\partial a_j(l+1)} \frac{\partial a_j(l+1)}{\partial a_i(l)} \\ &= \sum_{j=1}^{N_{l+1}} \delta_j(l+1) \frac{\partial a_j(l+1)}{\partial a_i(l)} \end{aligned} \tag{8}$$

Homogeneous Iterative ANN Model A special case of the generic iterative network is when there is a homogeneous set of parameters w_{ij} used for all the layers (iterations) with equal number of neurons at each layer, i.e., $w_{ij}(l) = w_{ij}, \forall l$. Usually, the derivative term in Eq. 6 is computed by either using only the top layer (last iteration) information without computing the back-propagated signals; $\frac{\partial E}{\partial w_{ij}} = \frac{\partial E}{\partial w_{ij}(L)}$, or it can be computed by taking into account the back-propagated signals by averaging the derivative values of all the layer;

$$\frac{\partial E}{\partial w_{ij}} = \sum_{l=1}^{L} \frac{\partial E}{\partial a_i(l)} \frac{\partial a_i(l)}{\partial w_{ij}(l)} \frac{\partial w_{ij}(l)}{\partial w_{ij}} = \sum_{l=1}^{L} \delta_i(l) \frac{\partial a_i(l)}{\partial w_{ij}(l)} \tag{9}$$

2.3 Neural Network Examples

In the following, we will summarize by Tables 1 and 2 that a wide variety of neural network models belong to the generic iterative ANN model and obey the unifying mathematical formulation in both of the retrieving and learning phases.

Learning Rules	Neural Networks	Iteration (Layer) l	Nonlinear Activation $f(\cdot)$	Ref.
Delta Learning	Single Layer Adaline	Single	Thresholding	[16]
	Memory & Learning Module	Time	Squashing	[10]
	Multilayer Adaline/ Committee Machine	Spatial	Thresholding	[15,11]
	Back-Propagation Network	Spatial	Sigmoid	[13]
	Recurrent Back-Propagation	Time	Sigmoid	[13]
Hebbian Learning	Parallel Hopfield Associative Network	Time	Thresholding	[4,5]
	Self-Organized Perceptual Network	Spatial	Linear	[9]
Competitive Learning	Self-Organized Feature Map	Single	Winner-Take-All	[6]
	Adaptive Resonance Theory	Single	Winner-Take-All	[3]
	Rumelhart Feature Detector	Spatial	Winner-Take-All	[14]
Stochastic Learning	Boltzmann Machine	Time	Stochastic	[1]
	Hidden Markov Model	Pattern	Stochastic	[12]

Table 1: Neural network examples belong to the generic iterative ANN model and obey the unifying mathematical formulation in the retrieving phase.

3 Unifying Ring Systolic Design for ANNs

An important consideration in the architectural design for ANNs is to ensure that the processing in both the retrieving phase and the learning phase can share the same storage and processing hardware. This will not only make it possible the on-line learning, but also avoid the difficulty of reloading of synaptic weights for retrieving. Another design consideration is to find a proper digital arithmetic technique (such as Cordic) to efficiently implement the neural processing units.

3.1 Ring Systolic ANN for the Retrieving Phase

The system dynamics in the retrieving phase of the generic iterative ANN model can be formulated as a consecutive matrix-vector multiplication problem interleaved with the nonlinear activation function (see Eqs. 1 and 2).

$$\begin{aligned} \mathbf{u}(l+1) &= \mathbf{W}(l+1)\mathbf{a}(l) + \theta(l+1) \\ \mathbf{a}(l+1) &= F[\mathbf{u}(l+1), \mathbf{a}(l)] \end{aligned} \tag{10}$$

where the $F[\mathbf{x}]$ operator performs the nonlinear activation function f on each element of the vector $\mathbf{x}$.

For the convenience of homogeneous architectural design, it is assumed that all the layers in the iterative ANN model have uniform size of N neural units (by artificially creating a certain number of pseudo no-operation neural units and fixed zero weights) to balance any inequality between two iterations (layers). This leads to a universal ring systolic architecture as shown in Figure 2 [8].

Neural Networks	Learning Recursion m	Measure Function E	Updating Formulation $w_{ij}(l) = \Phi(\cdot)$	Back-Propagated Signal $\delta_i(l)$	Comments
Single Layer Adaline	Pattern	$E = \sum_{i=1}^{N_1} (t_i - u_i)^2$	$w_{ij} + \eta (t_i - u_i) a_j(0)$	No	LMS Learning
Memory & Learning Module	Pattern	$E = \sum_{i=1}^{N} (\theta_i - \mu_i(L))^2$	$w_{ij}(L) + \eta (\theta_i - \mu_i(L))\, a_j(L)$	No	$\mu_i(L) = \sum_j w_{ij} a_j(L-1)$
Multilayer Adaline/ Committee Machine	Pattern	$E = \sum_{i=1}^{N_L} \lvert t_i - a_i(L) \rvert$	$w_{ij}(l) + \eta\, \psi(\frac{\Delta E}{\Delta a_i(l)}) a_j(l-1)$	Yes	$\psi(\frac{\Delta E}{\Delta x}) = \begin{cases} 0 & \text{if } \Delta E \geq 0, \\ \frac{\Delta E}{\Delta x} & \text{if } \Delta E < 0 \end{cases}$
Back-Propagation Network	Pattern	$E = \sum_{i=1}^{N_L} (t_i - a_i(L))^2$	$w_{ij}(l) - \eta \delta_i(l) f'(u_i(l)) a_j(l-1)$	Yes	$f'(x) = f(x)(1 - f(x))$, $\delta_i(L) = -(t_i - a_i(L))$
Recurrent Back-Propagation	Pattern	$E = \sum_{i=1}^{N} (t_i - a_i(L))^2$	$w_{ij} - \eta \sum_{l=1}^{L} \delta_i(l) f'(u_i(l)) a_j(l-1)$	Yes	$\Delta w_{ij} = \sum_l \Delta w_{ij}(l)$
Parallel Hopfield Associative Network	Sweep	$E = -\frac{1}{2} \sum_i^N \sum_j^N w_{ij} a_i(L) a_j(L) - \sum_i^N \theta_i a_i(L)$	$\sum_{m=1}^{P} (2a_i^{(m)}(L) - 1) \cdot (2a_j^{(m)}(L) - 1)$	No	No Adaptive Learning
Self-Organized Perceptual Network	Sweep	$E_i(l) = -\frac{1}{2} \sum_{j=1}^{N_{l-1}} \sum_{k=1}^{N_{l-1}} Q_{jk}(l) w_{ij}(l) w_{ik}(l) - \frac{c_5}{2} (\sum_{j=1}^{N_{l-1}} w_{ij}(l))^2 - c_6 \sum_{j=1}^{N_{l-1}} w_{ij}(l)$	$w_{ij}(l) + \eta [\sum_{k=1}^{N_{l-1}} Q_{jk}(l) w_{ik}(l) + c_5 \sum_{j=1}^{N_{l-1}} w_{ij}(l) + c_6]$	No	$Q_{jk}(l) = < (a_j^{(m)}(l-1) - \bar{a}_j(l-1)) \cdot (a_k^{(m)}(l-1) - \bar{a}_k(l-1)) >$
Self-Organized Feature Map	Pattern	$E = \frac{1}{2} \sum_{i=1}^{N} a_i(1) (a_j(0) - w_{ij})^2$	$w_{ij} + \eta\, a_i(1) (a_j(0) - w_{ij})$	No	Shrinking Neighborhood Weight Updating
Adaptive Resonance Theory	Pattern	$E = \frac{1}{2} \sum_{i=1}^{N} a_i(1) (a_j(0) - w_{ij})^2$	$w_{ij} + \eta\, a_i(1) (a_j(0) - w_{ij})$	No	Vigilance Test For New Nodes
Rumelhart Feature Detector	Pattern	$E_l = \frac{1}{2} \sum_{i=1}^{N} a_i(l) (a_j(l-1) - w_{ij}(l))^2$	$w_{ij}(l) + \eta\, a_i(l) (a_j(l-1) - w_{ij}(l))$	No	Leaky Learning To Avoid Unlearned Nodes
Boltzmann Machine	Sweep	$\mathrm{E} = \sum_{\forall \mathbf{a}_v} Pr^+(\mathbf{a}_v)\, ln\, \frac{Pr^+(\mathbf{a}_v)}{Pr^-(\mathbf{a}_v)}$	$w_{ij} + \eta (p_{ij}^+ - p_{ij}^-)$	No	$p_{ij}^{\pm} = \sum_{\forall \mathbf{a}} Pr^{\pm}(\mathbf{a})\, a_i a_j$
Hidden Markov Model	Sweep	$E = Pr(O \mid \lambda) = \sum_{i=1}^{N} a_i(L)$	$\eta\, w_{ij} \sum_{l=1}^{L} \delta_i(l) f_i(o_l) a_j(l-1)$	Yes	$w_{ij} \geq 0$, $\sum_{i=1}^{N} w_{ij} = 1$, $\eta = \frac{1}{\sum_{l=0}^{L-1} \delta_j(l)\, a_j(l)}$

Table 2: Neural network examples belong to the generic iterative ANN model and obey the unifying mathematical formulation in the learning phase.

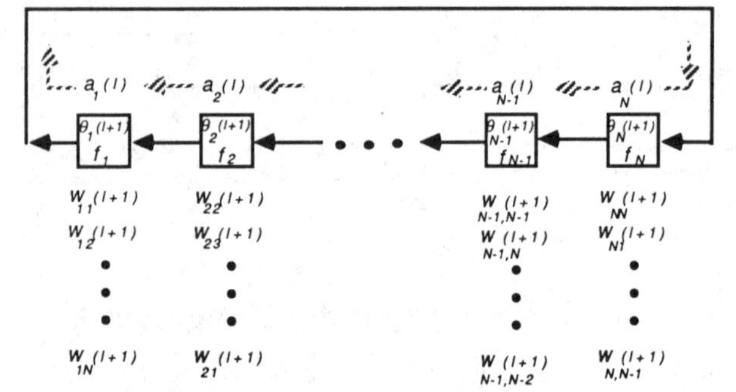

Figure 2: The universal ring systolic architecture for the retrieving phase of the generic iterative ANN models.

Retrieving Iterations in the Ring Systolic ANN At the $(l+1)$-th iteration of the retrieving phase, each processor element (PE), say the i-th PE, can be treated as a neuron at that layer, and the corresponding incoming synaptic weights $(w_{i1}(l+1), w_{i2}(l+1), \cdots, w_{iN}(l+1))$ are stored in the memory of the i-th PE in a circularly-shift-up order (by $i-1$ positions). The operations at the $(l+1)$-th iteration can be described as follows:

1. Each neuron activation value $a_j(l)$, created at j-th PE, will move counter-clockwise across the ring array and visit each of the other PEs once in N clock units.

2. When $a_j(l)$ arrives at the i-th PE, it is multiplied with $w_{ij}(l+1)$, and the product is added to the $\theta_i(l+1)$ to derive $u_i(l+1)$ (see Eq. 1). After N clock units, all the products are collected and the resulting $u_i(l+1)$ is ready for the nonlinear activation operation $f(\cdot)$ (see Eq. 2) to create $a_i(l+1)$ for the next iteration.

The above procedure can be executed in a fully pipelined fashion. Moreover, it can be recursively executed (with increased l) until L iterations are completed.

3.2 Ring Systolic ANN for the Learning Phase

The ring systolic array derived for the retrieving phase can be easily adapted to apply to the learning phase [8]. It is observed from Table 2 that two types of operations are required for most of the weight updating formulations: the correlation rule and the back-propagated rule. Both rules can be efficiently implemented by the ring systolic ANN based on the same storage and processing hardware in the retrieving phase. The correlation rule can be summarized by the following outer-product formulation.

$$\begin{aligned} \Delta w_{ij}(l+1) &= g(a_i(l+1),\ \delta_i(l+1),\ t_i) \cdot h(a_j(l),\ w_{ij}(l+1)) \\ \Delta \mathbf{W}(l+1) &= \mathbf{g}(l+1)\, \mathbf{h}(l+1)^T \end{aligned} \tag{11}$$

where $\mathbf{x}^T$ denotes the transpose of the vector $\mathbf{x}$. The back-propagated rule can be simply formulated as a consecutive vector-matrix multiplication operations [8];

$$\begin{aligned} \delta_i(l) &= \sum_{j=1}^{N} \delta_j(l+1)\, r(w_{ji}(l+1), f_j) \\ \mathbf{d}(l)^T &= \mathbf{d}(l+1)^T\, \mathbf{R}(l+1) \end{aligned} \tag{12}$$

where $\mathbf{R}(l+1) = \{r_{ij}(l+1) = r(w_{ij}(l+1), f_i)\}$, $\mathbf{d}(l) = [\delta_1(l), \cdots, \delta_N(l)]^T$.

Correlation Rule in the Ring Systolic ANN The operations of the correlation rule in the ring systolic ANN can be briefly described as follows (see Figure 3):

1. The value of $g_i(l+1)$ is computed and stored in the i-th PE. The value $h_j(l+1)$ produced at the j-th PE will be cyclically propagated to all other PEs in the ring systolic ANN during the N clocks.

2. When $h_j(l+1)$ arrives at the i-th PE, it is multiplied with the stored value $g_i(l+1)$ to yield $\Delta w_{ij}(l+1)$, which will then be incorporated with $w_{ij}(l+1)$ of previous recursion to produce the new $w_{ij}(l+1)$. Note that the old weight data $\{w_{ij}(l+1)\}$ are retrieved in a circularly-shift-up sequence, just like that used in the retrieving phase.

3. After N clocks, all the $N \times N$ new weights at $(l+1)$-th layer $\{w_{ij}(l+1)\}$ are generated. The ring systolic ANN is now ready for the weight updating of the next layer (l).

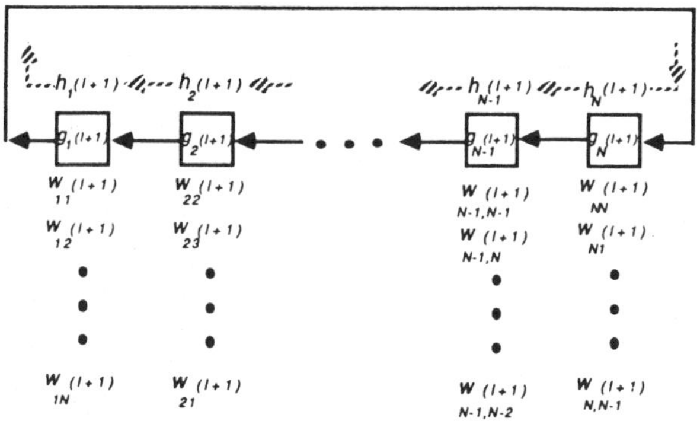

Figure 3: The universal ring systolic architecture for the correlation rule of the generic iterative ANN models.

Back-Propagated Rule in the Ring Systolic ANN When the correlation rule takes place for the weight updating of $(l+1)$-th layer, the weight value $w_{ji}(l+1)$ of the previous recursion should be retrieved for the modification, and it can be used to compute $r_{ji}(l+1)$. The operations of these two rules can thus be calculated at the same time. The operations of the back-propagation rule in the ring systolic ANN can be briefly described as follows [8] (see Figure 4);

1. The back-propagated signal $\delta_j(l+1)$ and the value $r_{ji}(l+1)$ are now available in the j-th PE at $(l+1)$-th iteration. The value $r_{ji}(l+1)$ is then multiplied with $\delta_j(l+1)$ at j-th PE.

2. The product is added to the newly arrived accumulator $acc_i(l)$, which is initiated at the i-th PE with zero initial value and circularly shifted leftward across the ring array.

3. After N such accumulation operations, the accumulator $acc_i(l)$ will return to i-th PE after accumulating all the products $\delta_i(l) = \sum_{j=1}^{N} \delta_j(l+1)\, r_{ji}(l+1)$.

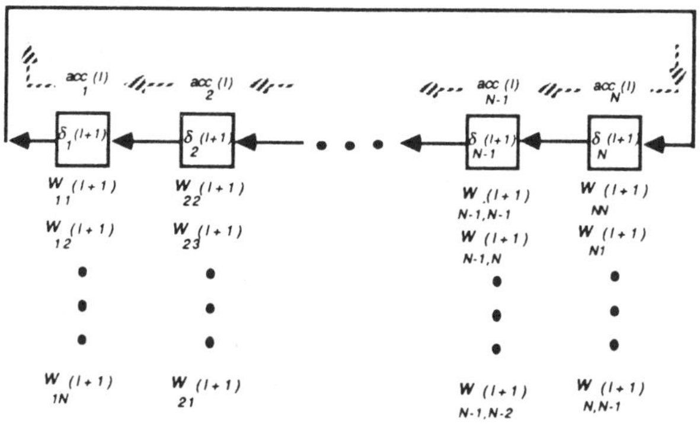

Figure 4: The universal ring systolic architecture for the back-propagation rule of the generic iterative ANN models.

3.3 Cordic Based Neural Processing Units

For a dedicated digital VLSI implementation of the neural processing units, the feasibility of the nonlinear sigmoid function and the area consumption are quite important, and a Cordic processor might be a good alternative [2]. A Cordic scheme is an iterative method based on bit-level shift-and-add operations. It is especially suitable for computing a class of rotations [7]. A 2-dimensional vector $\mathbf{v} = [x, y]$ can be rotated by an angle α by using a rotation operator R_α, $\mathbf{v}' = R_\alpha \mathbf{v}$.

In the linear coordinate system, the Cordic can be used for MAC (multiply and accumulation) operations (see Figures 5(a)). Given x, y, and α, we can get the Cordic output $y + x\alpha$ in the linear mode which is very useful for propagation rule operations in the neural processing units. The sigmoid activation function can be implemented by using the Cordic in the hyperbolic mode, where the inputs are set as $\mathbf{v} = [1, 1]$ and $\alpha = u/2$ (see Figures 5(b)).

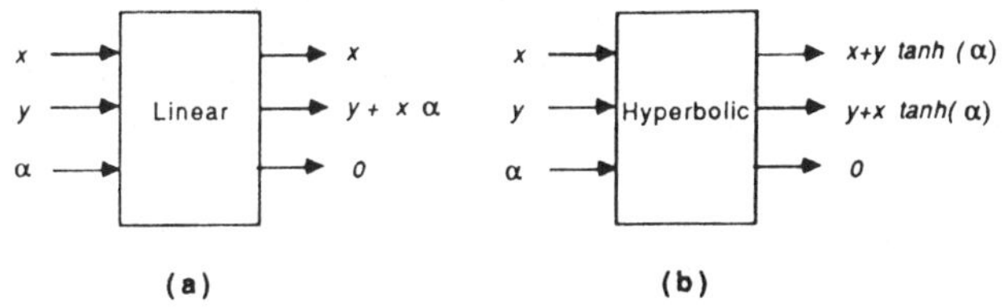

Figure 5: (a) The linear coordinate system of the Cordic processing. (b) The hyperbolic coordinate system of the Cordic processing.

4 Conclusion

For real time processing performance, the neural net architectures will require massive parallel processing. Fortunately, today's VLSI and CAD technologies facilitate practical and cost-effective implementation of large scale computing networks. In order to fully exploit VLSI's strength, a programmable universal ring systolic ANN design is derived based on the unifying mathematical formulations of the generic iterative ANN model. Thanks to the versatility of this systolic design, both of the retrieving and learning phases of most ANN models can be efficiently implemented.

References

[1] D. H. Ackley, G. E. Hinton, and T. J. Sejnowski. A learning algorithm for Boltzmann machines. *Cognitive Science*, 9:147–169, 1985.

[2] H.M. Ahmed. Alternative arithmetic unit architectures for VLSI digital signal processors. In *VLSI and Modern Signal Processing*, Chapter 16, pages 277–306, Prentice Hall, Inc., Englewood Cliffs, NJ, 1985.

[3] S. Grossberg. Adaptive pattern classification and universal recoding: Part 1. parallel development and coding of neural feature detectors. *Biological Cybernetics*, 23:121–134, 1976.

[4] J. J. Hopfield. Neural network and physical systems with emergent collective computational abilities. In *Proc. Natl'. Acad. Sci. USA*, pages 2554–2558, 1982.

[5] J. N. Hwang. *Algorithms/Applications/Architectures of Artificial Neural Nets*. Dept. of Electrical Engineering, University of Southern California, December 1988. Ph.D. Dissertation.

[6] T. Kohonen. Self-organized formation of topologically correct feature map. *Biological Cybernetics*, 43:59–69, 1982.

[7] S. Y. Kung. *VLSI Array Processors*. Prentice Hall Inc., N.J., 1988.

[8] S. Y. Kung and J. N. Hwang. Parallel architectures for artificial neural nets. In *IEEE, Int'l Conf. on Neural Networks, ICNN'88, San Diego*, pages Vol.2: 165–172, July 1988.

[9] R. Linsker. Self-organization in a perceptual network. *IEEE Computer Magazine*, 21:105–117, March 1988.

[10] J. L. McClelland and D. E. Rumelhart. Distributed memory and the representation of general and specific information. *Journal of Experimental Psychology: General*, 114:158–188, 1985.

[11] N. J. Nilsson. *Learning Machines*. McGraw-Hill Book Company, 1965.

[12] L. R. Rabiner and B. H. Juang. An introduction to hidden Markov models. *IEEE ASSP Magazine*, 3(1):4–16, January 1986.

[13] D. E. Rumelhart, G. E. Hinton, and R. J. Williams. Learning internal representations by error propagation. In *Parallel Distributed Processing (PDP): Exploration in the Microstructure of Cognition (Vol. 1)*, Chapter 8, pages 318–362, MIT Press, Cambridge, Massachusetts, 1986.

[14] D. E. Rumelhart and D. Zipser. Feature discovery by competitive learning. *Cognitive Science*, 9:75–112, 1985.

[15] B. Widrow and R. Winter. Neural nets for adaptive filtering and adaptive pattern recognition. *IEEE Computer Magazine*, 21:25–39, March 1988.

[16] G. Widrow and M. E. Hoff. Adaptive switching circuit. *IRE Western Electronic Show and Convention: Convention Record*, 96–104, 1960.

About the Author

Nelson Morgan is a research scientist at the International Computer Science Institute (ICSI), a non-profit research laboratory associated with the Electrical Engineering and Computer Science Department at the University of California, Berkeley. His interests include the design of algorithms, architectures, and systems for parallel signal processing and pattern recognition systems. He also admits having an interest in artificial neural networks. He is currently involved in the use of ANNs for machine recognition of continuous speech, as well as in the design of hardware to perform this task.

Over the last 8 years, Dr. Morgan has also worked on the application of ANN algorithms to the classification and processing of speech and biomedical signals. He is the author of a book on IC's for synthetic speech. He holds patents both for discrete-time signal processing hardware, and for brain-scanning technology.

Morgan received his Ph.D. from UC Berkeley in 1980. He received his B.S. and M.S. from UCB as well. His earlier history is shrouded in mystery.

Index

References

Ackley, D.H., Hinton, G.E., and Sejnowski, T.J., 1985. ''A learning algorithm for Boltzmann machines,'' Cognitive Science 9 (1985), pp.147-169.

Baker, T., and Hammerstrom, D., 1988, ''Modifications to Artificial Neural Networks Models for Digital Hardware Implementation,'' Oregon Graduate Center Technical Report No. CS/E 88-035.

Beck, J., Morgan, N., Allman, E., Beer, J., 1989. ''A Multi-DSP Ring Array for Connectionist Simulations,'' Proceedings of the 1989 Asilomar Conference on Signals, Systems, and Computers.

Brodersen, R.W., 1989. ''Evolution of VLSI Signal Processing Circuits,'' *Advanced Research in VLSI,* Proceedings of the 1989 Decennial Caltech Conference, Charles Seitz, editor.

Duranton, M., and Sirat, J.A., 1989. ''Learning on VLSI: A General Purpose Digital Microchip,'' Proceedings of 1989 International Neural Network Society Conference

Feldman, J.A., Fanty, M.A., Goddard, N., and Lynne, K., 1988. ''Computing with Structured Connectionist Networks,'' *Communications of the ACM,* 1988.

Gevins, A. and Morgan, N. (1986) ''Classifier-directed signal processing in brain research''. *IEEE Transactions on Biomedical Engineering, BME-33* (12), pp. 1054-1068.

Gevins, A., and Morgan, N., 1988. ''Applications of Neural Network (NN) Signal Processing in Brain Research,'' IEEE Transactions on Acoustics, Speech, and Signal Processing, July, 1988.

Hopfield, J.J., 1988. ''Artificial Neural Networks,'' IEEE Circuits and Devices Magazine, Vol. 4, No. 5, September, 1988.

Nillson, N.J., 1965. *Learning Machines,* McGraw-Hill, New York, 1965.

Ruetz, P., 1989. ''The Architectures and Design of a 20-MHz Real-Time DSP Chip Set,'' IEEE Journal of Solid State Circuits, April, 1989.

Rumelhart, D.E., Hinton, G.E. and Williams, R.J., 1986. ''Learning Internal Representations by Error Propagation,'' in *Parallel Distributed Processing.* vol. 1: Foundations, Ed. D.E.Rumelhart and J.L.McClelland, MIT Press, 1986.

Sinha P., and Morgan, N., 1989, ''VLSI Building Blocks for Connectionist Applications", ICSI Technical Report, In Progress.

Tuckerman, D.B., ''Laser-patterned interconnect for thin-film hybrid wafer-scale circuits,'' IEEE Elec. Dev. Let., EDL-8, No. 11, p.540, Nov. 1987

Viglione, S.S., 1970, ''Applications of pattern recognition technology,'' in *Adaptive Learning and Pattern Recognition Systems,* J.M. Mendel and K.S.Fu, Eds., New York, Academic Press, 1970, pp. 115-161.

Von Neumann, J., 1957. *The Computer and the Brain* New Haven and London, Yale University Press.

Weinfeld, M., Dreyfus, G., Johannet, A., Personnaz, L., 1988. '' A Fully Digital CMOS Integrated Feedback Network Including the Learning Process,'' Proceedings of Neural Networks for Computing, Snowbird, Utah, 1988.

Widrow, B. and Hoff, M.E., 1960. ''Adaptive Switching Circuits,'' *WESCON Convention Record,* 4:96-104.

IEEE Computer Society

Offices of the IEEE Computer Society

Headquarters Office
1730 Massachusetts Avenue, N.W.
Washington, DC 20036-1903
Phone: (202) 371-0101
Telex: 7108250437 IEEE COMPSO

Publications Office
P.O. Box
10662 Los Vaqueros Circle
Los Alamitos, CA 90720-1264
Membership and General Information: (714) 821-8380
Publications Orders: (800) 272-6657

European Office
13, Avenue de l'Aquilon
B-1200 Brussels, Belgium
Phone: 32 (2) 770-21-98
Telex: 25387 AVVALB

Asian Office
Ooshima Building
2-19-1 Minami-Aoyama, Minato-ku
Tokyo 107, Japan

IEEE Computer Society Press Publications

Monographs: A monograph is an authored book

Tutorials: A tutorial is a collection of original materials prepared by the editors and reprints of the best articles published in a subject area. They must contain at least five percent original material (15 to 20 percent original material is recommended).

Reprint Books: A reprint book is a collection of reprints divided into sections with a preface, table of contents, and section introductions that discuss the reprints and why they were selected. It contains less than five percent original material.

(Subject) Technology Series: Each technology series is a collection of anthologies of reprints, each with a narrow focus on a subset of a particular discipline, such as networks, architecture, software, robotics.

Submission of proposals: For guidelines on preparing CS Press Books, write Editor-in-Chief, IEEE Computer Society, P.O. Box 3014, 10662 Los Vaqueros Circle, Los Alamitos, CA 90720-1264 (telephone 714-821-8380).

Purpose

The IEEE Computer Society advances the theory and practice of computer science and engineering, promotes the exchange of technical information among 100,000 members worldwide, and provides a wide range of services to members and nonmembers.

Membership

Members receive the acclaimed monthly magazine *Computer,* discounts, and opportunities to serve (all activities are led by volunteer members). Membership is open to all IEEE members, affiliate society members, and others seriously interested in the computer field.

Publications and Activities

Computer. An authoritative, easy-to-read magazine containing tutorial and in-depth articles on topics across the computer field, plus news, conferences, calendar, interviews, and new products.

Periodicals. The society publishes six magazines and four research transactions. Refer to membership application or request information as noted above.

Conference Proceedings, Tutorial Texts, Standards Documents. The Computer Society Press publishes more than 100 titles every year.

Standards Working Groups. Over 100 of these groups produce IEEE standards used throughout the industrial world.

Technical Committees. Over 30 TCs publish newsletters, provide interaction with peers in specialty areas, and directly influence standards, conferences, and education.

Conferences/Education. The society holds about 100 conferences each year and sponsors many educational activites, including computing science accreditation.

Chapters. Regular and student chapters worldwide provide the opportunity to interact with colleagues, hear technical experts, and serve the local professional community.

Other IEEE Computer Society Press Texts

Monographs

Analyzing Computer Architecture
Written by J.C. Huck and M.J. Flynn
(ISBN 0-8186-8857-2); 206 pages

Desktop Publishing for the Writer: Designing, Writing, Developing
Written by Richard Ziegfeld and John Tarp
(ISBN 0-8186-8840-8); 380 pages

Integrating Design and Test: Using CAE Tools for ATE Programming
Written by K.P. Parker
(ISBN 0-8186-8788-6 (case)); 160 pages

JSP and JSD: The Jackson Approach to Software Development (Second Edition)
Written by J.R. Cameron
(ISBN 0-8186-8858-0); 560 pages

National Computer Policies
Written by Ben G. Matley and Thomas A. McDannold
(ISBN 0-8186-8784-3); 192 pages

Physical Level Interfaces and Protocols
Written by Uyless Black
(ISBN 0-8186-8824-6); approximately 272 pages

Protecting Your Proprietary Rights in the Computer and High Technology Industries
Written by Tobey B. Marzouk, Esq.
(ISBN 0-8186-8754-1); 224 pages

Tutorials

Advanced Computer Architecture
Edited by D.P. Agrawal
(ISBN 0-8186-0667-3); 400 pages

Advanced Microprocessors and High-Level Language Computer Architectures
Edited by V. Milutinovic
(ISBN 0-8186-0623-1); 608 pages

Advances in Distributed System Reliability
Edited by Suresh Rai and Dharma P. Agrawal
(ISBN 0-8186-8907-2); 352 pages

Computer Architecture
Edited by D.D. Gajski, V.M. Milutinovic, H. Siegel, and B.P. Furht
(ISBN 0-8186-0704-1); 602 pages

Computer Communications: Architectures, Protocols, and Standards (Second Edition)
Edited by William Stallings
(ISBN 0-8186-0790-4); 448 pages

Computer Graphics (2nd Edition)
Edited by J.C. Beatty and K.S. Booth
(ISBN 0-8186-0425-5); 576 pages

Computer Graphics Hardware: Image Generation and Display
Edited by H.K. Reghbati and A.Y.C. Lee
(ISBN 0-8186-0753-X); 384 pages

Computer Graphics: Image Synthesis
Edited by Kenneth Joy, Max Nelson, Charles Grant, and Lansing Hatfield
(ISBN 0-8186-8854-8); 384

Computer and Network Security
Edited by M.D. Abrams and H.J. Podell
(ISBN 0-8186-0756-4); 448 pages

Computer Networks (4th Edition)
Edited by M.D. Abrams and I.W. Cotton
(ISBN 0-8186-0568-5); 512 pages

Computer Text Recognition and Error Correction
Edited by S.N. Srihari
(ISBN 0-8186-0579-0); 364 pages

Computers for Artificial Intelligence Applications
Edited by B. Wah and G.-J. Li
(ISBN 0-8186-0706-8); 656 pages

Database Management
Edited by J.A. Larson
(ISBN 0-8186-0714-9); 448 pages

Digital Image Processing and Analysis: Volume 1: Digital Image Processing
Edited by R. Chellappa and A.A. Sawchuk
(ISBN 0-8186-0665-7); 736 pages

Digital Image Processing and Analysis: Volume 2: Digital Image Analysis
Edited by R. Chellappa and A.A. Sawchuk
(ISBN 0-8186-0666-5); 670 pages

Digital Private Branch Exchanges (PBXs)
Edited by E.R. Coover
(ISBN 0-8186-0829-3); 400 pages

Distributed Computing Network Reliability
Edited by Suresh Rai and Dharma P. Agrawal
(ISBN 0-8186-8908-0); 368 pages

Distributed Control (2nd Edition)
Edited by R.E. Larson, P.L. McEntire, and J.G. O'Reilly
(ISBN 0-8186-0451-4); 382 pages

Distributed Database Management
Edited by J.A. Larson and S. Rahimi
(ISBN 0-8186-0575-8); 580 pages

Distributed-Software Engineering
Edited by S.M. Shatz and J.-P. Wang
(ISBN 0-8186-8856-4); 304 pages

DSP-Based Testing of Analog and Mixed-Signal Circuits
Edited by M. Mahoney
(ISBN 0-8186-0785-8); 272 pages

Fault-Tolerant Computing
Edited by V.P. nelson and B.D. Carroll
(ISBN 0-8186-0677-0 (paper) 0-8186-8667-4 (case)); 432 pages

Gallium Arsenide Computer Design
Edited by V.M. Milutinovic and D.A. Fura
(ISBN 0-8186-0795-5); 368 pages

Human Factors in Software Development (2nd Edition)
Edited by B. Curtis
(ISBN 0-8186-0577-4); 736 pages

Integrated Services Digital Networks (ISDN) (Second Edition)
Edited by W. Stallings
(ISBN 0-8186-0823-4); 404 pages

For Further Information:

IEEE Computer Society, 10662 Los Vaqueros Circle, P.O. Box 3014,
Los Alamitos, CA 90720-1264

IEEE Computer Society, 13, Avenue de l'Aquilon, 2,
B-1200 Brussels, BELGIUM

IEEE Computer Society,
Ooshima Building, 2-19-1 Minami-Aoyama,
Minato-ku, Tokyo 107, JAPAN

Interconnection Networks for Parallel and Distributed Processing
Edited by C.-L. Wu and T.-Y. Feng
(ISBN 0-8186-0574-X); 500 pages

Local Network Equipment
Edited by H.A. Freeman and K.J. Thurber
(ISBN 0-8186-0605-3); 384 pages

Local Network Technology (3rd Edition)
Edited by W. Stallings
(ISBN 0-8186-0825-0); 512 pages

Microprogramming and Firmware Engineering
Edited by V. Milutinovic
(ISBN 0-8186-0839-0); 416 pages

Modeling and Control of Automated Manufacturing Systems
Edited by A.A. Desrochers
(ISBN 0-8186-8916-1); 384 pages

Modern Design and Analysis of Discrete-Event Computer Simulations
Edited by E.J. Dudewicz and Z. Karian
(ISBN 0-8186-0597-9); 486 pages

New Paradigms for Software Development
Edited by William Agresti
(ISBN 0-8186-0707-6); 304 pages

Object-Oriented Computing--Volume 1: Concepts
Edited by Gerald E. Peterson
(ISBN 0-8186-0821-8); 214 pages

Object-Oriented Computing--Volume 2: Implementations
Edited by Gerald E. Peterson
(ISBN 0-8186-082108); 214 pages

Office Automation Systems (Second Edition)
Edited by H.A. Freemand and K.J. Thurber
(ISBN 0-8186-0822-6); 324 pages

Parallel Architectures for Database Systems
Edited by A. R. Hurson, L.L. Miller, and S.H. Pakzad
(ISBN 0-8186-8838-6); 478 pages

Programming Productivity: Issues for the Eighties (Second Edition)
Edited by C. Jones
(ISBN 0-8186-0681-9); 472 pages

Recent Advances in Distributed Database Management
Edited by C. Mohan
(ISBN 0-8186-0571-5); 500 pages

Reduced Instruction Set Computers (Second Edition)
Edited by W. Stallings
(ISBN 0-8186-8943-9); 448 pages

Reliable Distributed System Software
Edited by J.A. Stankovic
(ISBN 0-8186-0570-7); 400 pages

Robotics Tutorial (2nd Edition)
Edited by C.S. G. Lee, R.C. Gonzalez, and K.S. Fu
(ISBN 0-8186-0658-4); 630 pages

Software Design Techniques (4th Edition)
Edited by P. Freeman and A.I. Wasserman
(ISBN 0-8186-0514-0); 736 pages

Software Engineering Project Management
Edited by R. Thayer
(ISBN 0-8186-0751-3); 512 pages

Software Maintenance
Edited by G. Parikh and N. Zvegintzov
(ISBN 0-8186-0002-0); 360 pages

Software Management (3rd Edition)
Edited by D.J. Reifer
(ISBN 0-8186-0678-9); 526 pages

Software-Oriented Computer Architecture
Edited by E. Fernandez and T. Lang
(ISBN 0-8186-0708-4); 376 pages

Software Reusability
Edited by Peter Freeman
(ISBN 0-8186-0750-5); 304 pages

Software Risk Management
Edited by B.W. Boehm
(ISBN 0-8186-8906-4); 508 pages

Standards, Guidelines, and Examples on System and Software Requirements Engineering
Edited by Merlin Dorfman and Richard H. Thayer
(ISBN 0-8186-8922-6); 626 pages

System and Software Requirements Engineering
Edited by Richard H. Thayer and Merlin Dorfman
(ISBN 0-8186-8921-8); 740 pages

Test Generation for VLSI Chips
Edited by V.D. Agrawal and S.C. Seth
(ISBN 0-8186-8786-X); 416 pages

VSLI Technologies: Through the 80s and Beyond
Edited by D.J. McGreivy and K.A. Pickar
(ISBN 0-8186-0424-7); 346 pages

VLSI Testing and Validation Techniques
Edited by H. Reghbati
(ISBN 0-8186-0668-1); 616 pages

Reprint Collections

Dataflow and Reduction Architectures
Edited by S.S. Thakkar
(ISBN 0-8186-0759-9); 460 pages

Expert Systems: Software Methodology
Edited by Peter Raeth
(ISBN 0-8186-8904-8); 476 pages

Logic Design for Testability
Edited by C.C. Timoc
(ISBN 0-8186-0573-1); 324 pages

Microprocessors and Microcomputers (3rd Edition)
Edited by J.T. Cain
(ISBN 0-8186-0585-5); 386 pages

Software (3rd Edition)
Edited by M.V. Zelkowitz
(ISBN 0-8186-0789-0); 440 pages

VLSI Technologies and Computer Graphics
Edited by H. Fuchs
(ISBN 0-8186-0491-3); 490 pages

Artifical Neural Networks Technology Series

Artificial Neural Networks: Concept Learning
Edited by J. Diederich
(ISBN 0-8186-2015-3); 140 pages

Artificial Neural Networks: Electronic Implementation
Edited by Nelson Morgan
(ISBN 0-8186-2029-3); approximately 192 pages

Artificial Neural Networks: Theoretical Concepts
Edited by V. Vemuri
(ISBN 0-8186-0855-2); 160 pages

Software Technology Series

Computer-Aided Software Engineering (CASE)
Edited by E.J. Chikofsky
(ISBN 0-8186-1970-8); 110 pages

Communications Technology Series

Multicast Communication in Distributed Systems
Edited by Mustaque Ahamad
(ISBN 0-8186-1970-8); 110 pages

Robotic Technology Series

Multirobot Systems
Edited by Rajiv Mehrotra and Murali R. Varanasi
(ISBN 0-8186-1977-5); 122 pages